AF469062

PORTRAIT OF
THE HEBRIDES

A JOURNEY TO SCOTLAND'S WESTERN SEABOARD AND BEYOND

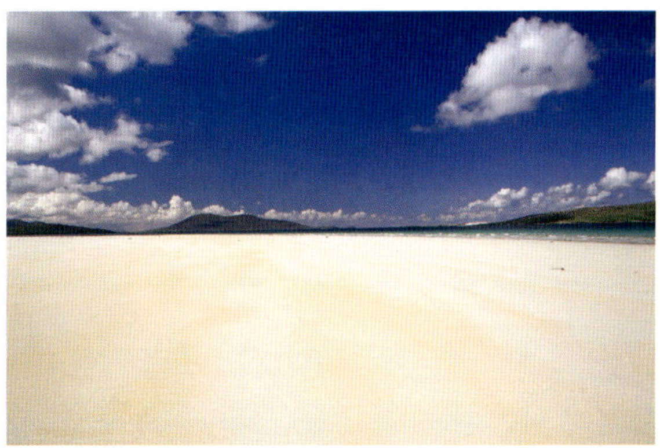

IAIN McGOWAN

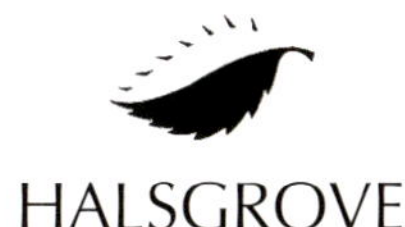

HALSGROVE

First published in Great Britain in 2008
Reprinted 2011

Title page photograph: *Tràigh Rosamol, Luskentyre, Harris*

British Library Cataloguing-in-Publication Data
A CIP record for this title is available from the British Library

ISBN 978 1 84114 740 6

HALSGROVE
Halsgrove House,
Ryelands Business Park,
Bagley Road, Wellington, Somerset TA21 9PZ
Tel: 01823 653777 Fax: 01823 216796
email: sales@halsgrove.com

Part of the Halsgrove group of companies
Information on all Halsgrove titles is available at: www.halsgrove.com

Printed and bound in China by Everbest Printing Co Ltd

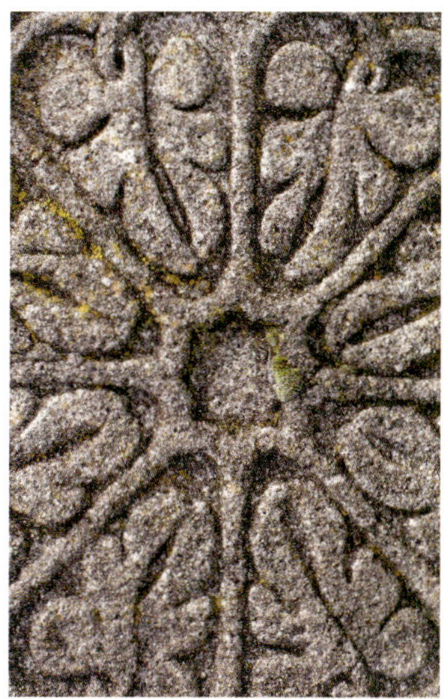

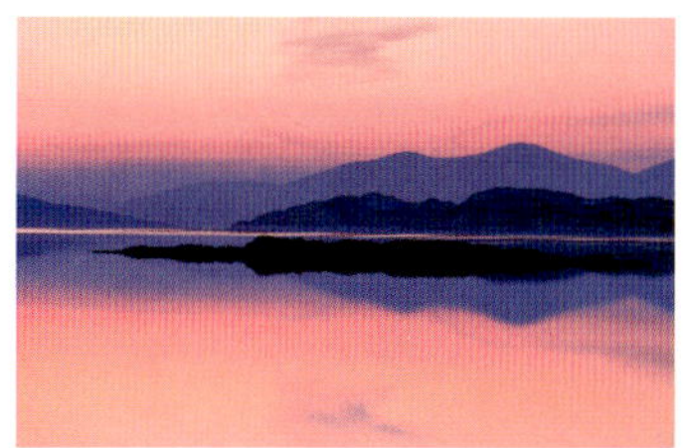

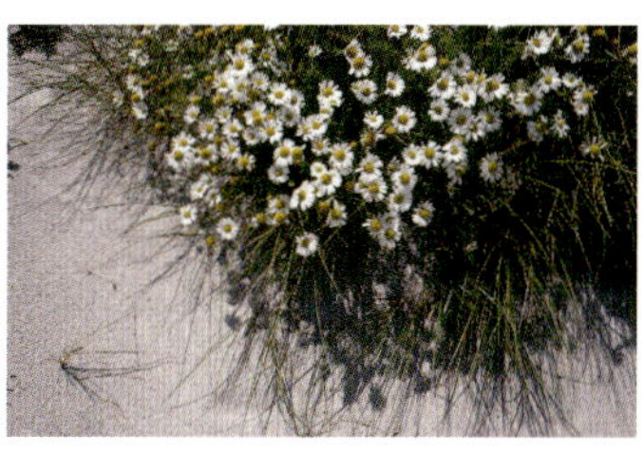

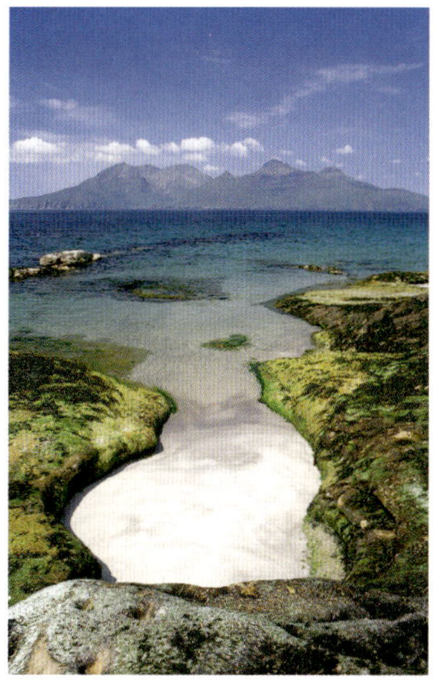

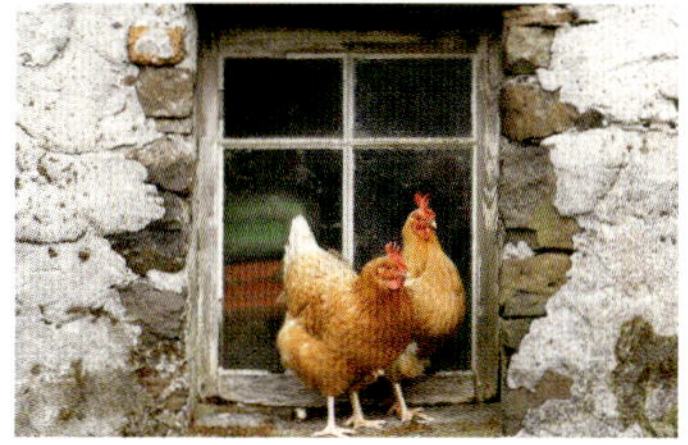

CONTENTS

MAP OF THE HEBRIDES AND SCOTLAND'S WESTERN SEABOARD

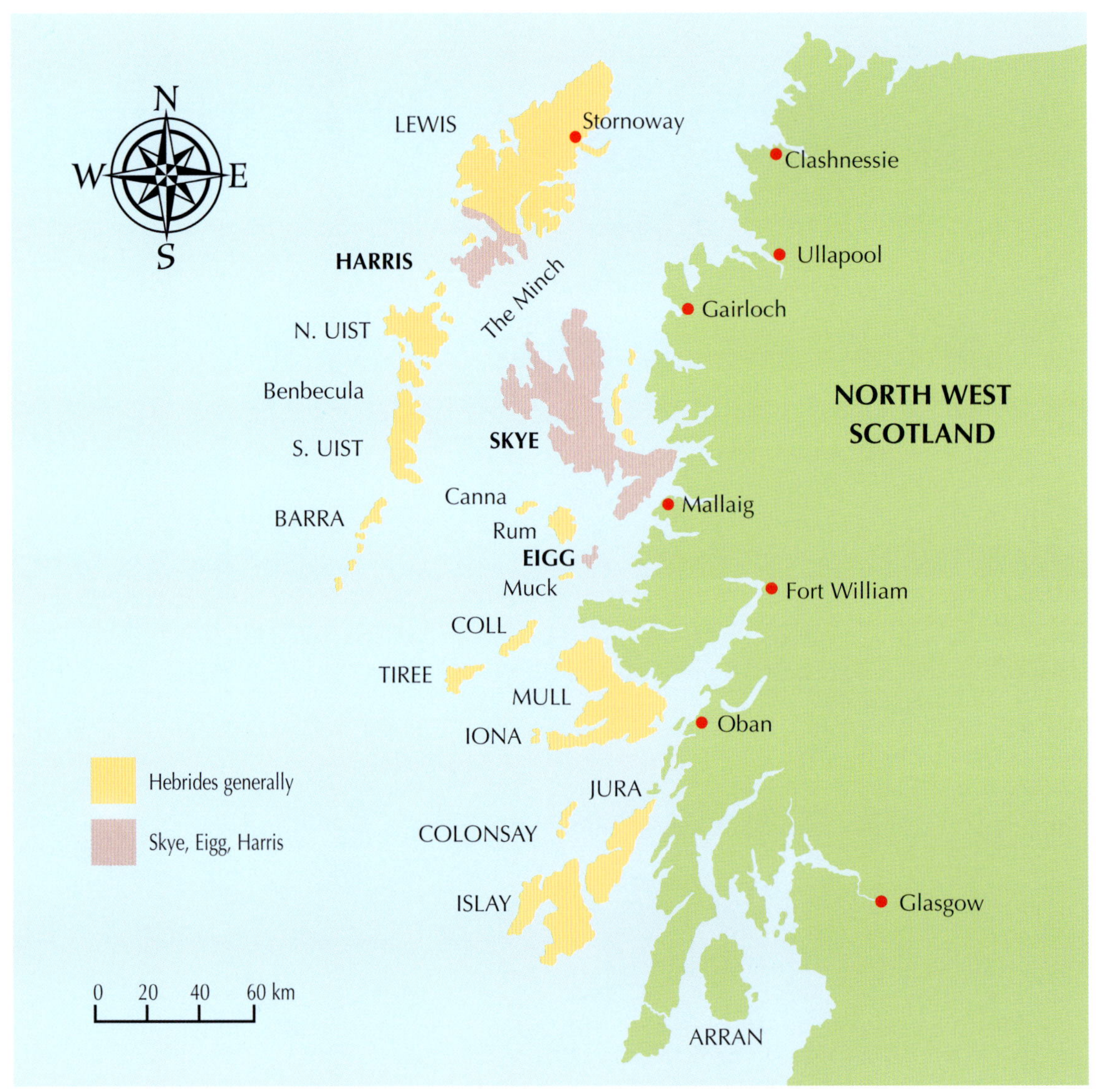

INTRODUCTION

You sing: and my soul is borne; to the isles of the outer seas –
To the far, wind-scarred, wave torn Wild Hebrides

Wilfred Wilson Gibson – *To the singer of the Isles*

For centuries people have sung of the Hebrides; the islands have been written about, fought over, dreamt of, longed for and to this day are still the subject of quite intense curiosity. In an ever-changing and rapidly shrinking world there are few places which still possess such a mystery and fascination as the waters around Scotland. In 1785 James Boswell in his *Journal of a Tour to the Hebrides* wrote: 'Doctor Johnson had for many years given me hope that we should go together and visit the Hebrides. Martin's account of these islands had impressed us with a notion that we might there contemplate a system of life almost totally different from what we had been accustomed to see; and to find simplicity and wildness, and all the circumstances of remote time or place, so near to our native great island, was an object within the reach of reasonable curiosity.' In certain respects it could almost have been written yesterday. Robert Buchanan in *The Hebrid Isles* written in 1873 describes numerous aspects of the Hebridean islands coming to the conclusion: 'A little, a very little has been said about these Isles; but to all ordinary people they are less familiar than Cairo, and further off than Calcutta'.

Unbelievably, it is only two hundred or so years since the Hebrides were first 'discovered' and even then by just the intrepid few. Before the nineteenth century only two reasonably descriptive books (Dean Monro, 1549 and Martin Martin, 1703) had been written about the Isles. The barrier of an uncertain storm-tossed sea, the natives' strange language and wild wind-swept landscapes were just too much of a challenge. For those brave enough to make the journey, the gulf between themselves and the Hebridean islanders, with their strong individual identity and Celtic ancestry, must have seemed enormous.

However things change and life moves on – we now regard the Hebrides as an area of breathtaking beauty, a kaleidoscope of colour, light and mood with a character created not only by the ever-changing sea and sky but by the complex geology, the climate and the numerous still-visible signs of the region's unique social history. Forming a shattered, splintered arc of some 360 km, the islands wrap around mainland Scotland's northwest coast in a double line – the Inner and Outer Hebrides. Of a total of at least 500 islands, less than 30 are now inhabited, these generally being the largest. In almost all however, there is that unique quality and fascination – the 'away from it all, edge of the world' atmosphere with each individual island possessing its own distinctive character. In many parts the landscape is totally barren and treeless, the sea is never far away and often the wind seems constant. Yet a sense of space and freedom prevails, here can be found the surviving heartland of Gaelic, still spoken as a first language by a considerable proportion of the native islanders.

This book is not intended as a definitive guide to the Hebrides; there are numerous places and islands not recorded here and in any case there are far better books available for such a purpose. What this book aims to achieve with its images and brief text is to bring out that certain, yet sometimes indefinable atmosphere and perhaps quality of life that is unique within the Hebrides.

To achieve this aim, considerable emphasis has been placed on the three highly contrasting islands of Skye, Eigg and Harris with more general observations of several of the remaining islands in the final chapter. The islands themselves are placed in their unique geographical context by an initial chapter featuring mainland Scotland's western seaboard. Using both detail and more general scenes, all these parts add up to a whole, somewhere to be recorded before too many values are eroded, somewhere that is literally a place beyond.

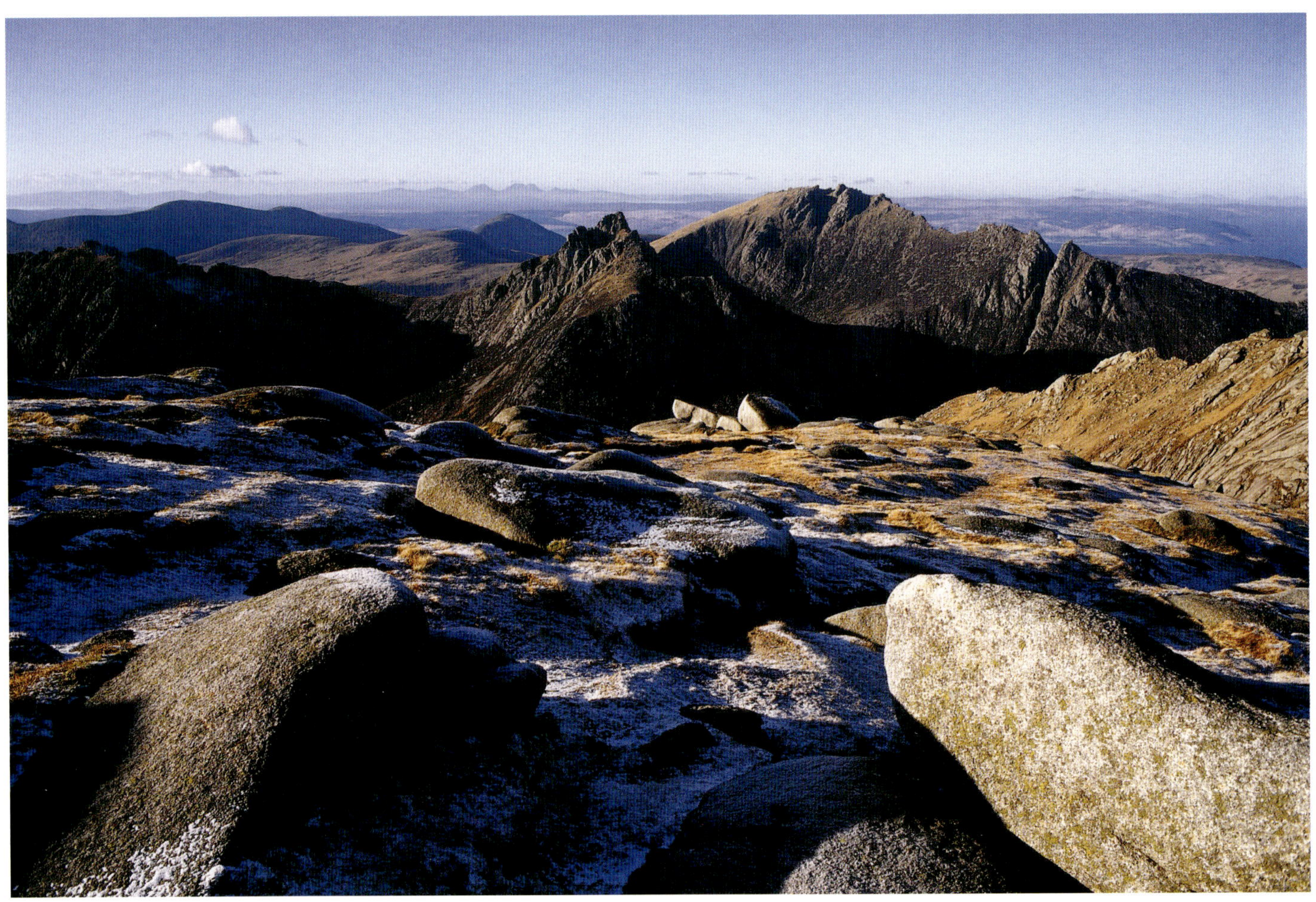

Towards the Hebrides. A wintry view from the 874m granite summit of Goat Fell, Arran's highest mountain, looking north west over the Kintyre peninsula to the distant Hebridean islands of Islay, Jura, Colonsay and Mull. Itself an island of considerable and diverse geological interest with high jagged mountains, wild glens, sweeping moorland, lonely forests and numerous bays and inlets, Arran is extremely accessible from the Scottish mainland and thus highly popular particularly with summer visitors. It is often referred to as 'Scotland in miniature' but with the neighbouring islands of Bute and Cumbrae is not strictly regarded as being part of the Hebrides.

Arran to Clashnessie

THE WESTERN SEABOARD

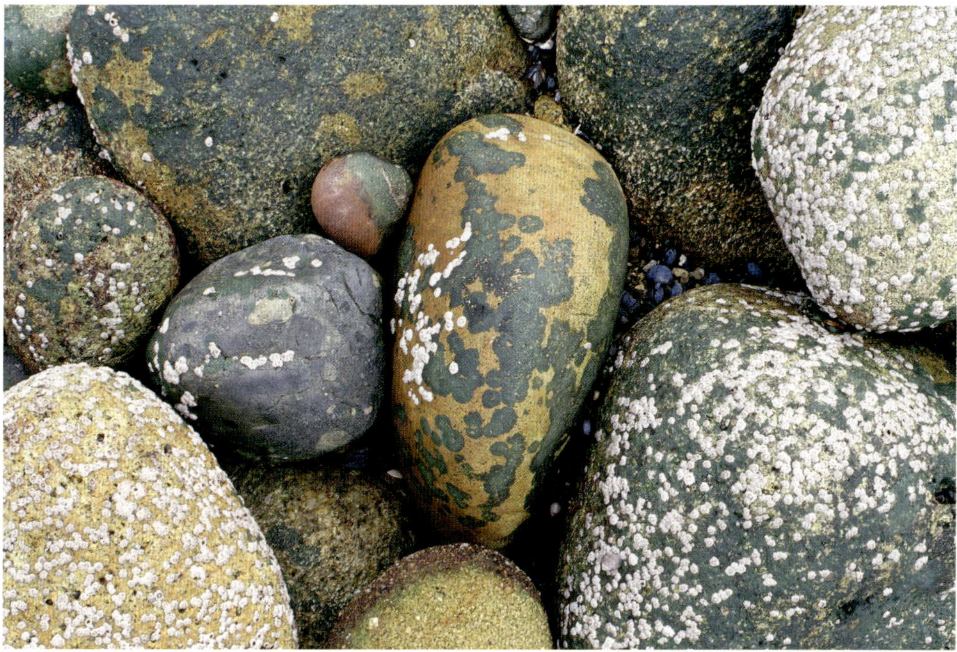

Coloured and encrusted boulders, Machrie Bay, Arran

The Scottish Western Seaboard stretches nearly 500km from the Mull of Galloway in the south to Cape Wrath in the north. If one accounted for the incredibly fretted nature of the coastline with its often deep, fjord-like lochs and inlets, then the true length of the coast is probably ten times this distance. The central section facing the Hebridean Islands, taken for the purposes of this book as being from Arran to Clashnessie Bay in Sutherland, is undoubtedly the most dramatic and scenically exciting coastline in Britain and acts as a marvellous starting point for Hebridean exploration. It sets the scene to describe the Hebrides and places the islands in their true context of being at the very western edge of European civilisation.

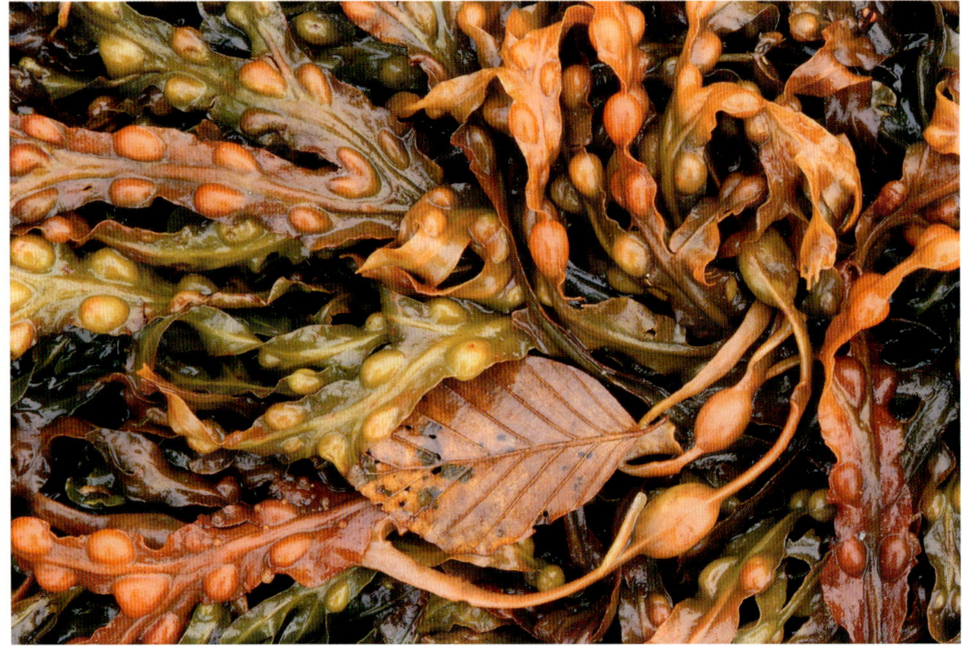

Seaweed and beech leaf, Portnacroish, Appin.

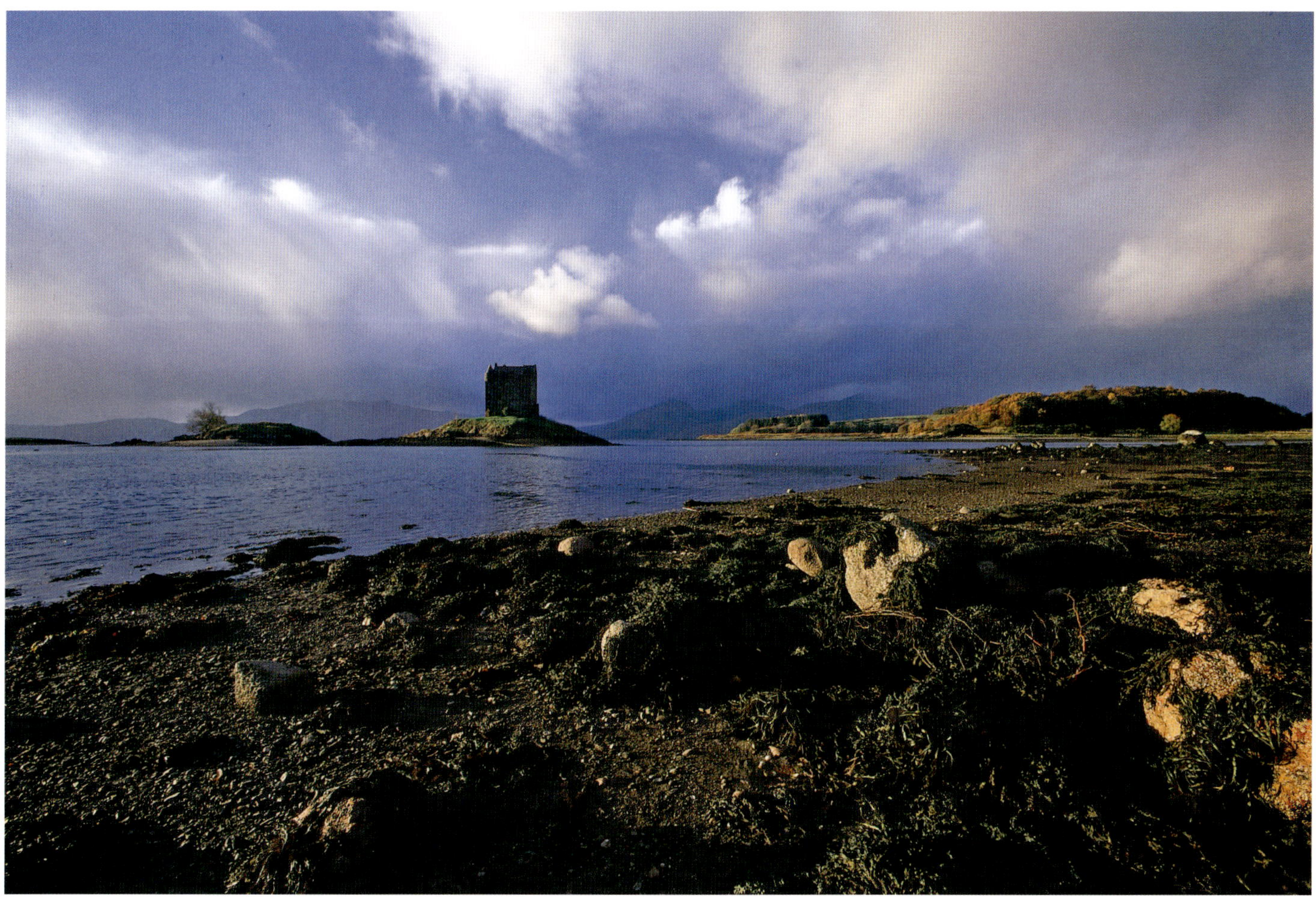

Sunlight and showers, Castle Stalker, Appin. Situated on its own minute and rocky island tantalisingly only a few metres from the Appin coast and lapped by the waters of Loch Linnhe and Loch Laich, the castle with its rectangular keep was built in the thirteenth century by the MacDougalls but like most Scottish castles was at the centre of a history of considerable feuding and inter-clan rivalry with much blood-letting in the process. To the west, opposite the now restored building, Loch Linnhe reaches the shores of Morvern and the islands of Lismore and Mull.

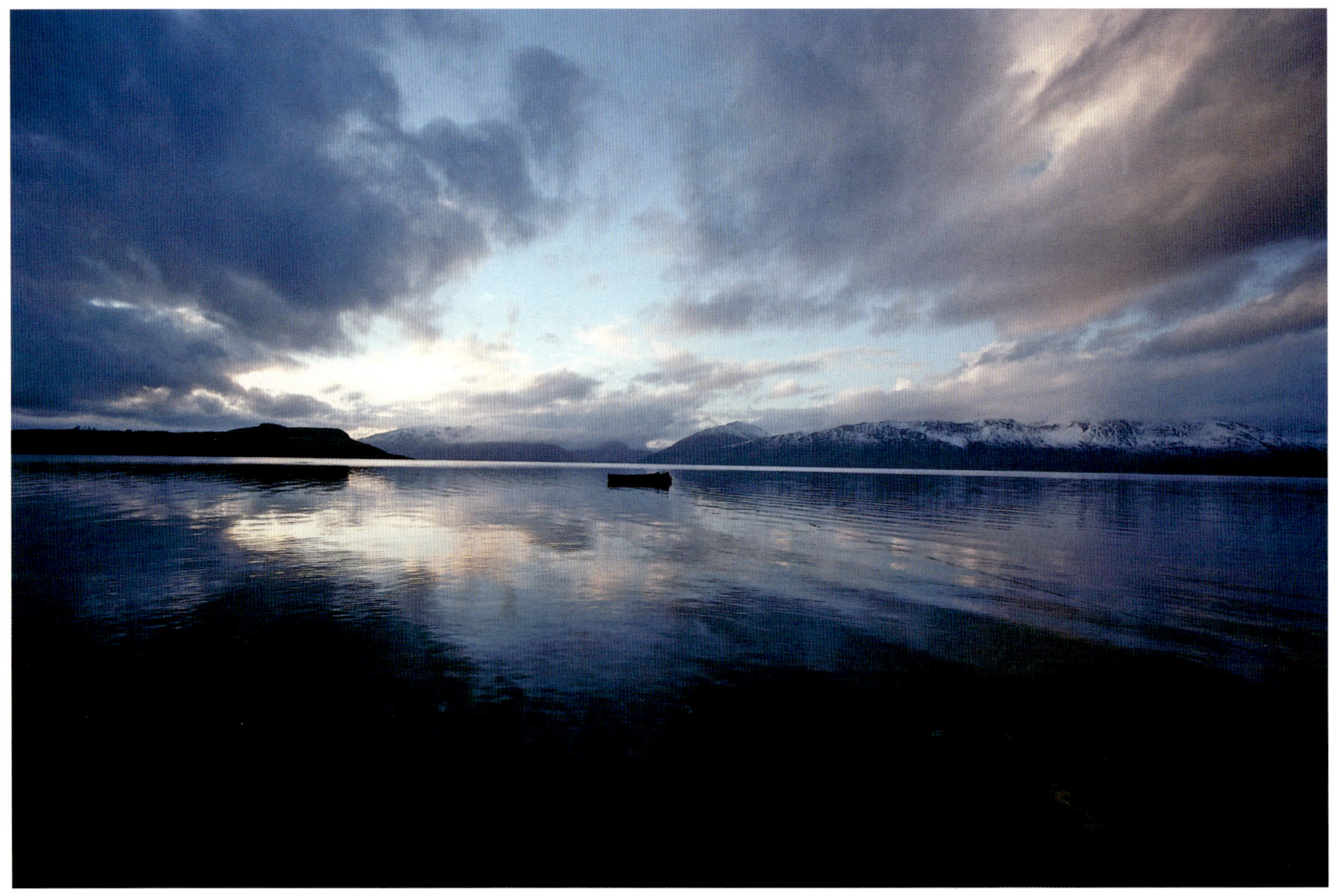

Late afternoon light on Loch Linnhe looking west towards the distant snow-capped hills of Morvern and Mull and with the northern shore of Shuna Island to the left of the photograph.

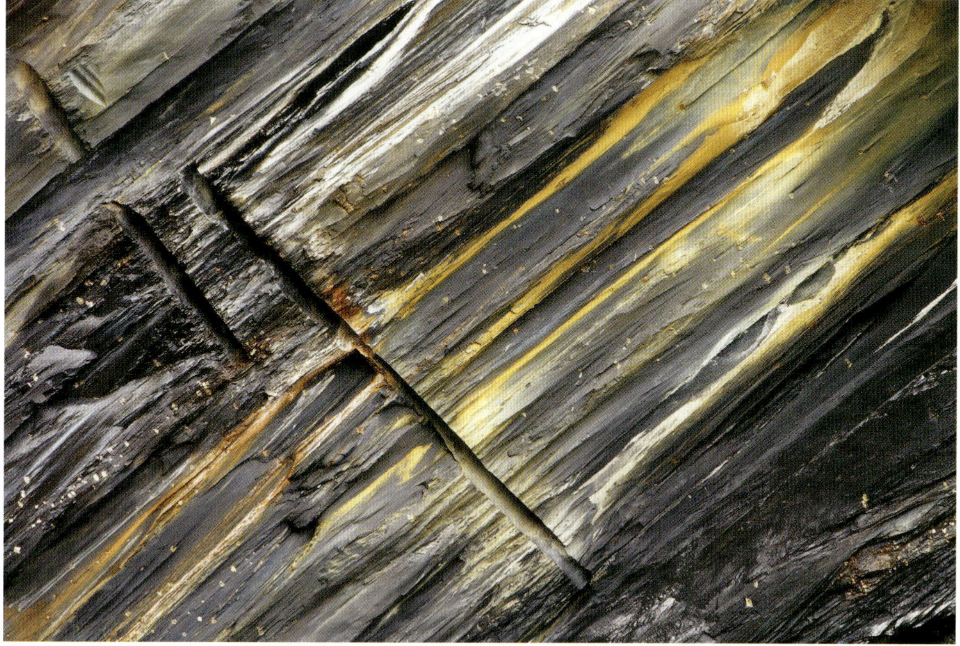

Rock section with drilling marks, Ballachulish slate quarry. The straggling village of Ballachulish is set on the shores of Loch Leven near the loch's outlet through the narrow straits of Ballachulish to Loch Linnhe. At one time the village was particularly famed for its slate quarries, opened in the seventeenth century but now closed and partly landscaped. On the shores of Loch Leven and surrounding the deep quarries, heaps of refuse slate still give an indication of the extent of the industry once carried out here. Only a short distance inland from the village lies the foot of the dramatic and infamous Glencoe.

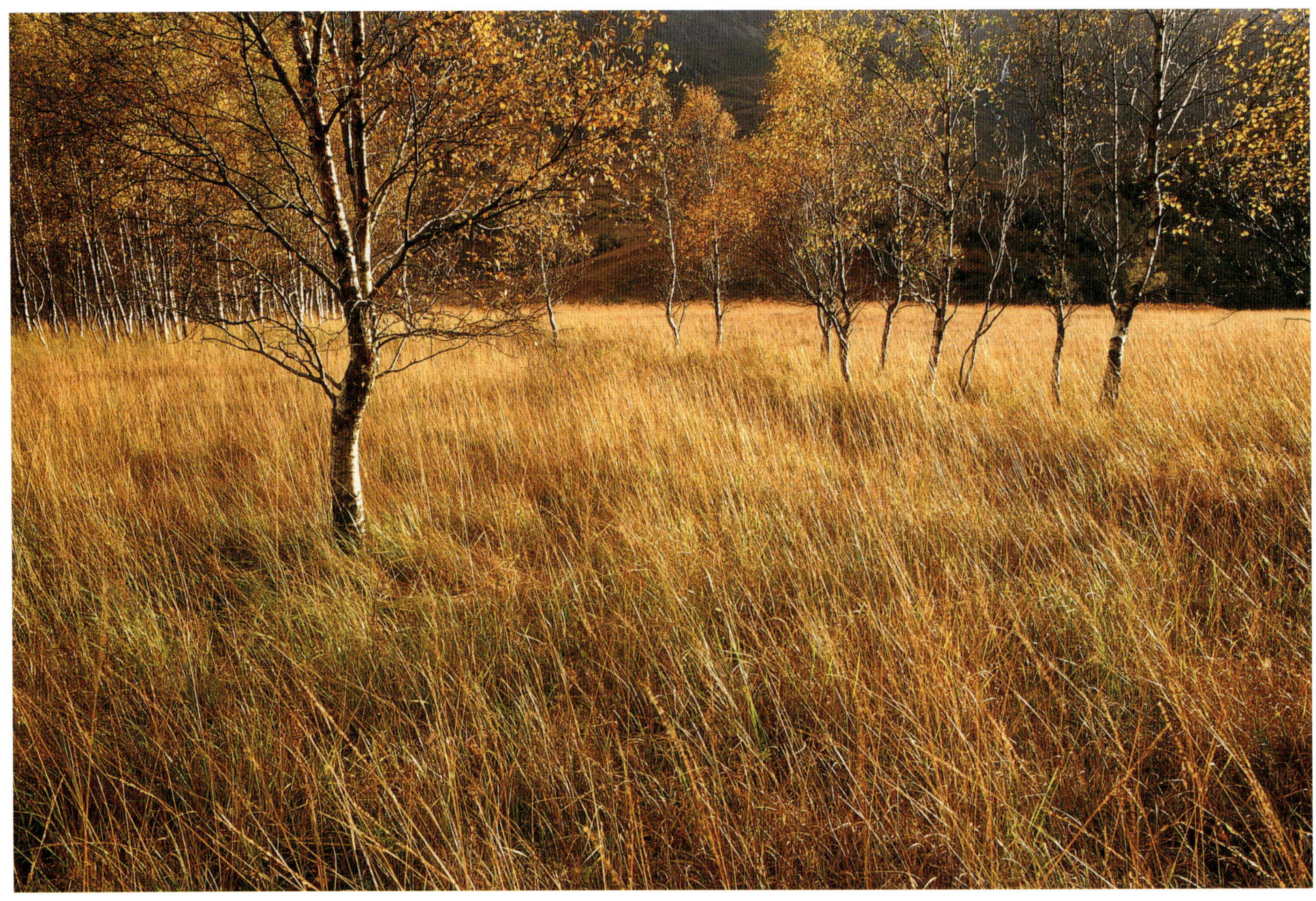

Golden colour and autumnal light on a stand of silver birch trees near the shores of Loch Leven.

Opposite: Early morning reflections in Loch Leven looking towards the 742m Pap of Glencoe from the Ballachulish shore. The loch extends inland on the left as far as Kinlochleven whilst on the right the hills rise steadily towards nearby Glencoe.

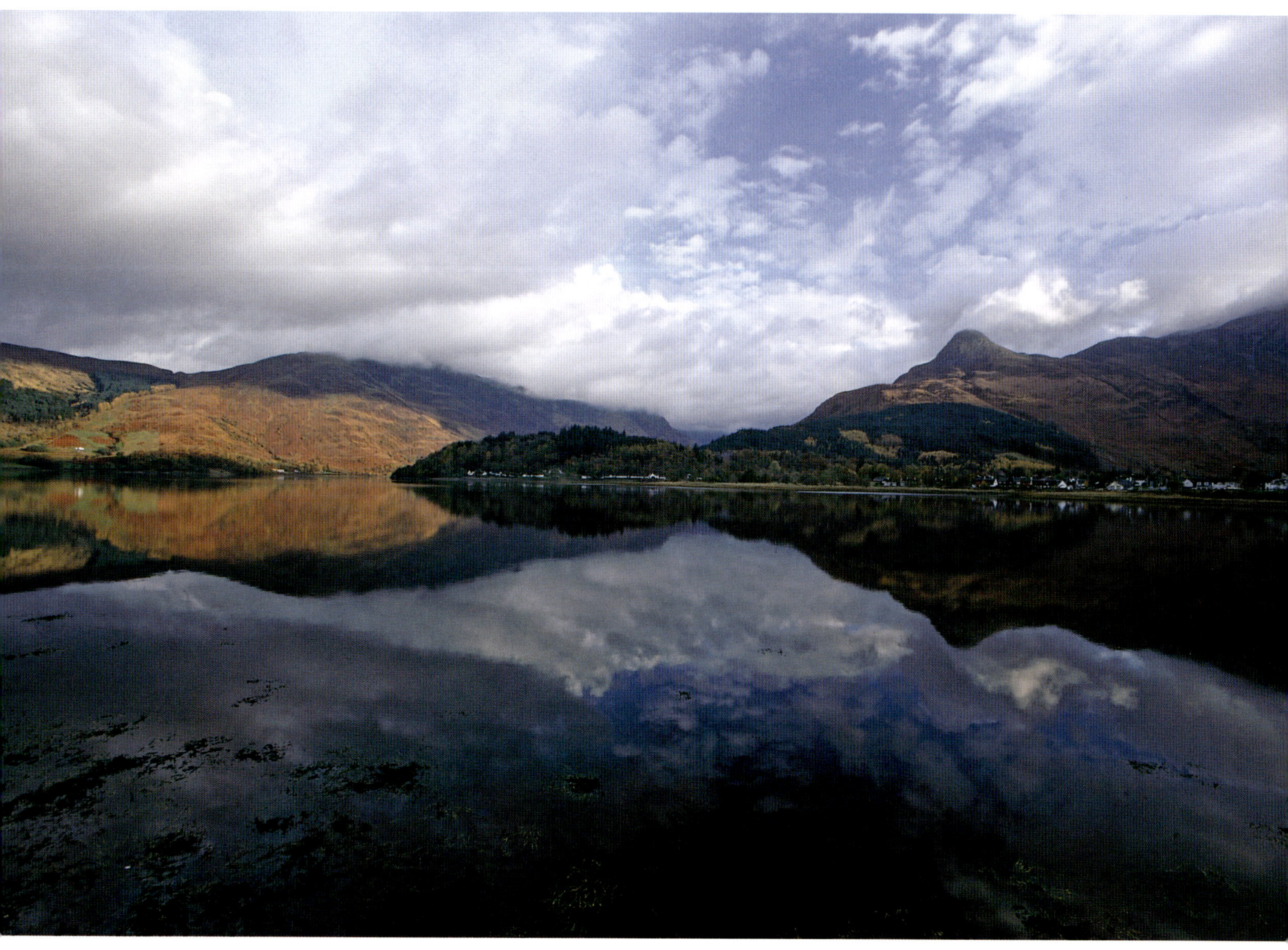

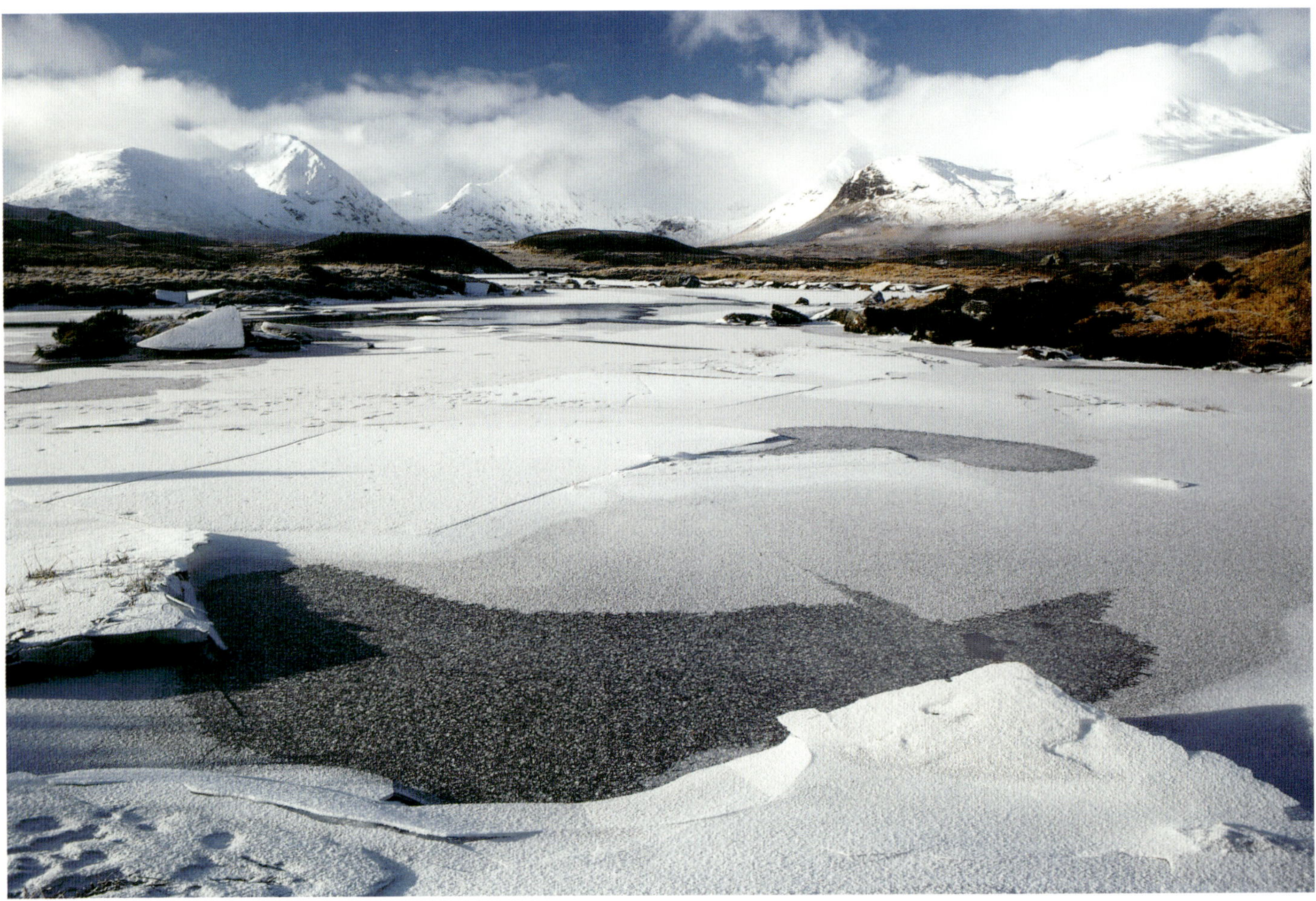

Approaching the Glencoe region from inland and the south involves the crossing of the desolate Rannoch Moor via the A82 trunk road. Normally shrouded in low cloud or swept by almost horizontal rain the moor can, on occasions, have a magical quality, particularly during the winter when its numerous lochans are often frozen and the surrounding moorland and mountains are covered in a fresh mantle of snow. The photograph shows the view looking west across Lochan na Stainge towards the sunlit peaks of Clach Leathad, Stob Ghabhar and Meall Odhar.

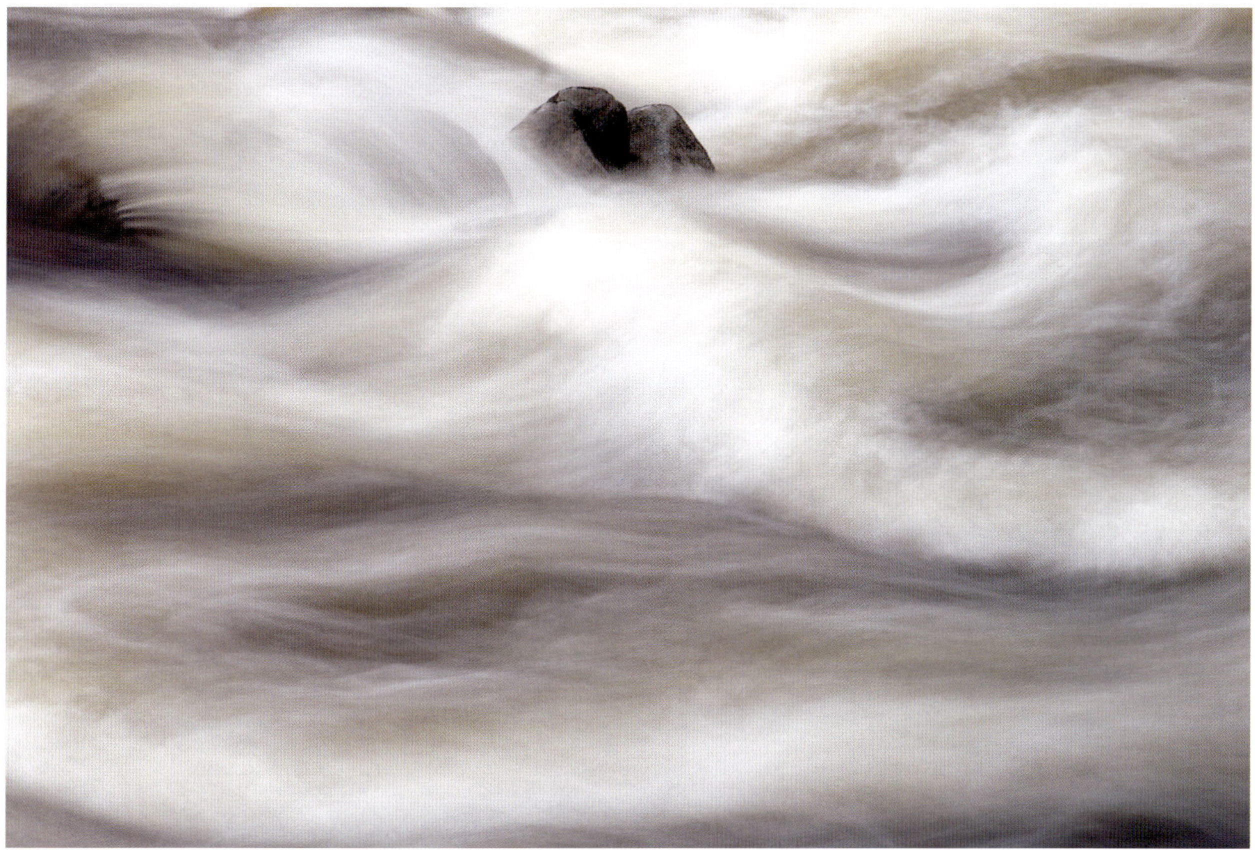

Melt water on the River Etive.

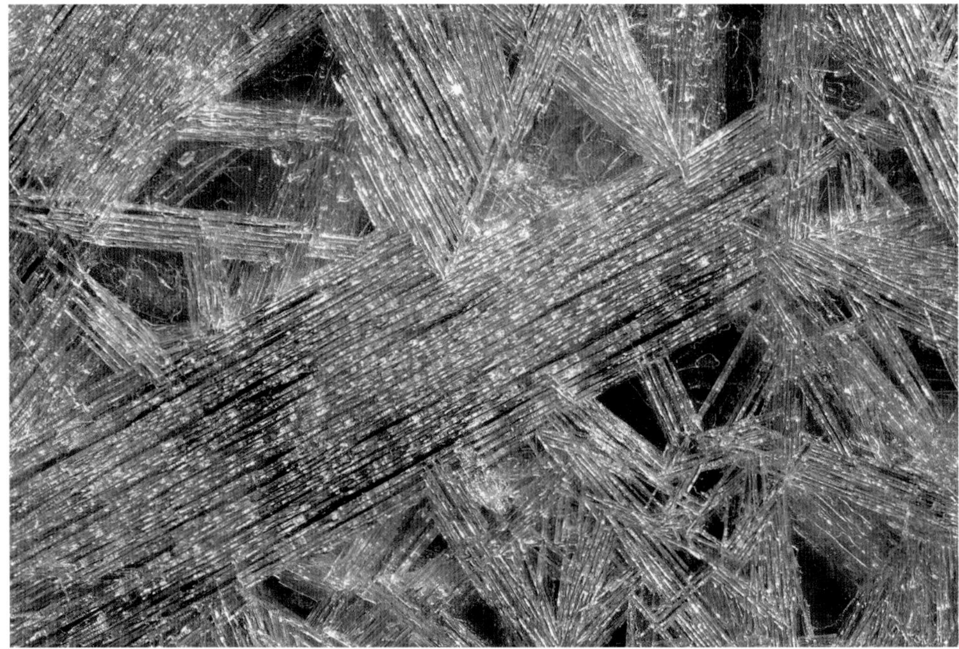

Ice design near Alltchaorunn, Glen Etive.

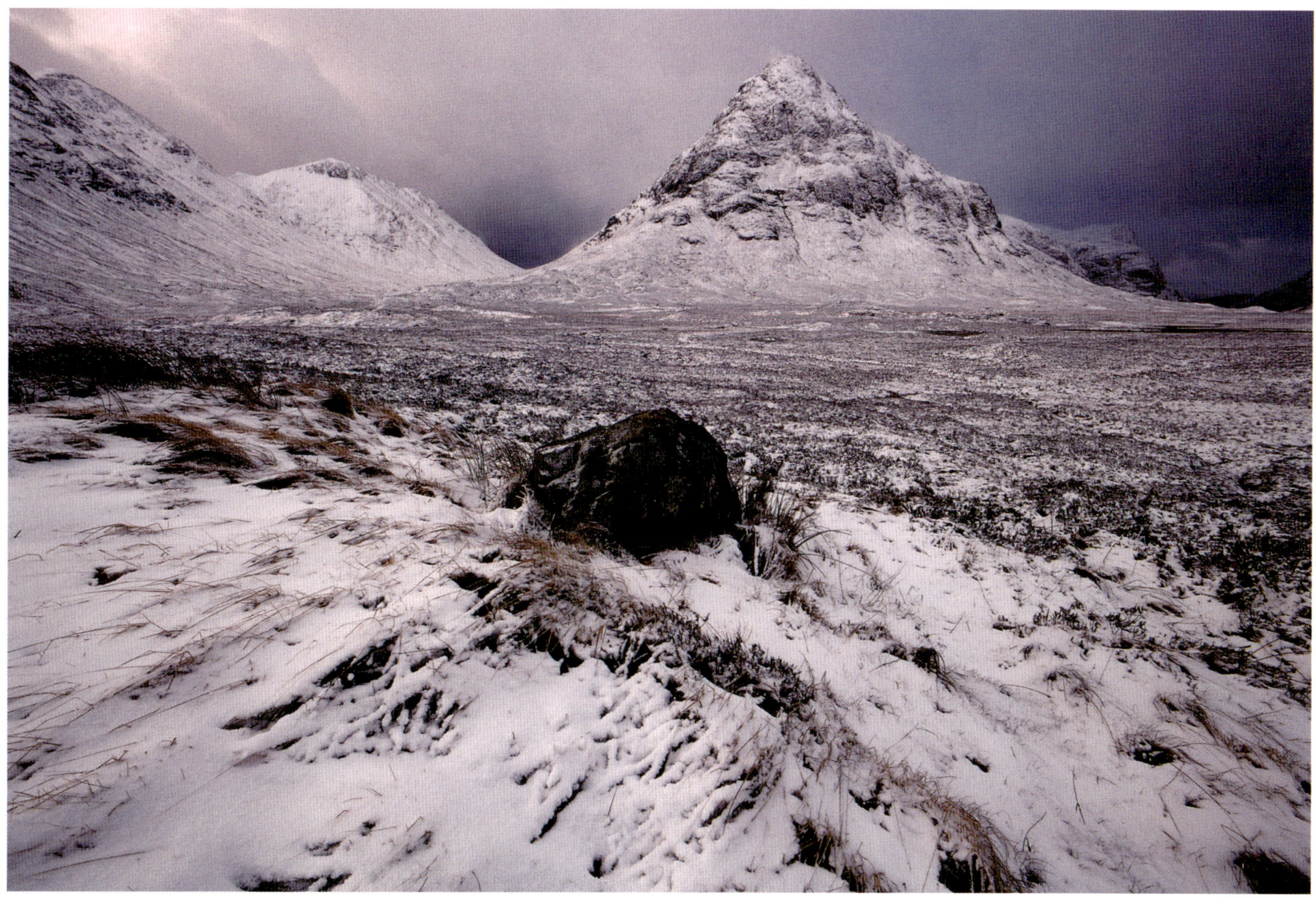

A ghostly warm early morning light on wintry Buachaille Etive Beag at the entrance to Glencoe heralds approaching sleet showers. One of Scotland's wildest and most famous glens, Glencoe has also been known as the 'Glen of Weeping' due to the infamous massacre in 1692 of the MacDonalds by soldiers under a Campbell commander. Acting as a deep trough within magnificent mountain scenery and with dramatic rock buttresses either side, the glen is often filled with cloud or mist adding to the pathos of its notorious history. In sunshine and clear light however, it is a mecca for climbers and walkers enjoying the surrounding peaks such as the 1150m Bidean nam Bian, Argyll's highest mountain or the narrow 6km long precipitous Aonach Eagach ridge on the north face of the glen.

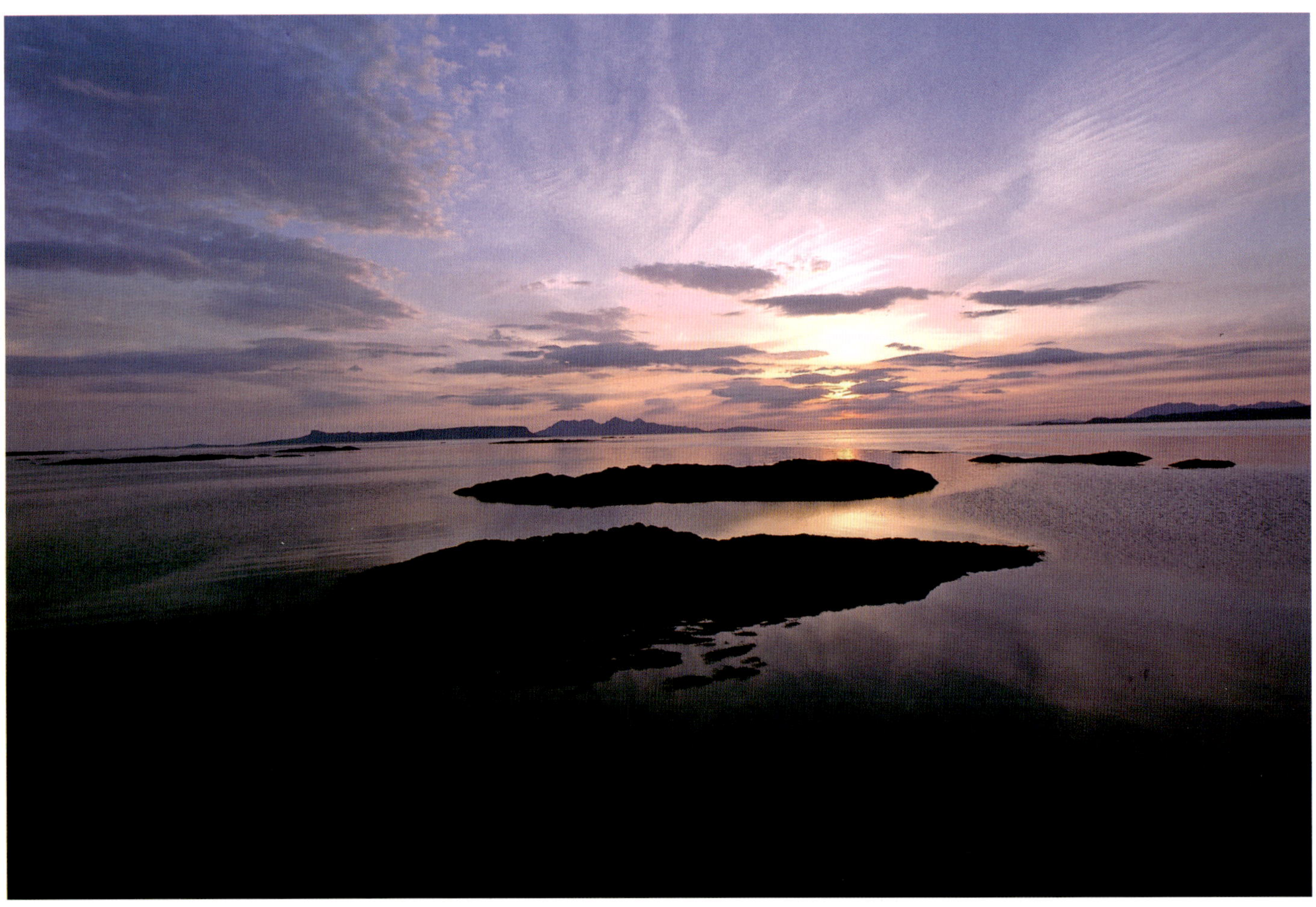

Sunset over the islands of Rum and Eigg viewed from Portnaluchaig near Arisaig. Between here and the Morar estuary the numerous bays and coves are often described as 'the silver sands of Morar' where the dunes, machair and outstanding sea views begin to take on a certain Hebridean character. It was near Arisaig that Prince Charles Edward Stuart landed in July 1745 to subsequently lead the 1745 Jacobite rising. He later fled from here in September 1746 after the disaster of Culloden. Loch Morar has the distinction of having the deepest inland water in Britain.

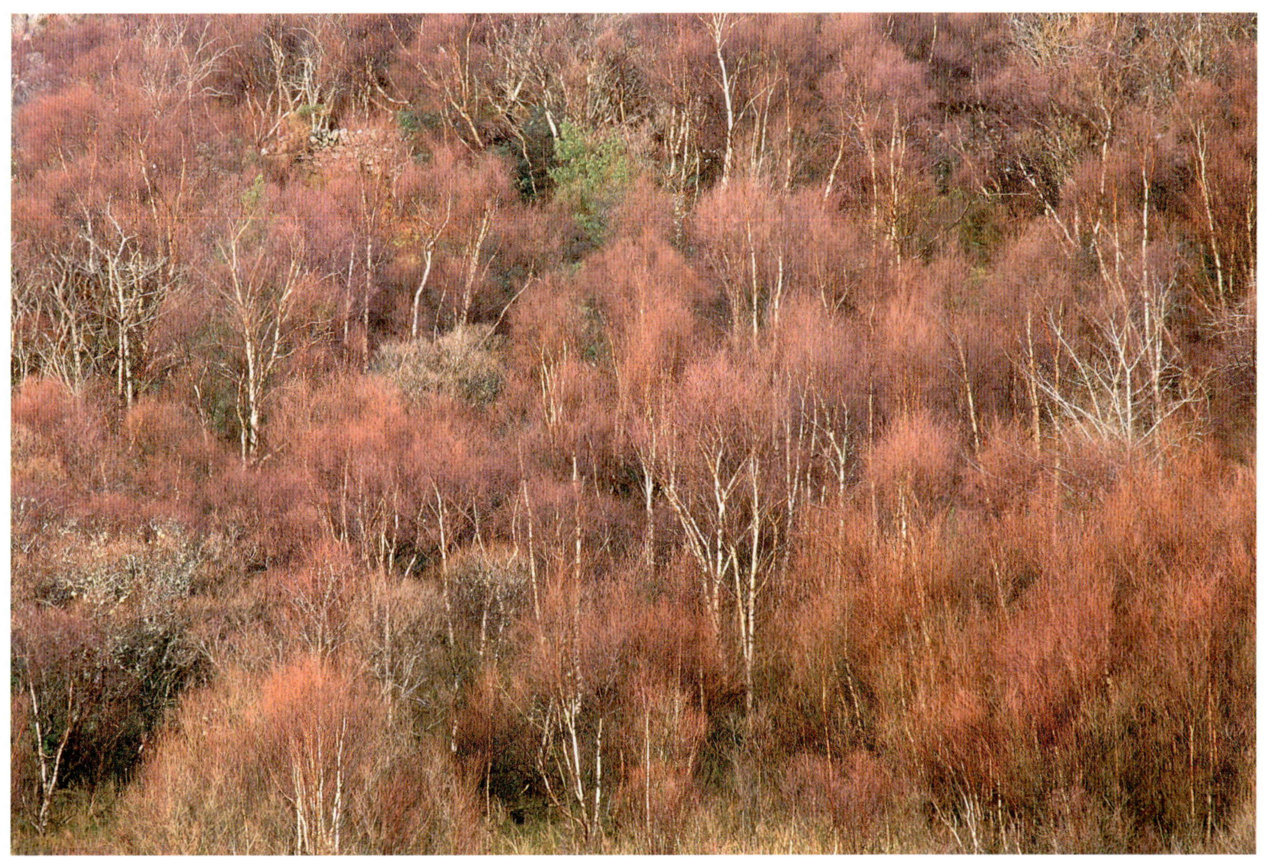

Silver birch trees in winter tones, Plockton.

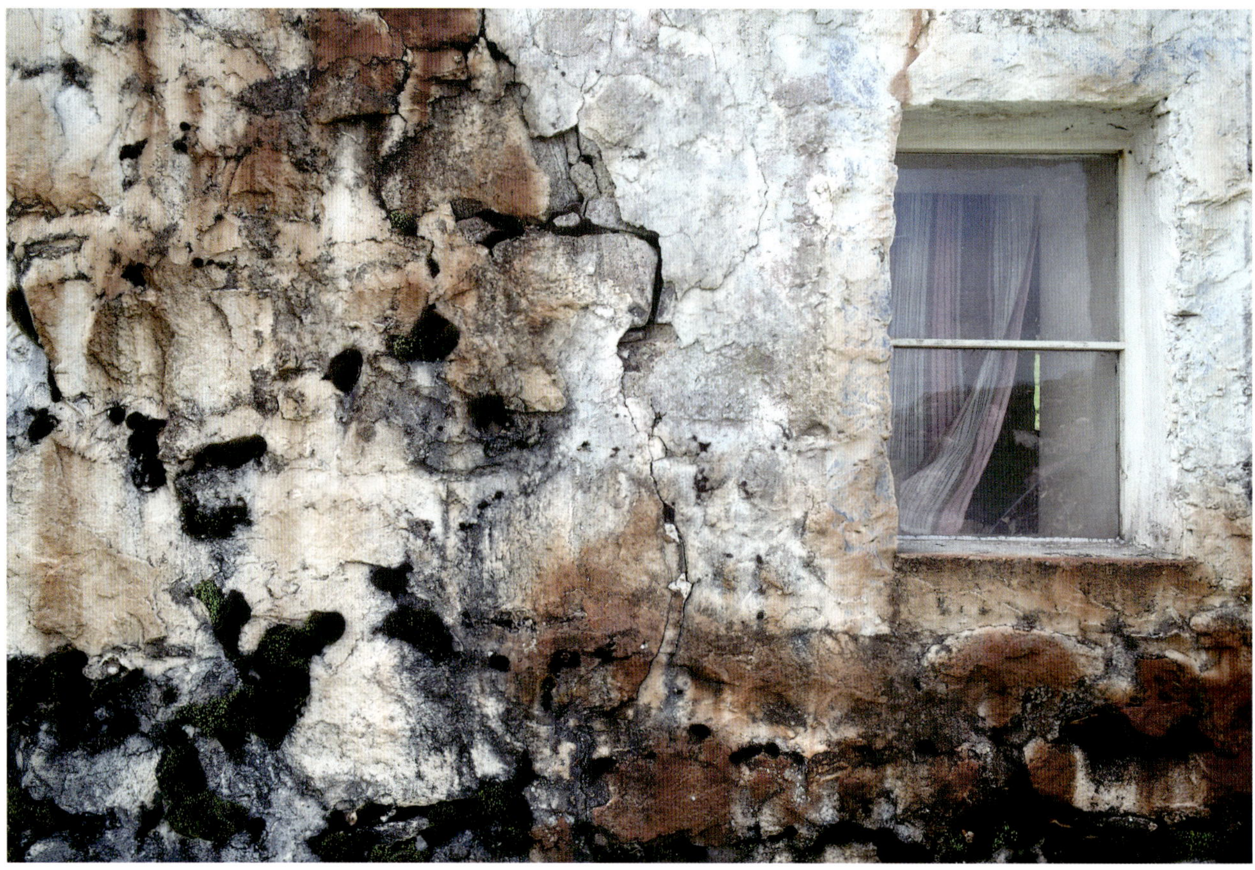

Deserted croft cottage, Applecross peninsula. North of Loch Carron the Highlands start to take on a harder character. The soil becomes increasingly infertile and the landscape wilder, more windswept and devoid of human civilisation. The dramatic road over the Bealach na Bà pass to Applecross with its numerous hair pin bends and steep gradients leads onward to the peninsula coast where a few scattered and isolated hamlets still struggle against the wilder elements for existence.

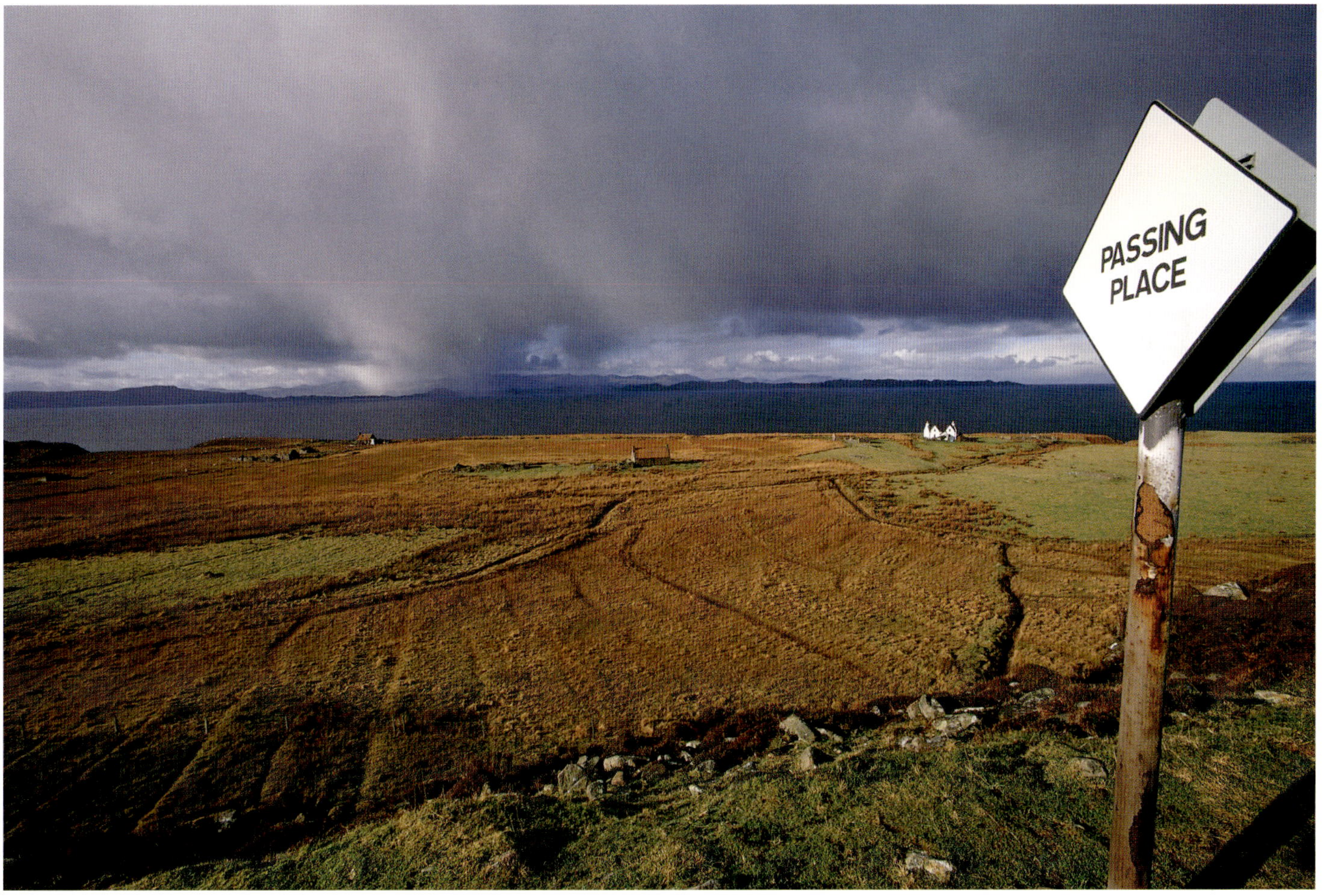

Travelling north from Applecross, the undulating coastal road continues on to Sheildaig within the Torridon region. This view near Lonbain looking towards the islands of Raasay and Skye gives an impression of the nature of this lonely area with its often empty crumbling buildings and abandoned croft land.

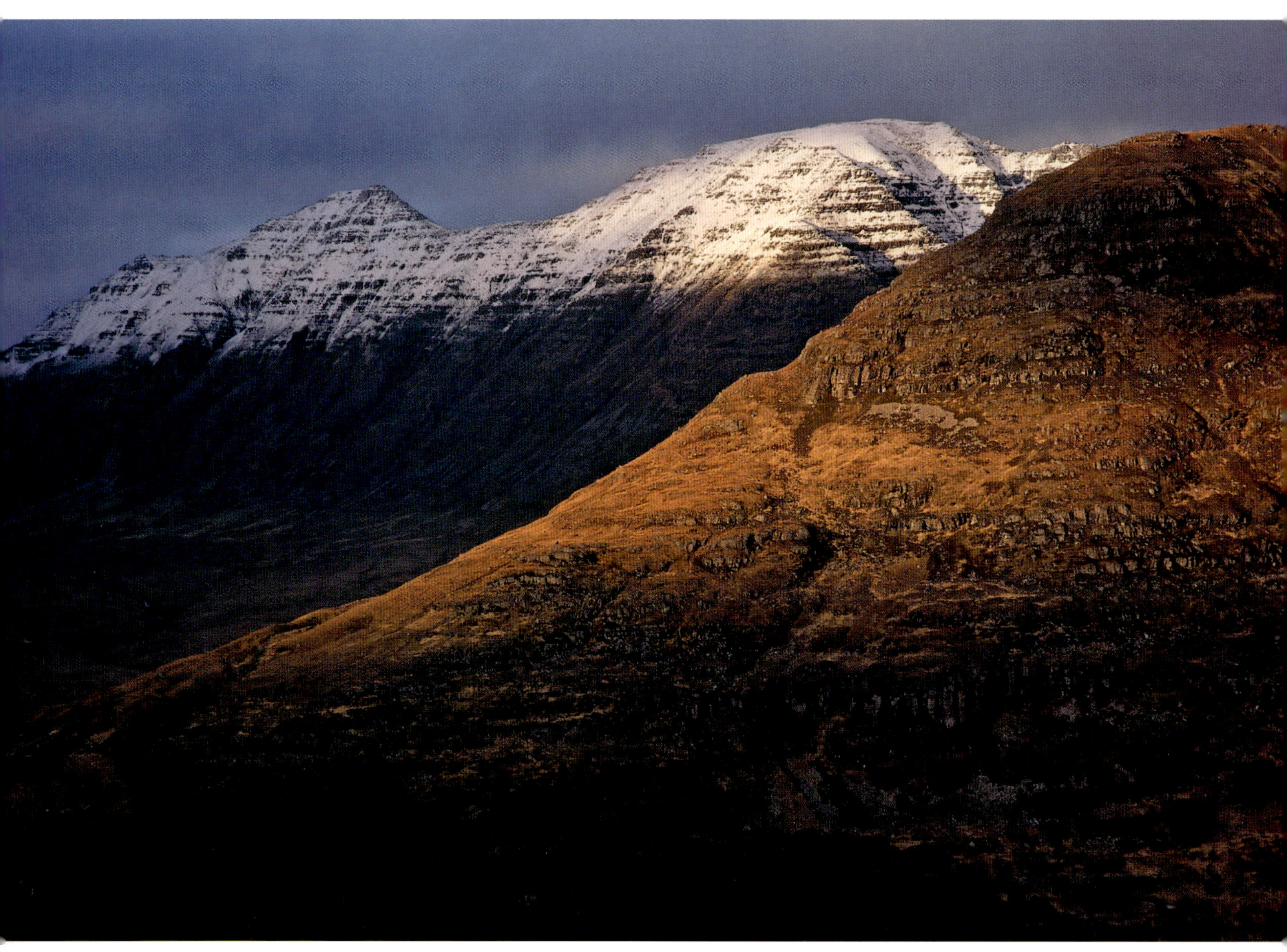

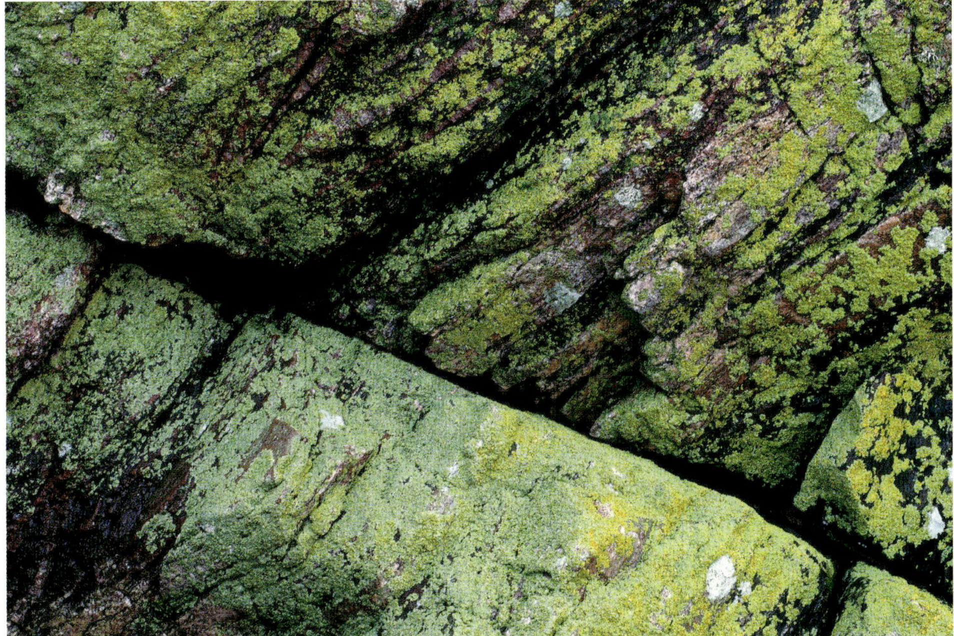

Rock colours, Lower Diabaig.

Opposite: Late afternoon sunshine on the shoulders of Liathach (1024m), and snow-capped Beinn Alligin (985m) viewed from near Sheildaig across Upper Loch Torridon. These mountains together with neighbouring Beinn Eighe form some of the most dramatic scenery in the North West Highlands. For geologists their main interest is the rock itself where the Torridonian sandstone of the mountains rises from platforms of Lewisian Gneiss thought to be the oldest rock known. Another unique feature is the reflective white quartzite capping to many of the higher summits.

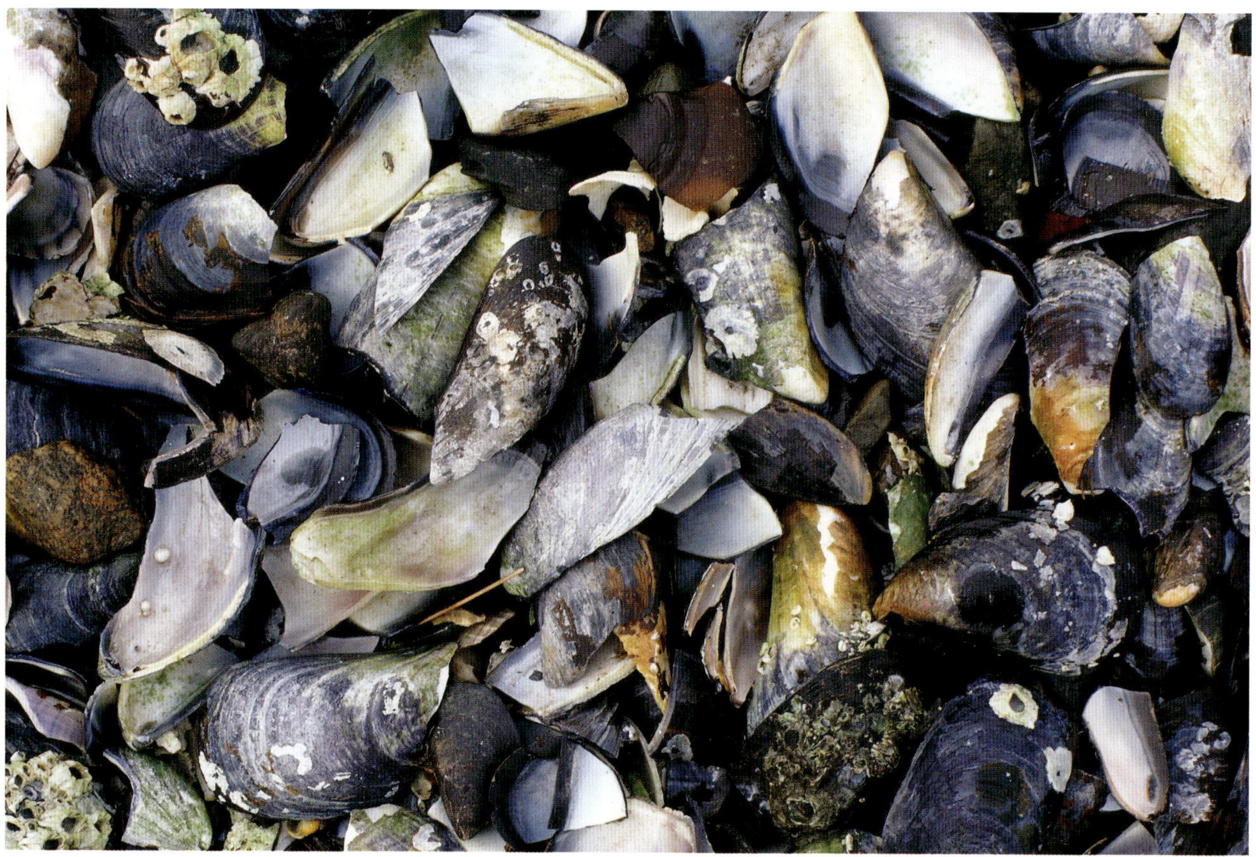

Sea harvest, Lower Diabaig.

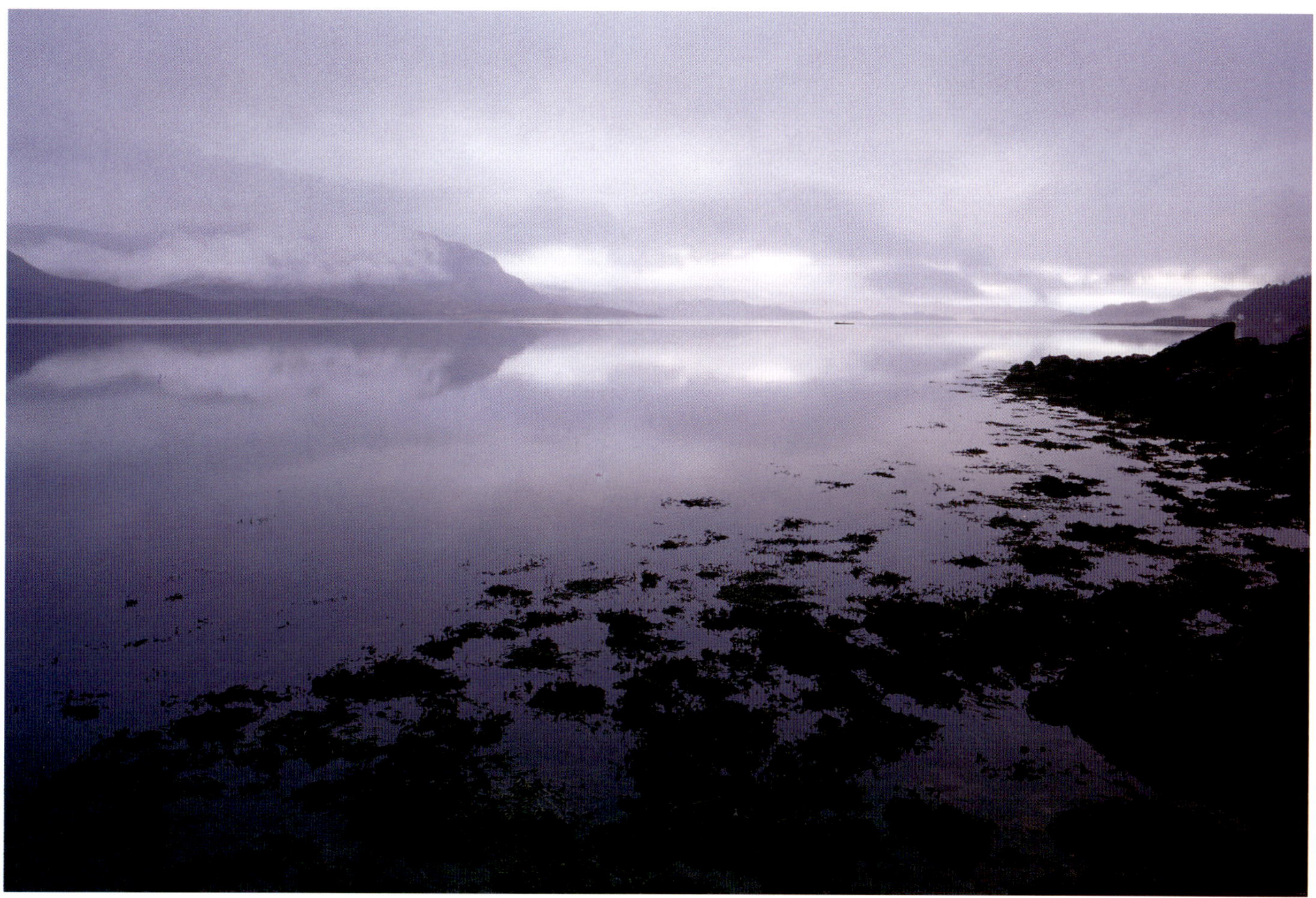

A 'soft' afternoon, Upper Loch Torridon.

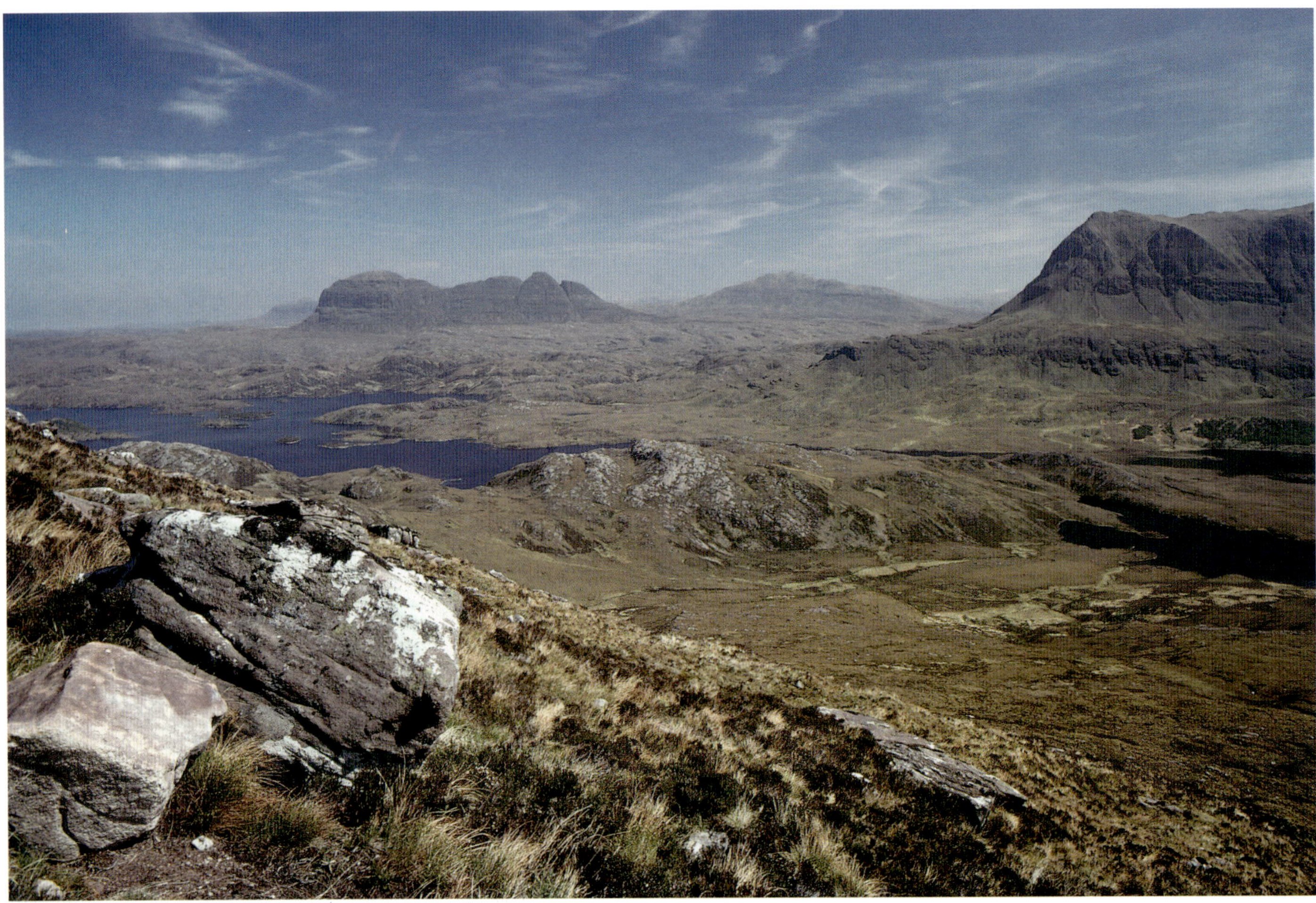

High summer in Sutherland. On a clear day from the 613m, splintered and spired summit of Stac Pollaidh, north of Ullapool, one can see almost to the top of Scotland. From this superb viewpoint the real nature of the Sutherland landscape becomes apparent with its desert of moorland and rock broken only by numerous small rivers and lochans and the strange upstanding silhouettes of the isolated mountains rearing up from their surrounds. In this view the peaks of Suilven, Cul Mor, Canisp and Quinag can be clearly seen.

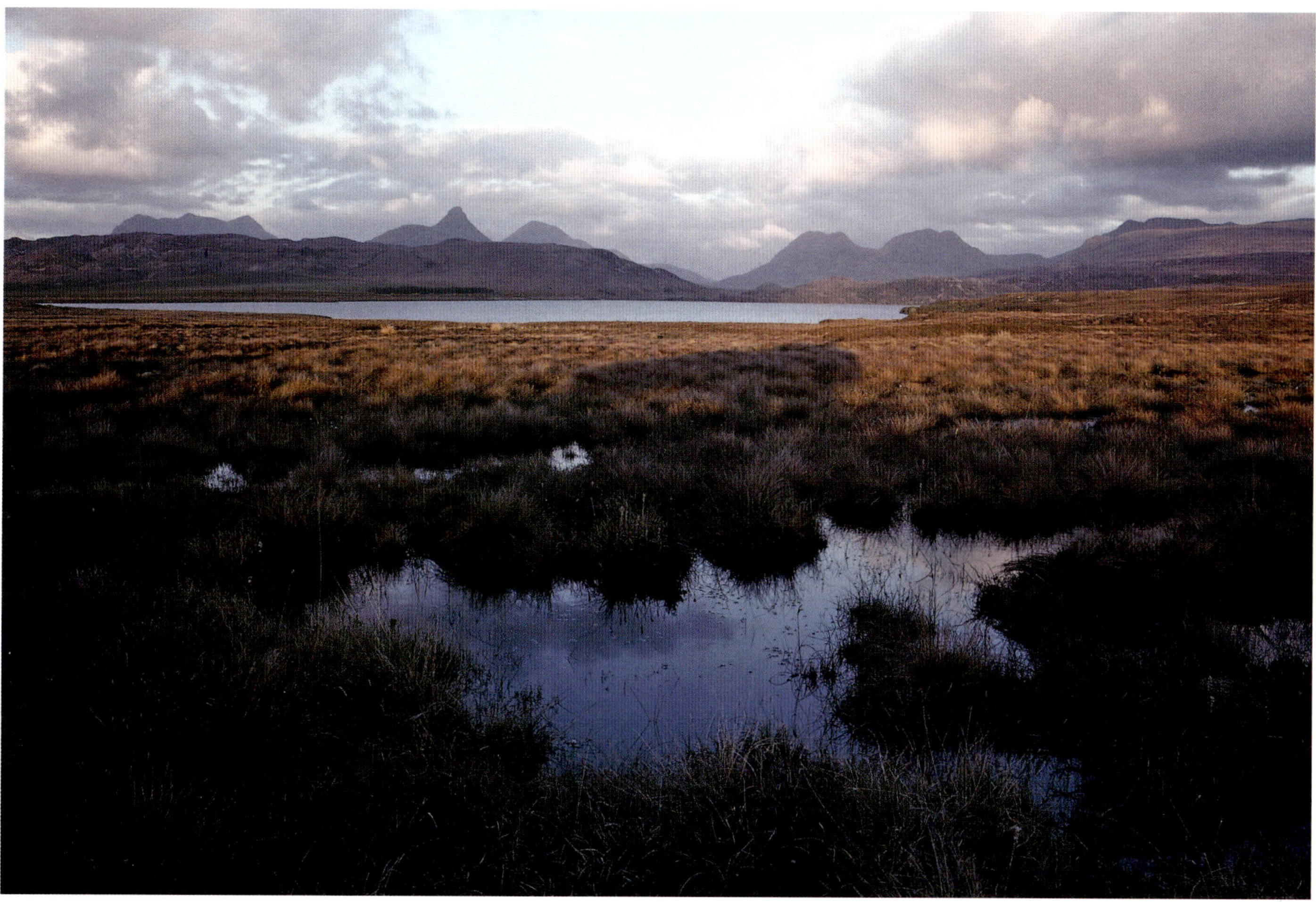

Another more distant view looking north east from Achnahaird on the Coigach peninsula across typically boggy Sutherland ground towards the same mountains. The wild, desolate landscape of this entire area is for many one of the most unspoilt regions of Scotland and one of the last great areas of wilderness left in Britain. At nearby Achiltibuie, boat trips can be taken to the now deserted Summer Isles.

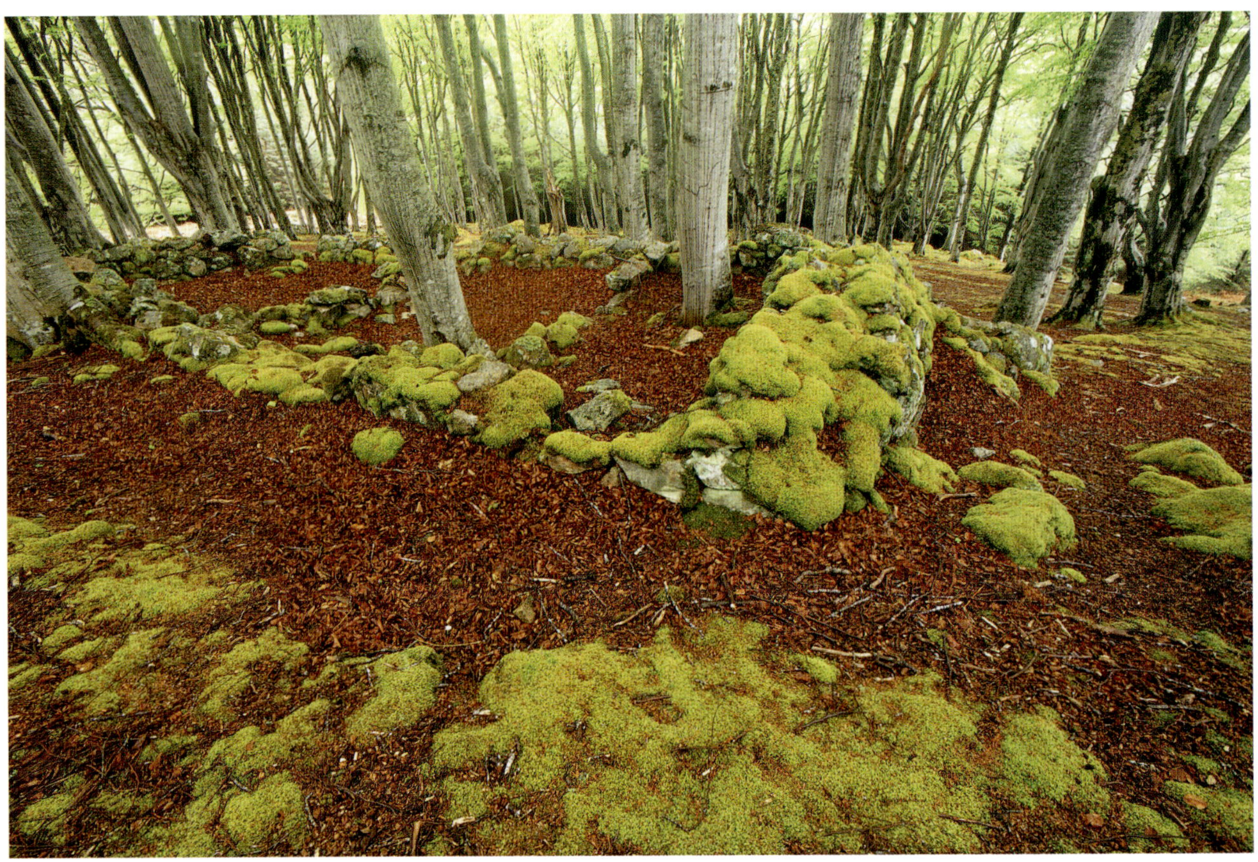

Trees grow up through moss-covered walls and remains of abandoned buildings in a small wood near Little Gruinard above the coast of Gruinard Bay. Many of these structures would once have been occupied by tenants subsequently cleared from their homes during the infamous Highland Clearances of the nineteenth century when people were forcibly evicted from their land in favour of sheep farming. Now regarded as one of the most shameful episodes of British history, the effect of the clearances is still apparent all over the Highlands and Islands where signs of original habitation can be found and where the memories, passed down through generations, still live on.

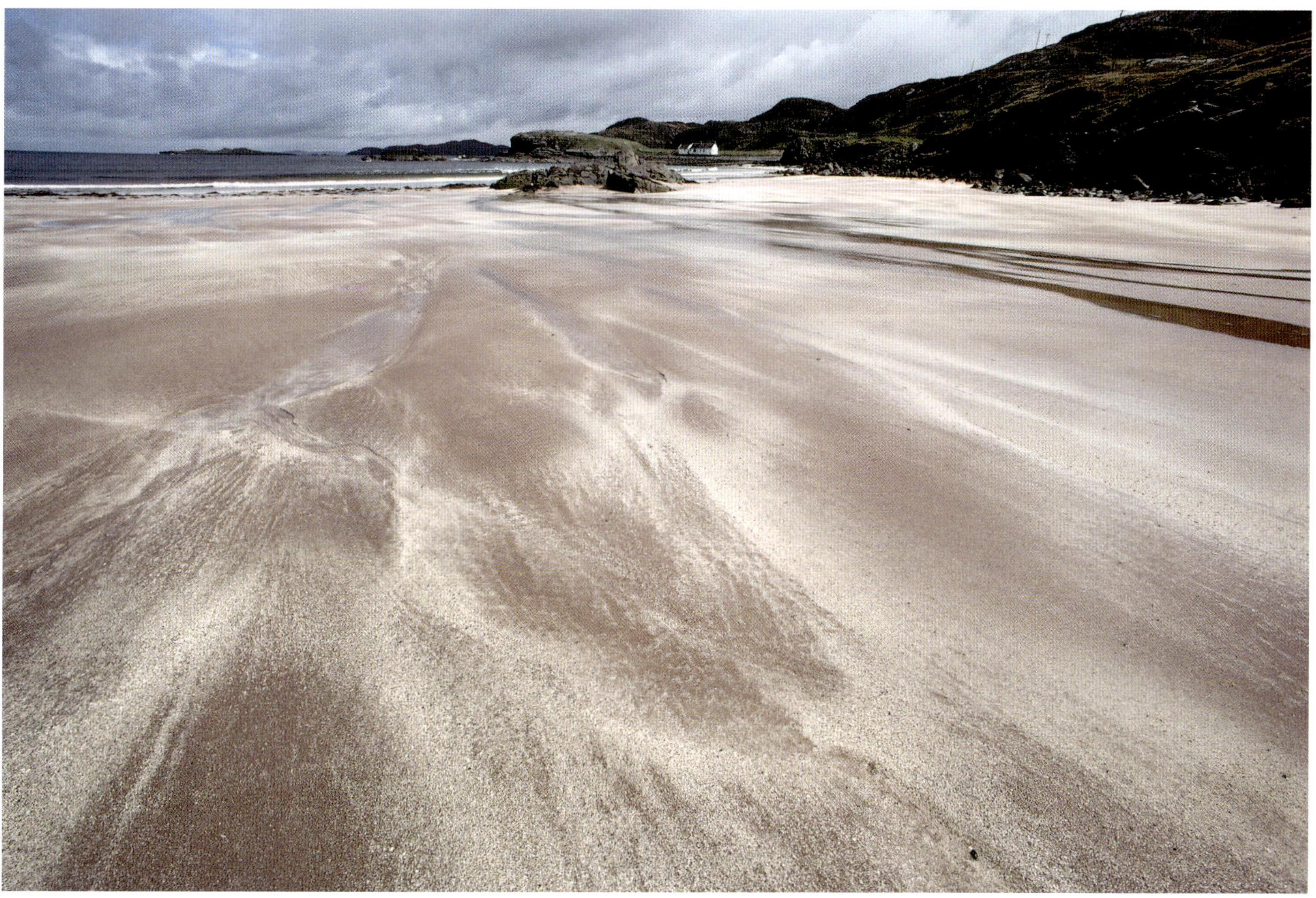

The broad pinkish sands of Clashnessie Bay on the Rhu Stoer peninsula face outwards to the larger Eddrachillis Bay studded with small islands and a favourite haunt of lobster fishermen. From here onwards the Sutherland coastline stretches via Scourie, Kinlochbervie and in particular the bays of Oldshoremore and Sandwood to its final turning point at Cape Wrath. Only the Faeroe Islands lie further to the north but to the west the Hebrides await.

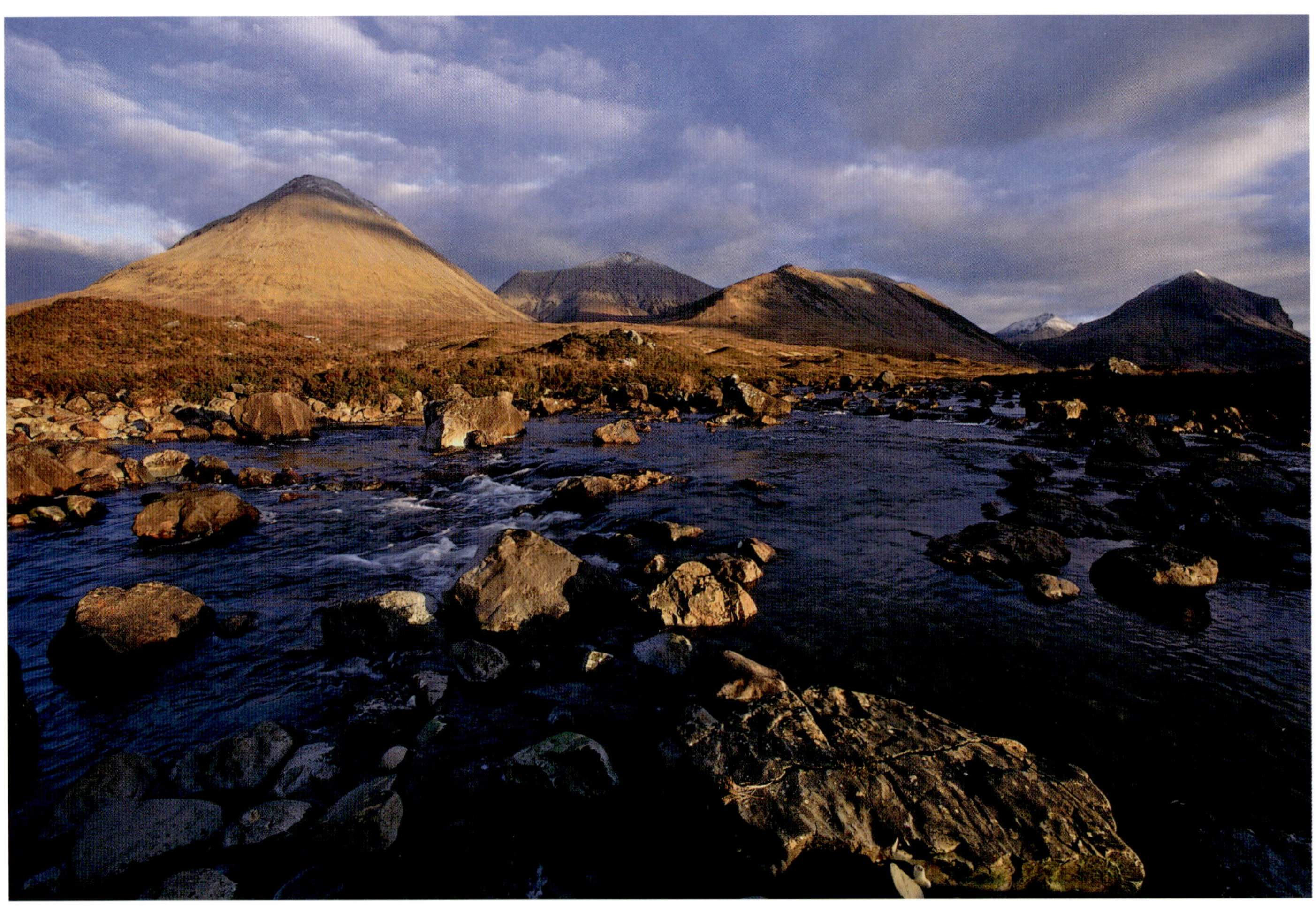

Clearing skies at Sligachan as the late afternoon light bathes the slopes of Glamaig and the Red Hills. In the distance Marsco and Bla Bheinn still have a dusting of snow on their summits. With easy access to both the Red Hills and the dramatic Black Cuillin range, Sligachan is one of the most popular centres on Skye for climbers and walkers although in recent years the emphasis for climbers has possibly shifted to Glen Brittle. Numerous walks radiate out from Sligachan, most notably the track through Glen Sligachan to Loch Scavaig whilst only 5km away the most northerly of the Cuillin peaks, Sgurr nan Gillean rises to a height of 964m.

Mountain, Moor and Mood
SKYE

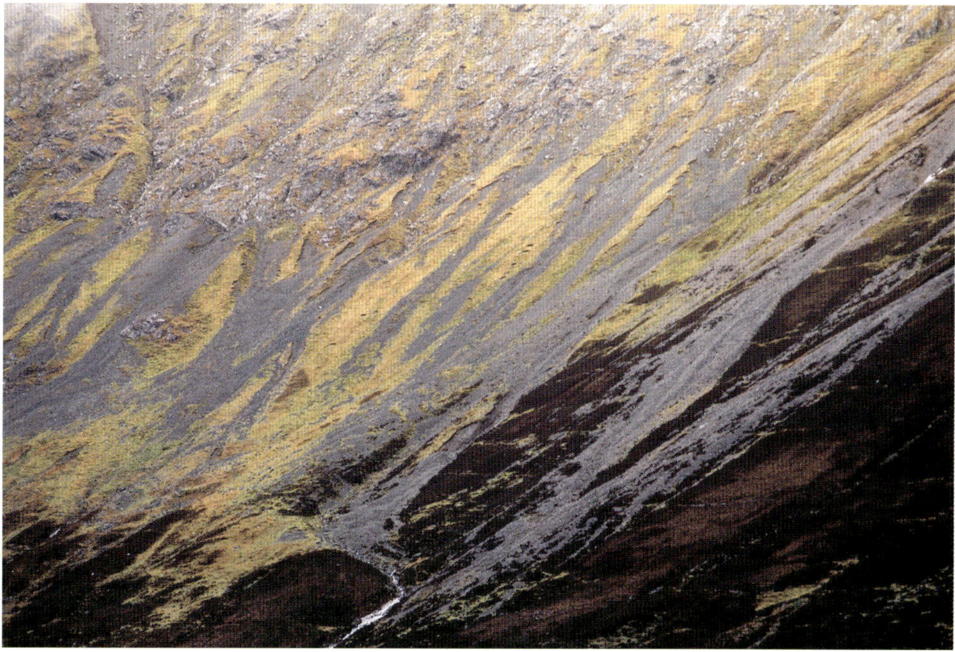

Colour and texture on the slopes of Glamaig.

Skye is undoubtedly the most well known of the Hebridean Islands and since being linked to the mainland at Kyle of Lochalsh by the new Skye bridge, it has become even more popular and accessible. It is often the first Hebridean island to be explored by the visitor. The island is almost 120km long yet no part of the land is more than 10km from the sea due to its deeply riven coastline. Often known as the 'misty isle' it is for the greater part bare and treeless with a high moorland interior dominated by the horseshoe-shaped Black Cuillin range of mountains with their spiky, jagged peaks rising almost 1000m. In the south the peninsula of Sleat (the garden of Skye) proves the exception with its many small deciduous and coniferous woodlands reaching almost down to the sea. In the north the slightly softer but more windblown Duirinish, Waternish and Trotternish peninsulas with their dramatic cliffs and stacks point the way towards the Outer Hebrides (or Western Isles) some 30km to the west. Unusually for a Hebridean island, most of the beaches are an unattractive grey/black stone or sand.

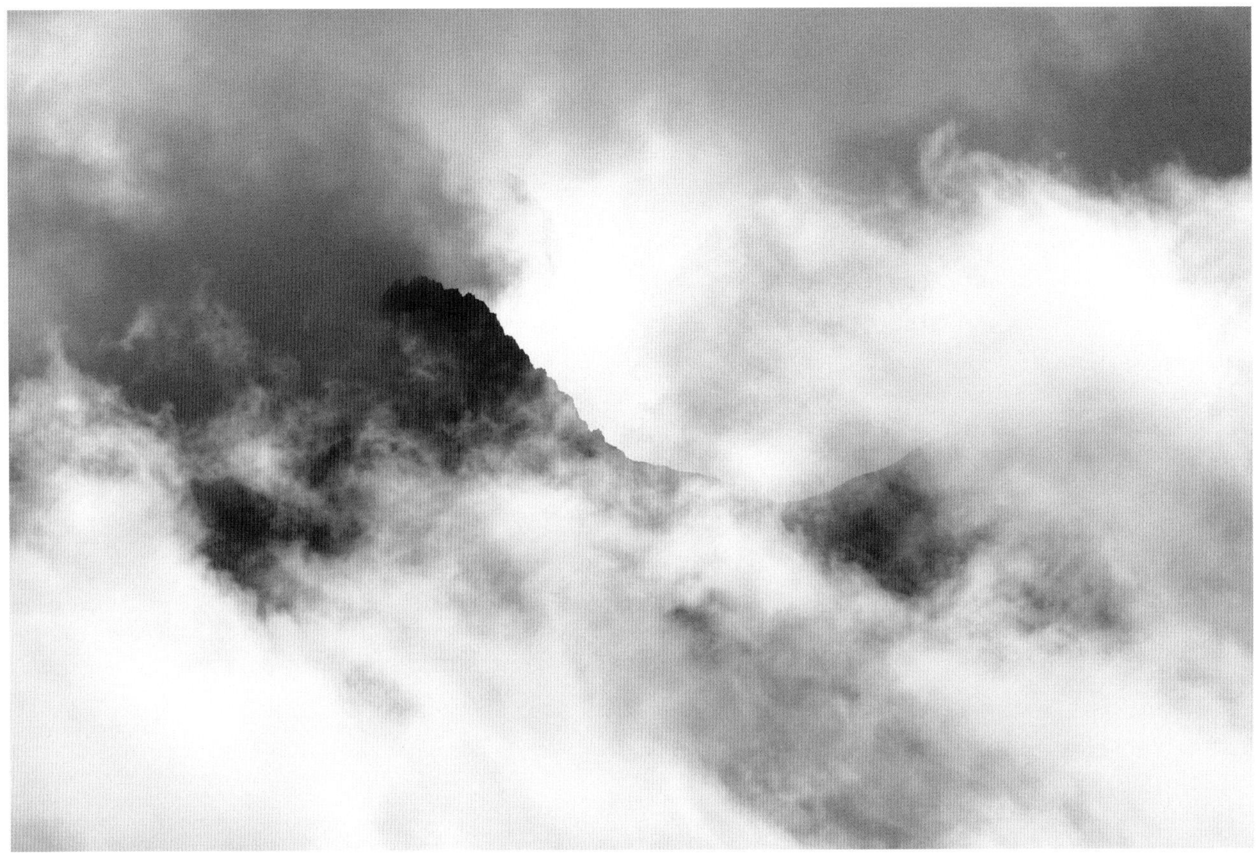

One of the craggy Black Cuillin summits appears tantalisingly through a break in low cloud seen from above Sligachan. Described as the most exciting mountains in Britain, the 13km traverse of the main ridge is generally regarded as the finest days' mountaineering in the country. Few of the peaks can be reached without rock climbing skills and therefore most walkers adhere to the surrounding valleys or lower slopes. The summit of Bruach na Frithe (958m) is one of the principal exceptions reached after a 7km walk from Sligachan. Over the centuries these ice-carved hills have provided inspiration for numerous artists, writers, poets and photographers. The late Gaelic poet Sorley MacLean wrote of 'the exact and serrated blue ramparts' of the Cuillins and it is this interplay of cloud, light and colour together with the very profiles of the peaks that provides so much fascination.

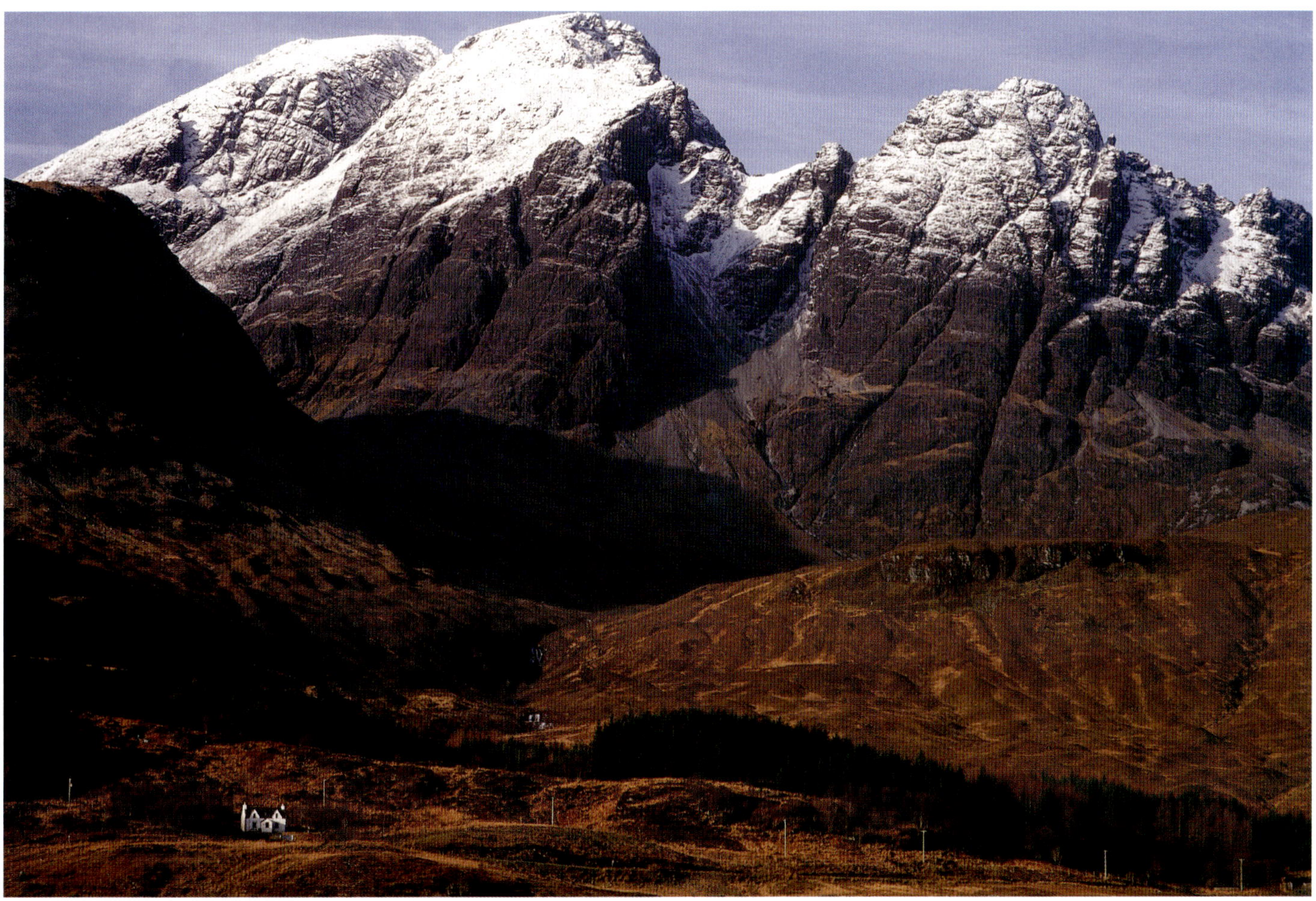

On a glorious winter's day the snow-capped summit of Bla Bheinn rears up from the shores of Loch Slapin. Although isolated by Glen Sligachan from the main Cuillin ridge, this outlying mountain is generally classified as one of the Black Cuillin and popular with both walkers and climbers. From its 928m summit the view is one of the very best in the entire Highlands and Islands extending over the whole of Skye, much of the nearby mainland and out towards many of the other Hebridean islands.

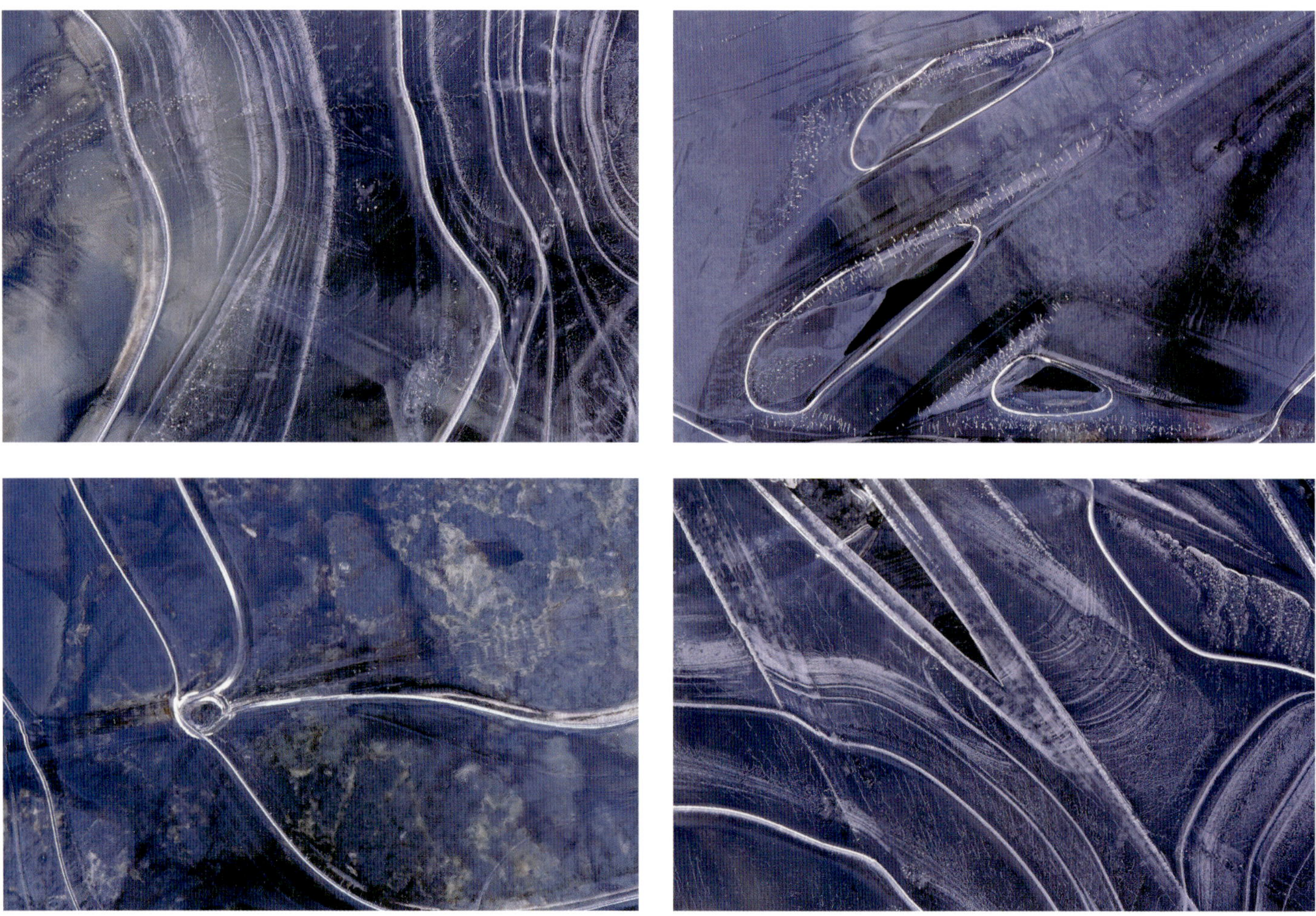

Ice patterns at Sligachan.

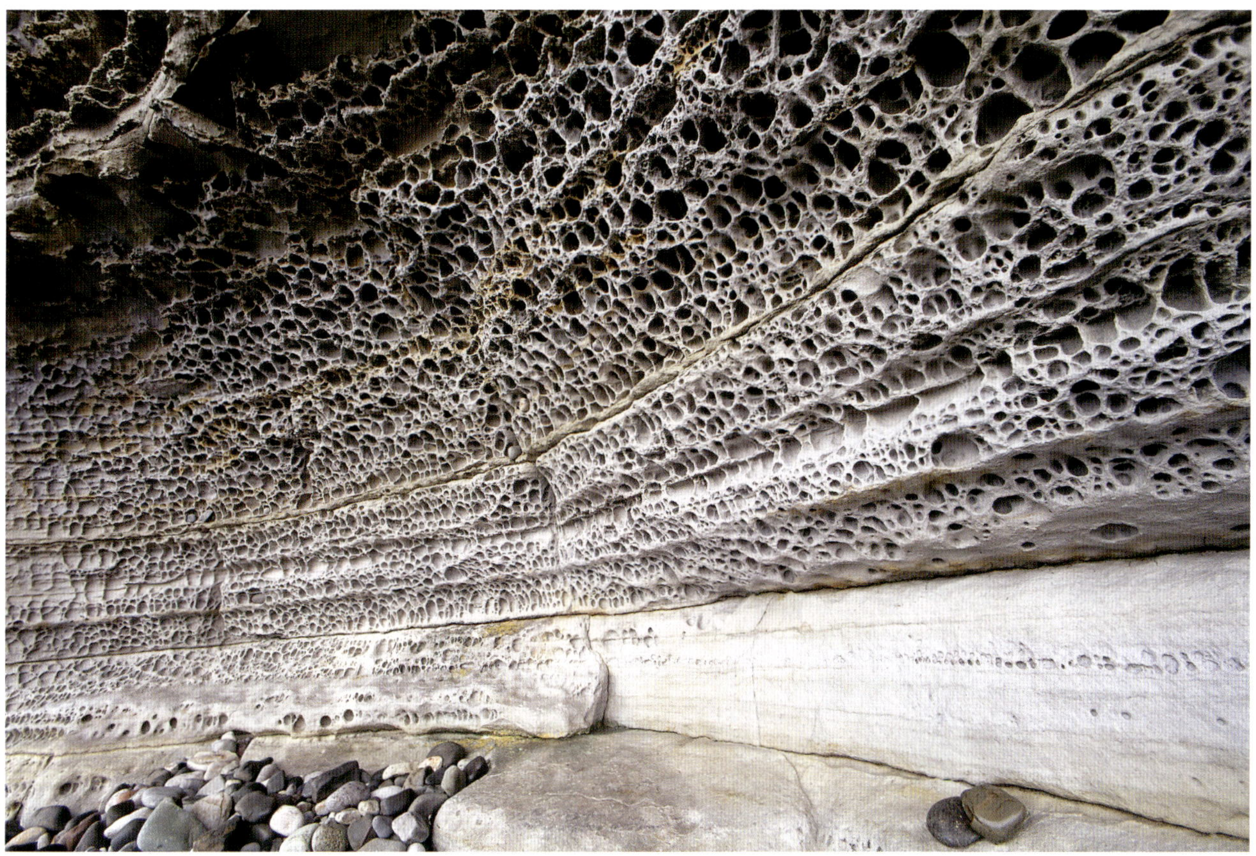

The road from Broadford passing Loch Slapin with its views to Bla Bheinn ends at Elgol. From here boat trips can be taken across Loch Scavaig enabling tourists, walkers and climbers to reach the isolated Loch Coruisk set in the very heart of the Black Cuillin horseshoe. Of this place Walter Scott wrote in 1814:

'Rarely human eye has known
A scene so stern as that dread lake
With its dark ledge of barren stone ...'

Many, however, will be content to stay at Elgol just to admire the classic view across Loch Scavaig to the Cuillin range or to study the fascinating geology of the nearby cliffs. The photograph here shows the remarkable honeycombed Jurassic sandstone ceiling where the cliffs overhang part of the rocky beach.

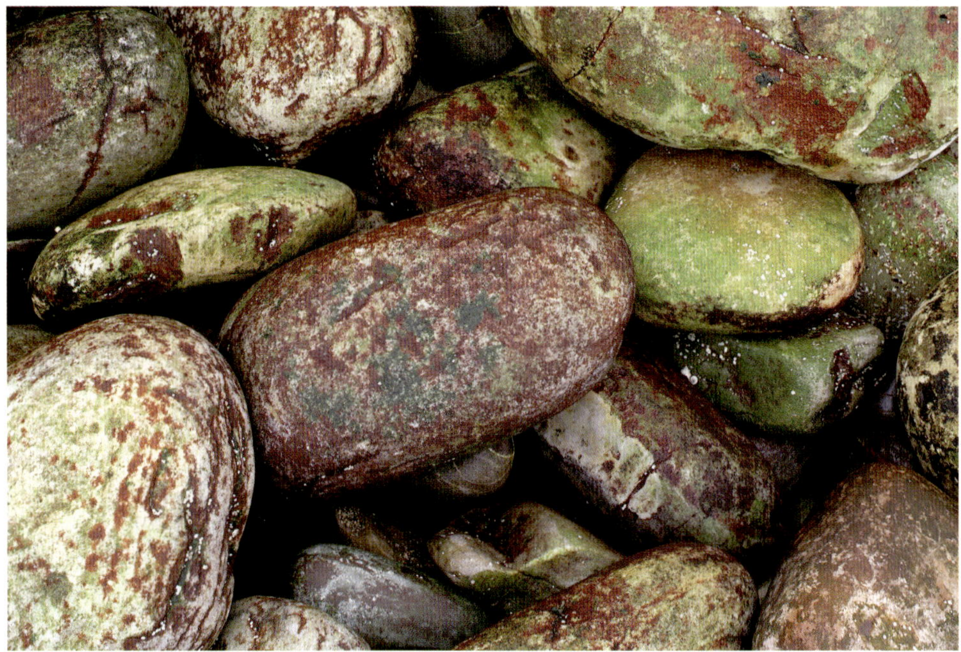

Coloured boulders, Elgol.

Morning calm across Broadford Bay looking towards the small island of Pabbay and the distant mainland Applecross peninsula and Torridon. Broadford, Skye's largest crofting community, straggles the main A87 road through the island and with its shops, hotel and hospital acts as the major centre for the southern part of Skye. In 1843 it was noted as having just three houses and an inn!

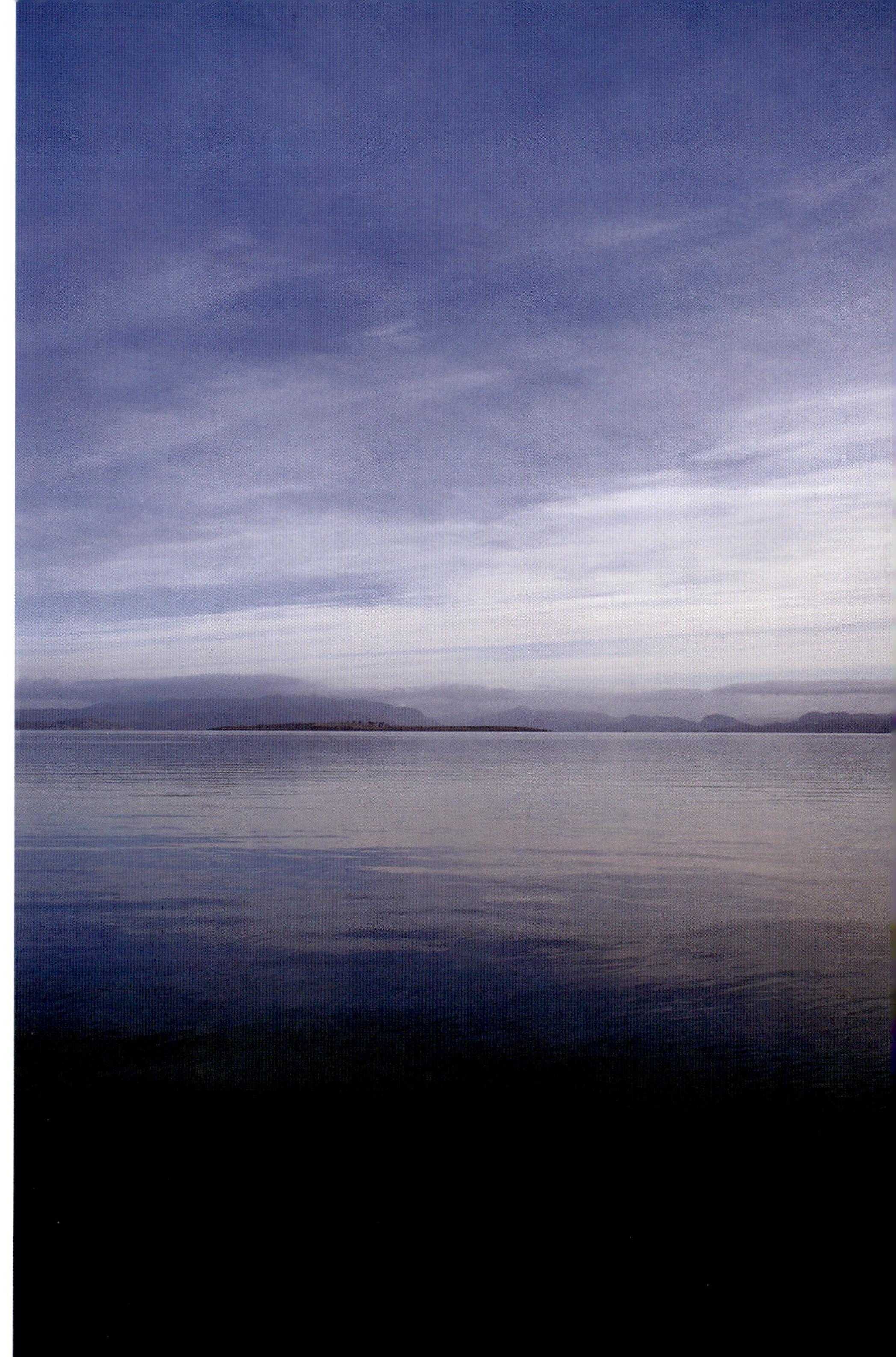

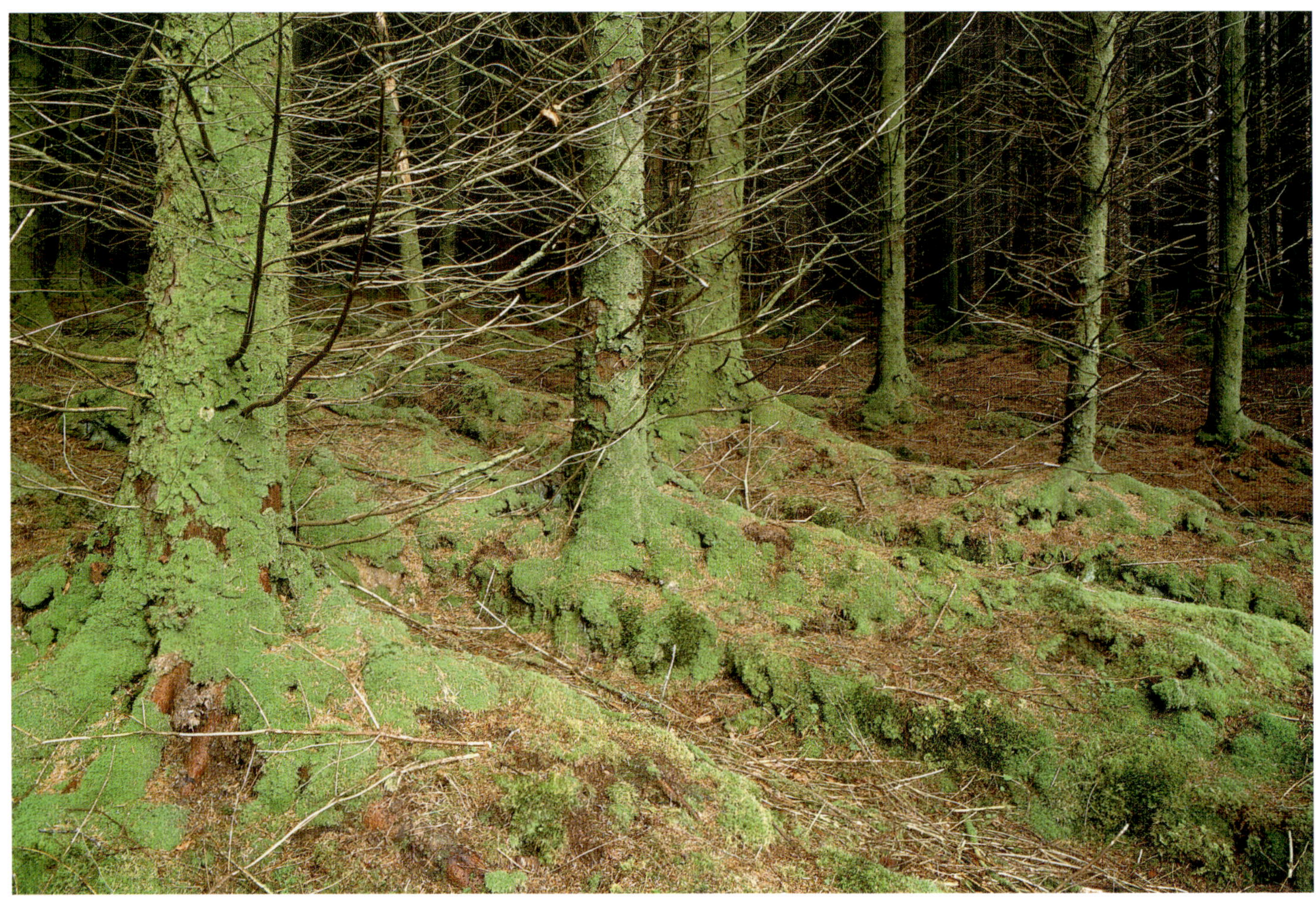

Colour and shade, forest edge, Aird of Sleat.

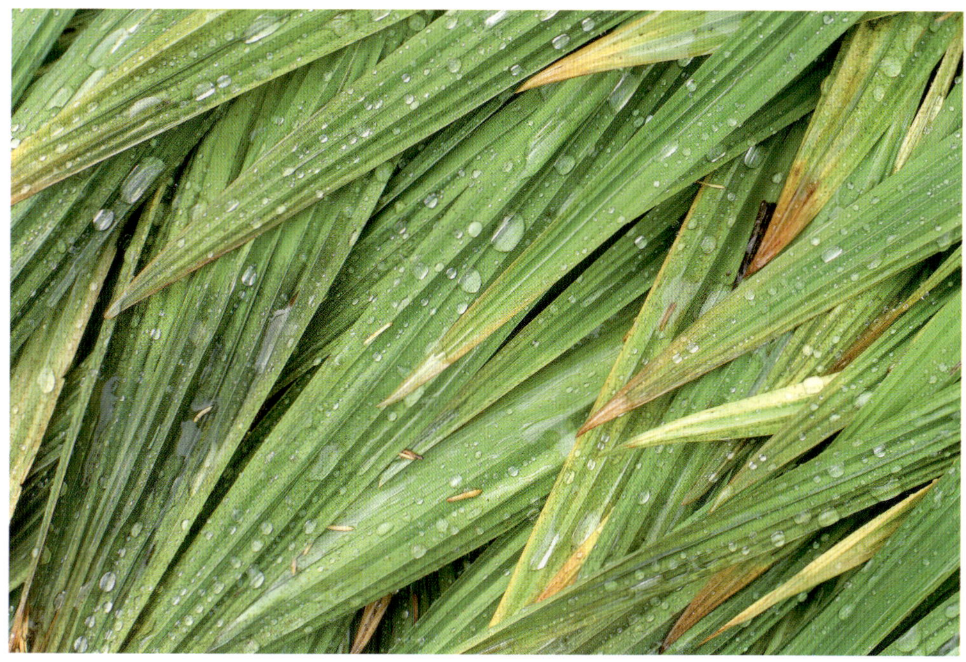

Montbretia leaves covered in rain drops make a splash of bright green on a roadside verge, Sleat.

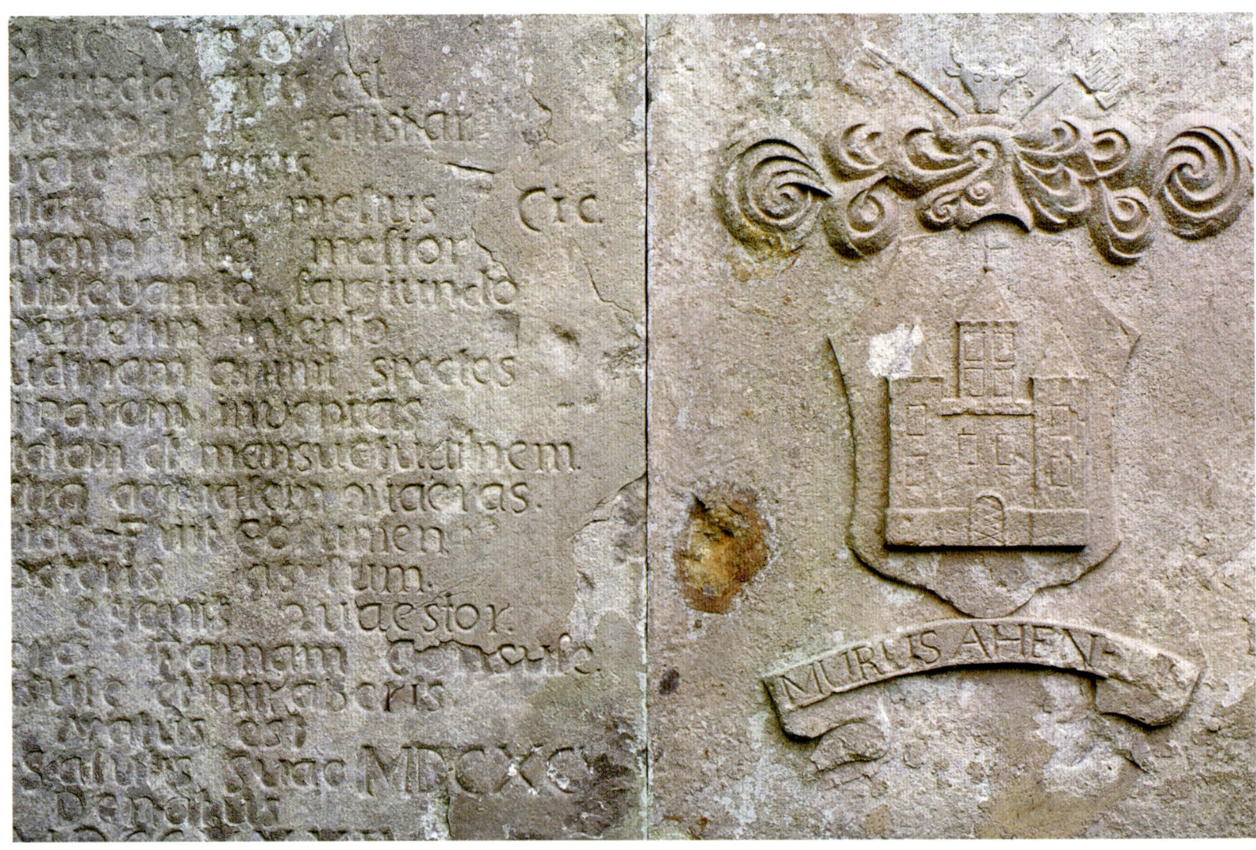

Tombstone, Borline, Loch Eynort. In the shadow of Beinn Buidhe na Creige and at the end of the road from Carbost are two ruined churches surrounded by a single graveyard carpeted with snowdrops in early springtime. The larger building is thought to be of eighteenth-century construction but the smaller measuring only about 8m x 5m is of a much earlier origin. This ornately carved memorial stone is set within its walls. Less than 4km around the coast on the northern shores of Loch Eynort can be found the abandoned crofting township of Tuasdale. Here, with its numerous often grass-covered stone walls and foundations, are the final remnants of a once thriving community cleared from their homes in 1840.

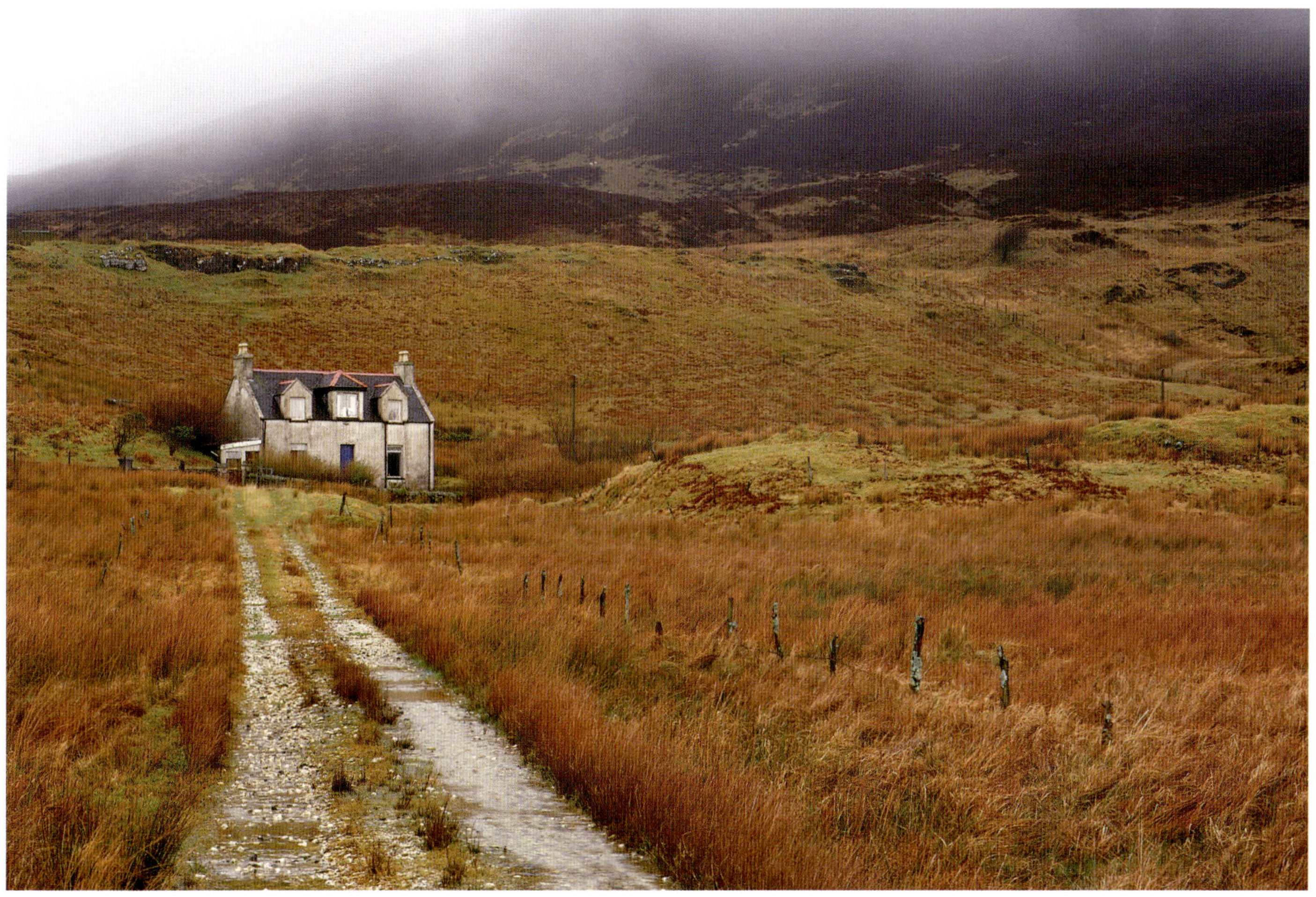

There are many empty croft cottages to be seen all over Skye deserted either through deaths of elderly inhabitants or perhaps the hard nature of the land where any fight against the often difficult elements has simply been lost. This empty cottage with its rough stony track and broken fencing together with the wild, coloured moorland and low mist over the surrounding hills tells a story familiar in many of the Hebridean islands.

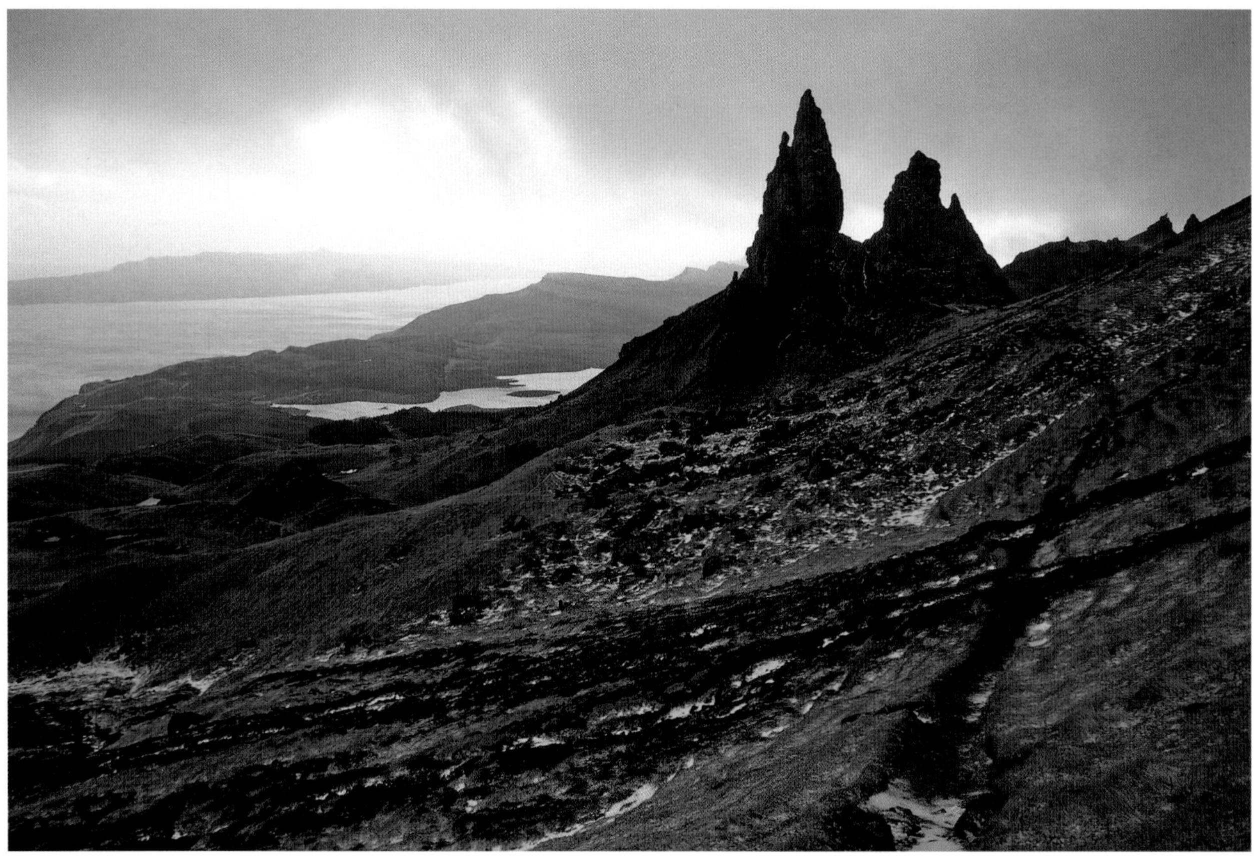

Late afternoon wintry light on the Old Man of Storr. Beyond Portree, the island's capital, the Trotternish peninsula stretches north some 40km to Duntulm and Rubha Hunish. With a spine of high hills and steep cliffs, the eastern flank of the peninsula is a geologist's paradise where numerous signs of vast landslips occurring over thousands of years can be found. One of the principal features is The Storr, 719m high, below which are a series of remarkable monolithic rock pinnacles, the Old Man being the largest and first climbed in 1955. Balanced on a rock plinth and backed by 200m cliffs, it is one of Skye's major attractions.

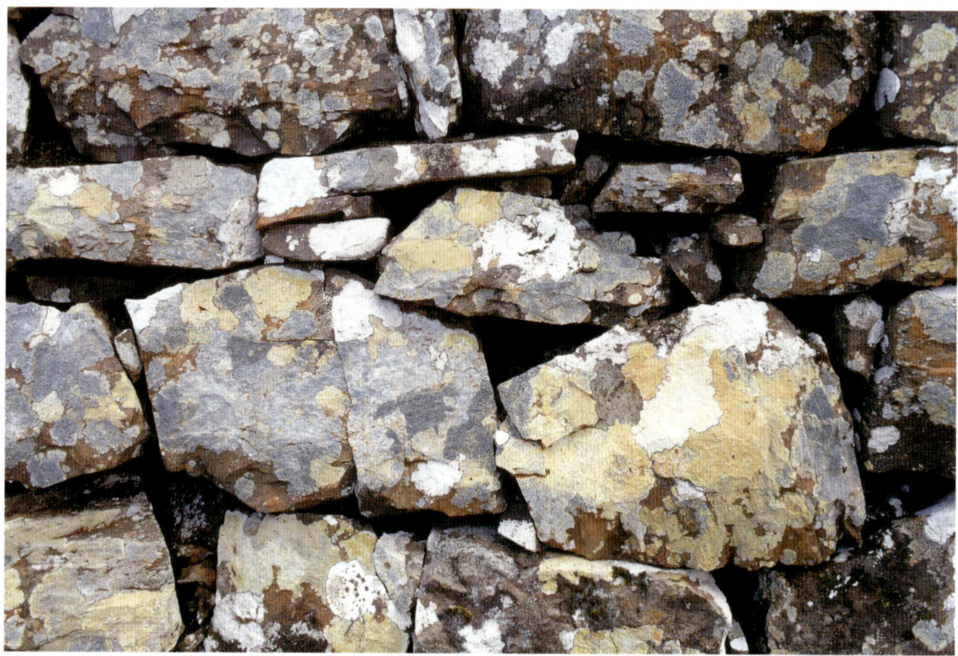

Stone wall and lichen near Staffin.

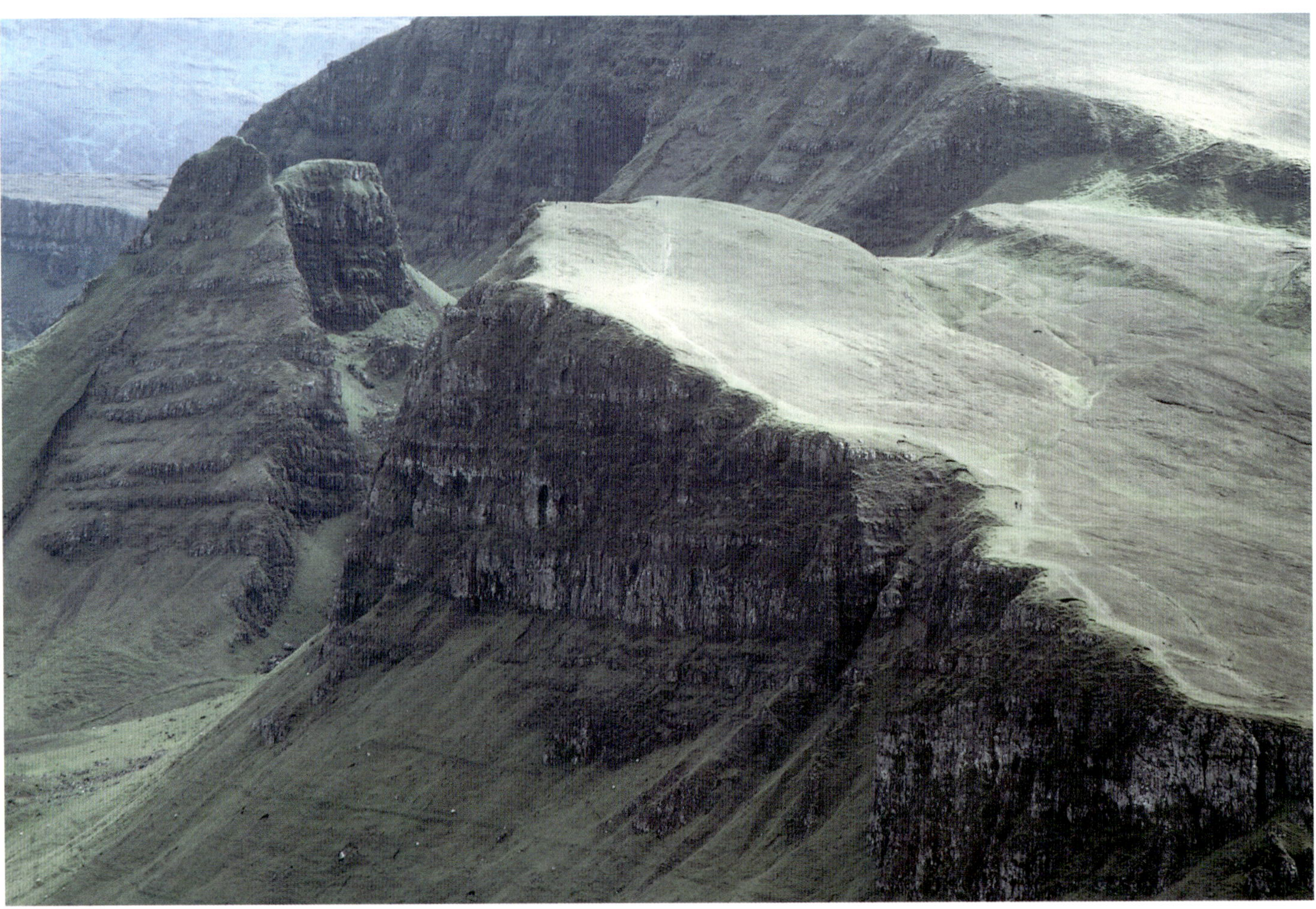

Trotternish cliffs above Staffin.

Opposite: Towards the Quiraing. A light dusting of snow following a brief blizzard covers the Trotternish cliffs near the Quiraing. Consisting of a series of castellated crags known as The Prison, another pinnacle named The Needle and a higher flattened grassy platform encased by rock walls called The Table, the Quiraing means a pillared stronghold and is another result of side-slipping from the summit cliffs. Annual midsummer games of shinty were once played on The Table.

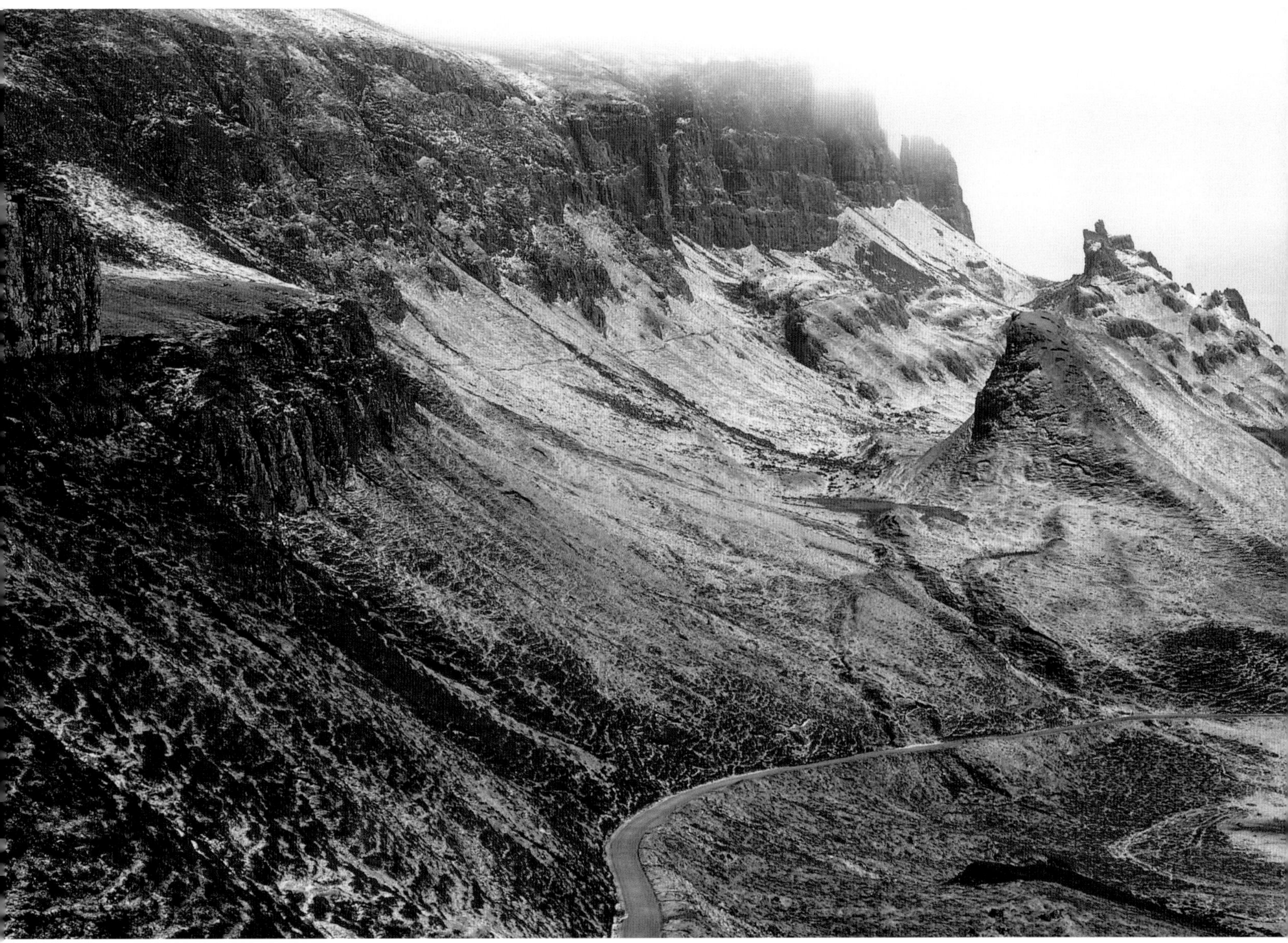

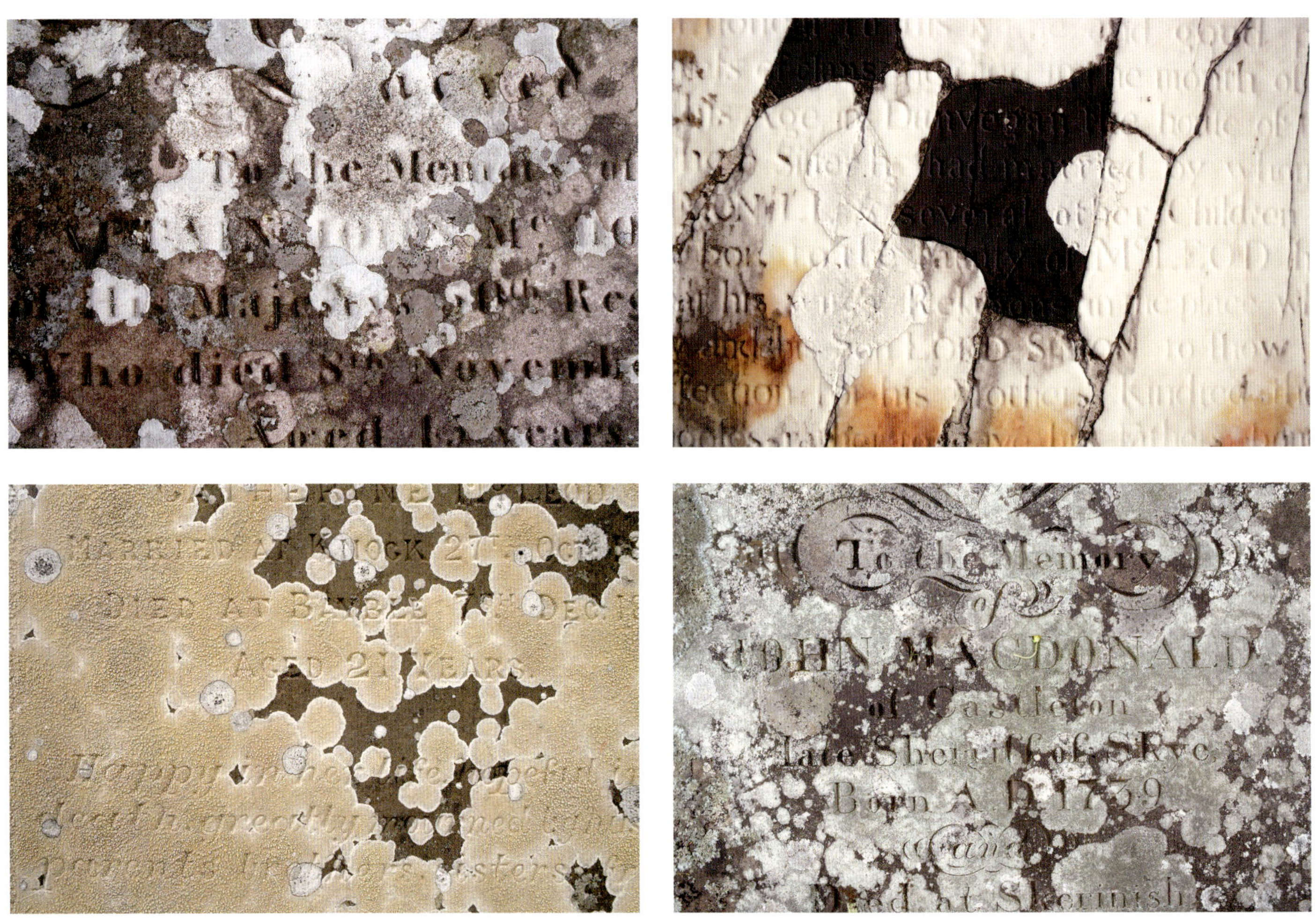

Lichen in its many colours spreads slowly over weatherworn gravestones in Skye burial grounds to take on a map-like appearance of the past.

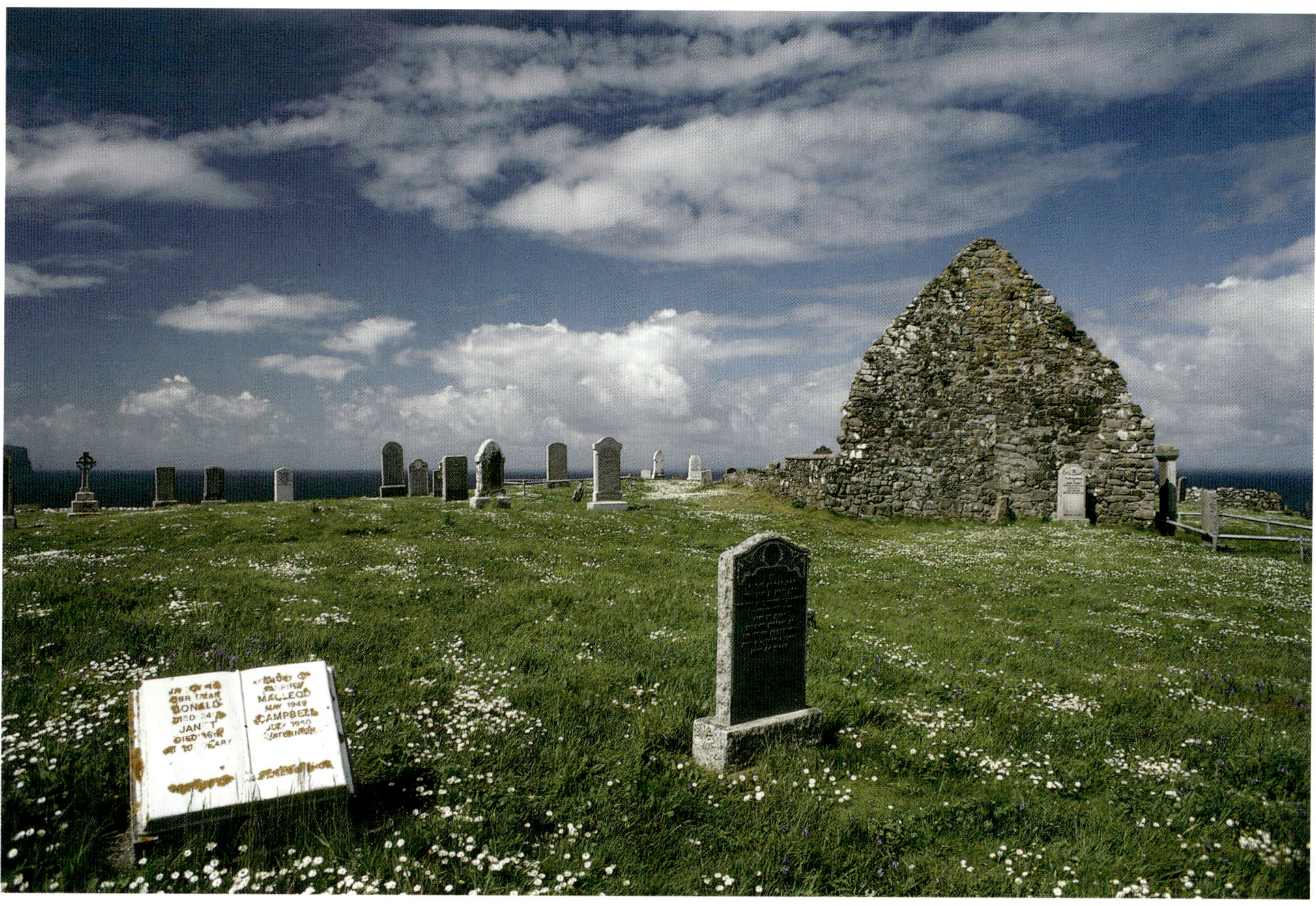

Trumpan Church, Waternish. Once known as Kilconan church, the remains of the building and its surrounding graves lie on top of a small hill almost at the extremity of the Waternish peninsula near Ardmore Point. With its outstanding views to the outer islands of Harris and the Uists, this peaceful place is for many one of the most beautiful parts of Skye. However, it has not always been so for here in 1578 most of the local inhabitants were murdered by the MacDonalds, the building being set alight during a church service. The MacDonalds themselves retreating too slowly were subsequently killed by the MacLeods acting in revenge, their bodies being buried under the tumbling of a nearby earthen dyke and known as 'The Battle of the Spoiling of the Dyke'. An adjacent stone still displays the marks from the sharpening of swords.

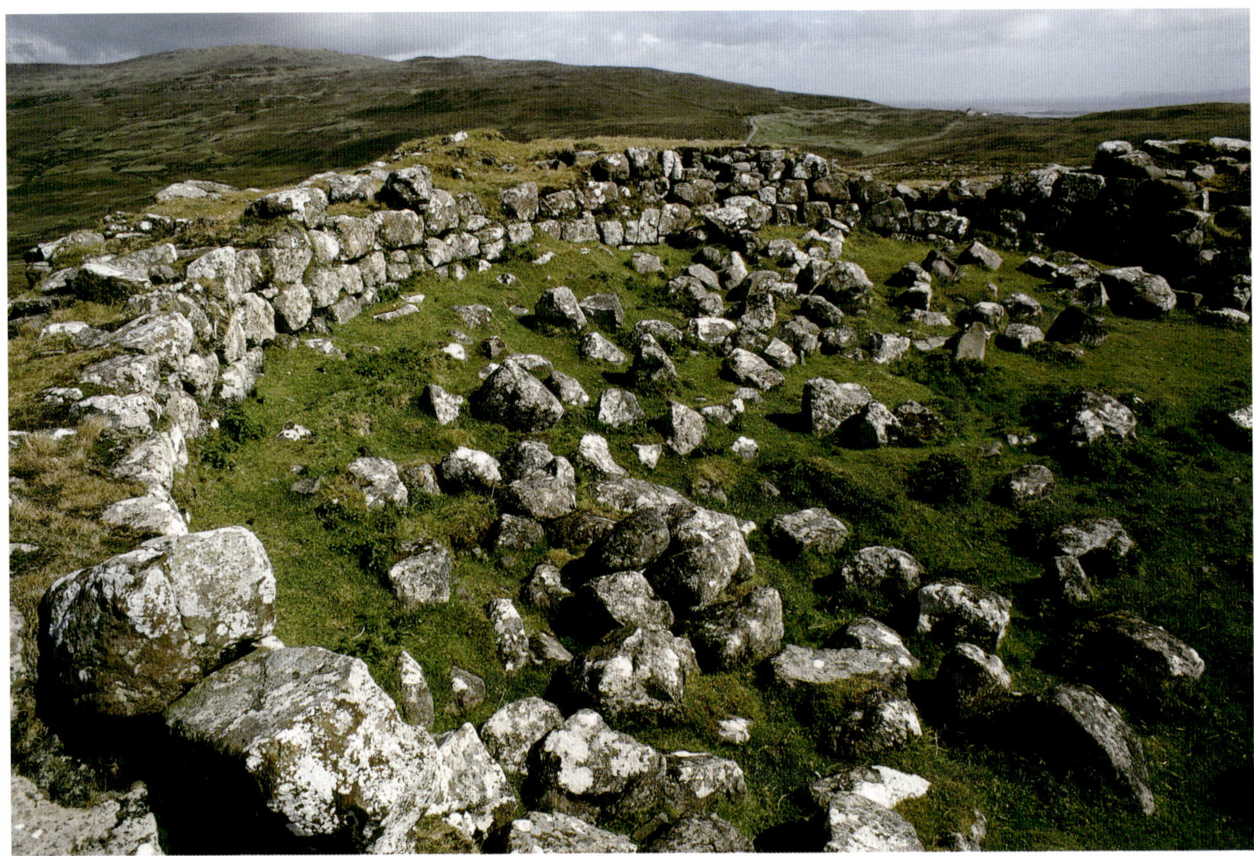

The remains of the broch of Dun Halin look out over the townships of Halin, Halistra and Gillen mid-way along the Waternish peninsula. Probably built about the 1st century BC initially for defensive purposes and then as a communal refuge it would once have consisted of a tapering circular double-stone wall with galleries and staircases within. Using a smooth faced outer wall, pierced only by a small entrance passage, brochs were almost impregnable. When built it would have been at least 12m high but removal of stones over the centuries for various domestic purposes has reduced the walls to about 3m.

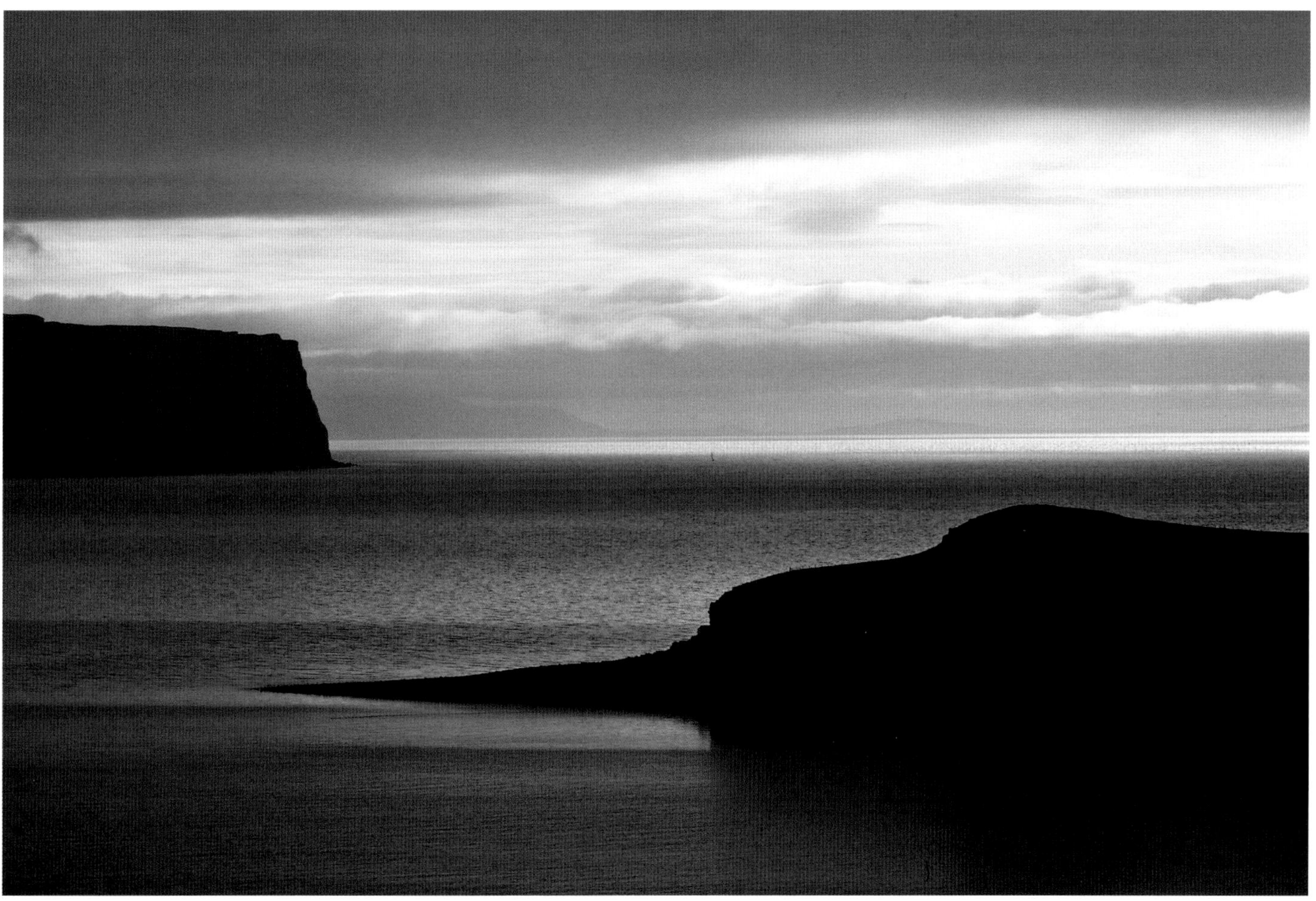

Low light across Loch Bay looking out from Waternish towards Ardmore Point and Dunvegan Head. The Outer Hebridean islands of North and South Uist lie on the horizon.

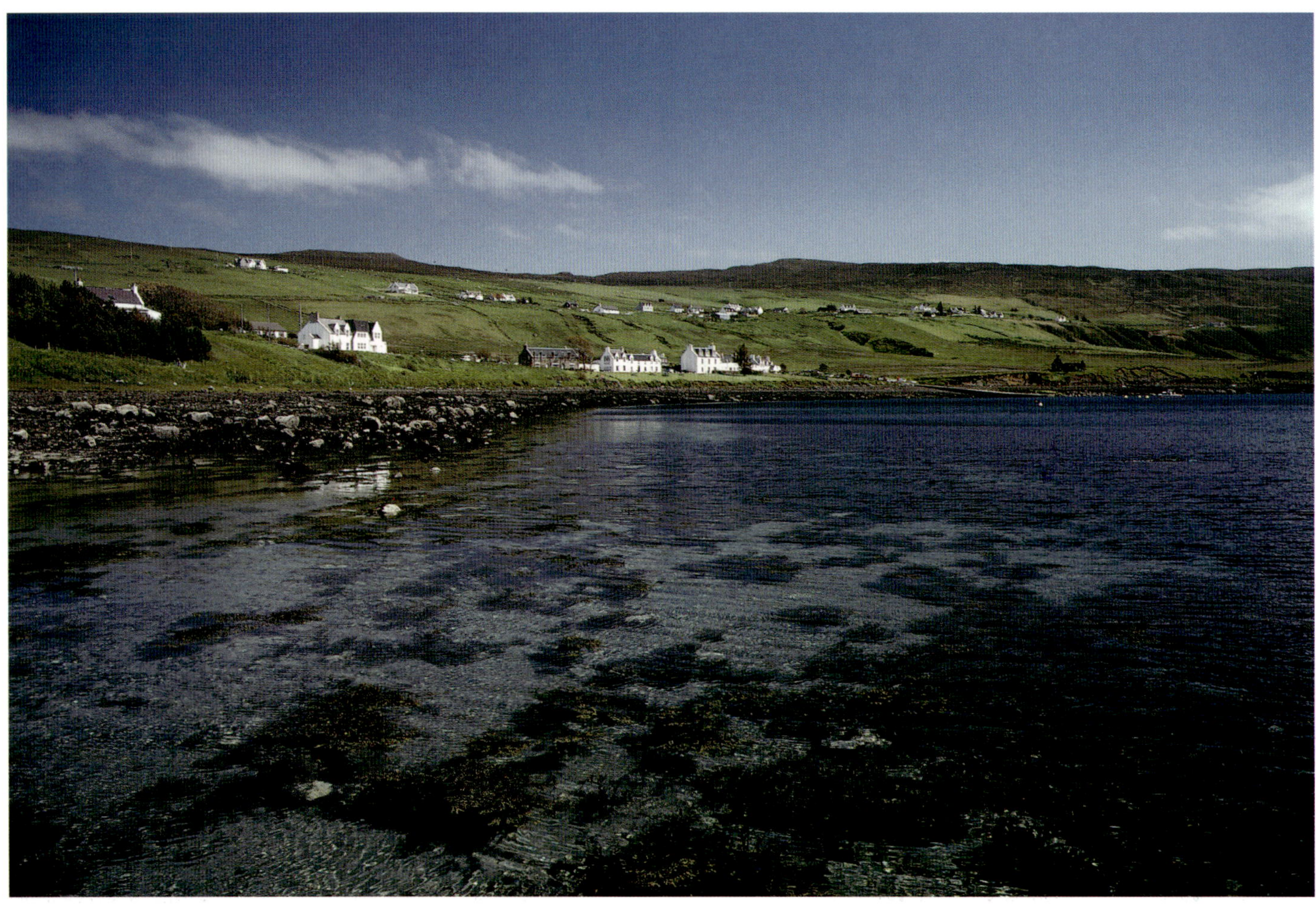

Stein. The village of Stein was founded at Waternish in 1787 by the British Fisheries Society with provision of boats, nets, pier etc. in order to promote a new fishing industry. However, with little enthusiasm from local inhabitants and the vagaries of fish movements the venture failed. By the mid nineteenth century the village had been abandoned and only in more recent years has it again come to life partly due to the folk singer Donovan whose purchase of several buildings initially injected much needed finance and enthusiasm back into the area and by the comparatively new appreciation of this beautiful part of Skye.

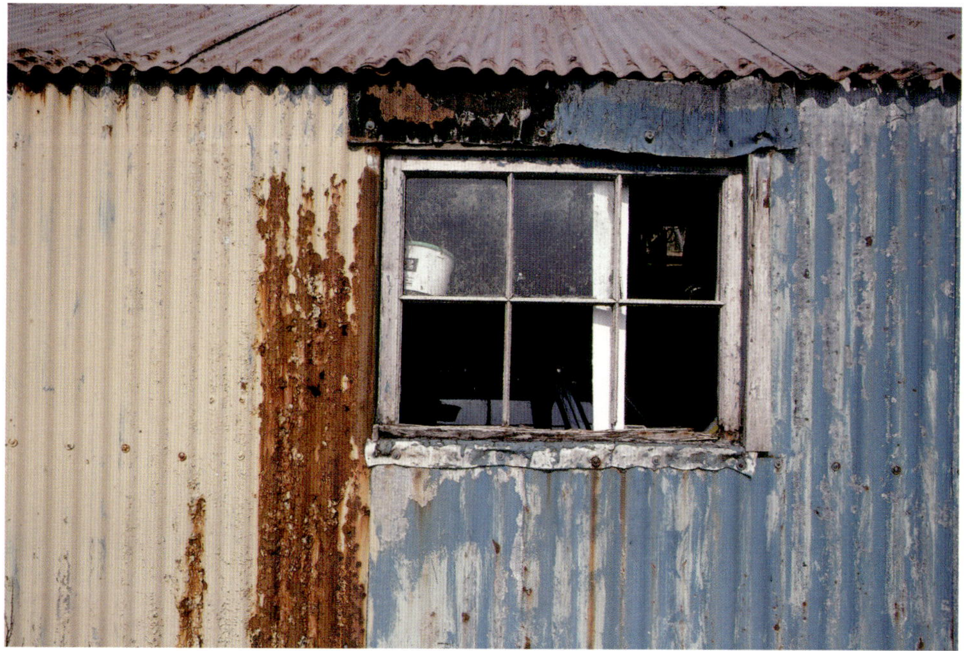

A corrugated iron garage near Stein displays a different colour scheme to that of the normal white.

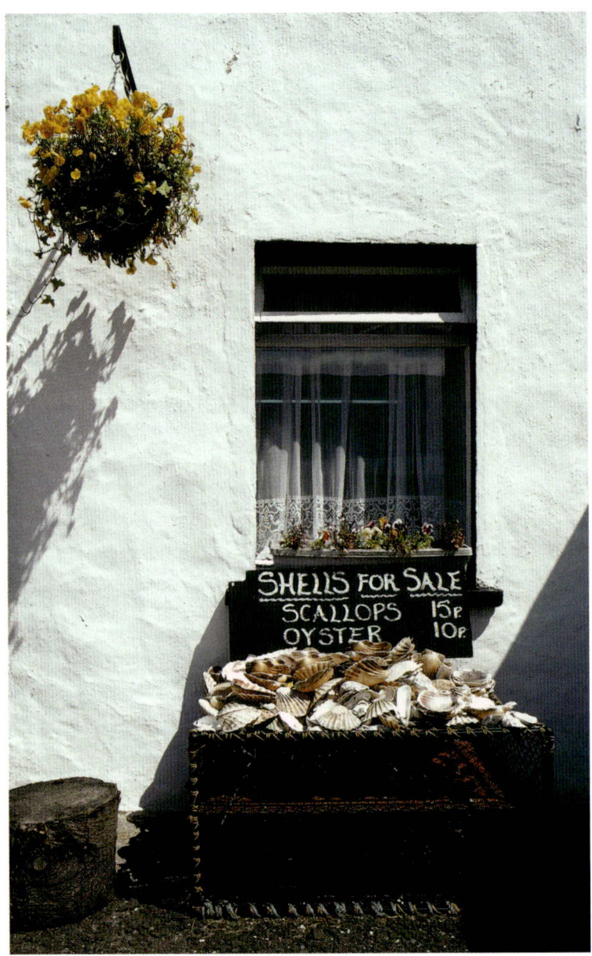

Shells for sale, Stein.

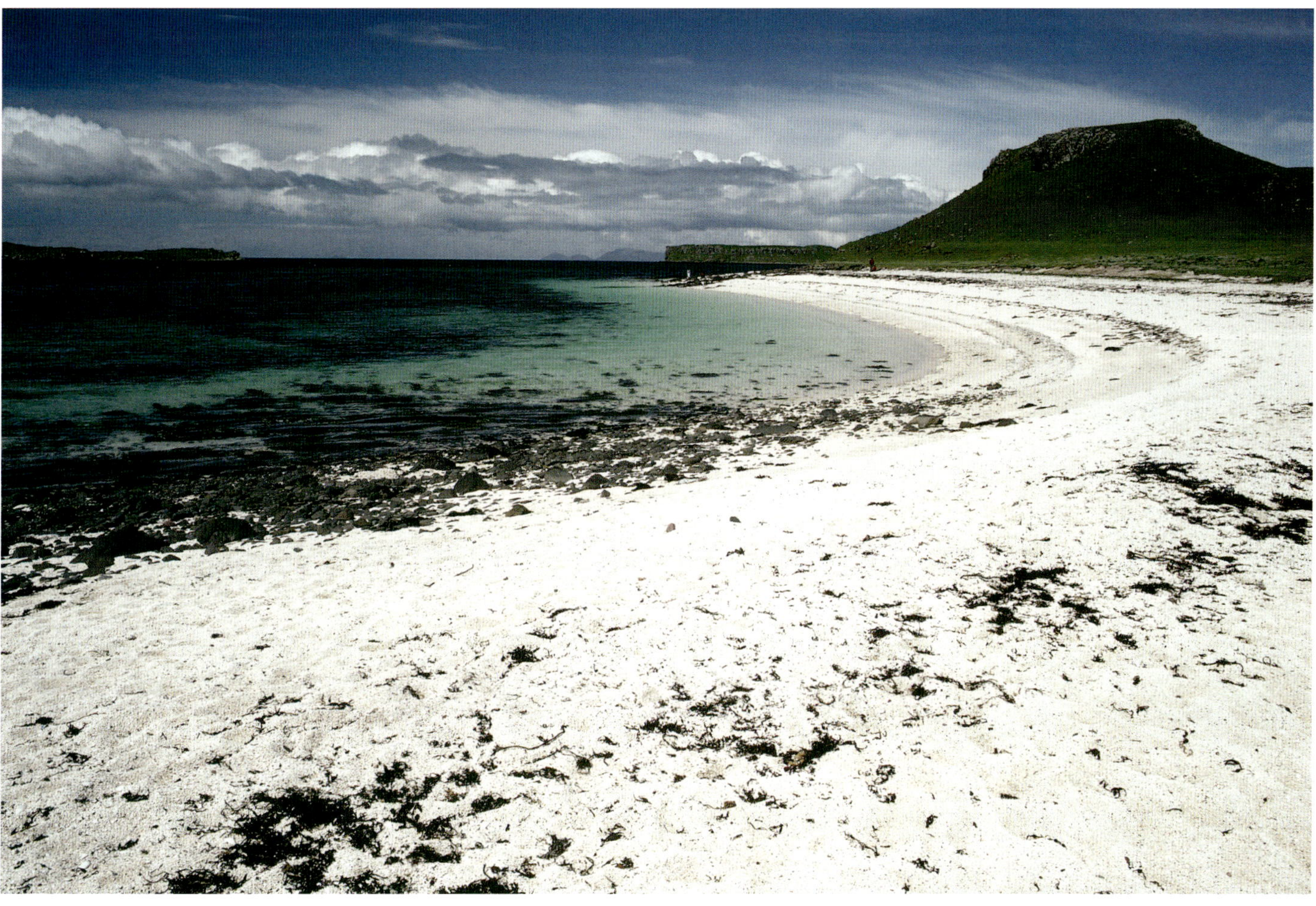

Coral beach, Claigan. On the west coast of Skye the main road reaches the village of Dunvegan to then turn eastwards toward Trotternish. However, 8km north of Dunvegan Castle, the MacLeod family seat, a minor road becoming a track continues to two small beaches near Claigan. These beautiful beaches are formed entirely of coral, generally fragmented to coarse sand and often covered with shells of many varieties and colours. As a result these beaches, and a similar one at Staffin, are a delightful contrast to the dull grey stone and sand normally found on Skye. The coral itself grows offshore and pieces broken by wave action are cast up to form the beaches.

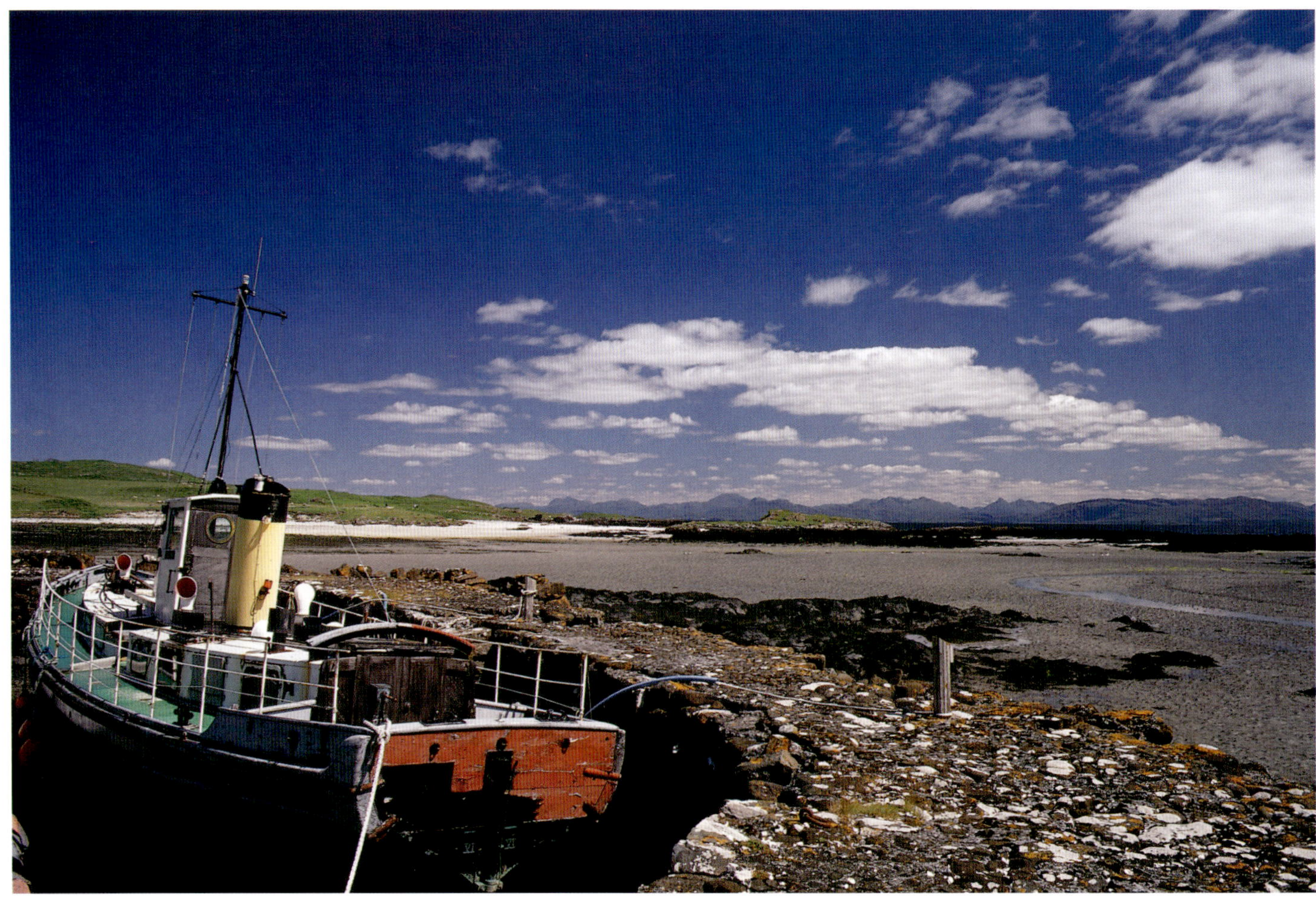

A perfect summer's day over Eigg harbour at low tide with the privately-owned ex-naval harbour launch *Talisman* moored up against the old Clanranald Pier and with the mainland hills of Morar, Knoydart, Glenelg and Kintail in the far distance. To the right, just out of the photograph, is the new pier opened in 2004 now enabling the Caledonian MacBrayne ferry to berth at the island itself rather than requiring the use of a 'flit' boat between ferry and shore. The island is also served by direct ferry from Arisaig. Eigg, together with the neighbouring islands of Muck, Rum and Canna form the geographical and social group known as the Parish of the Small Isles and these various ferries linking the islands together are literally a lifeline to the outside world.

Sunshine, Shadow and Solitude

EIGG

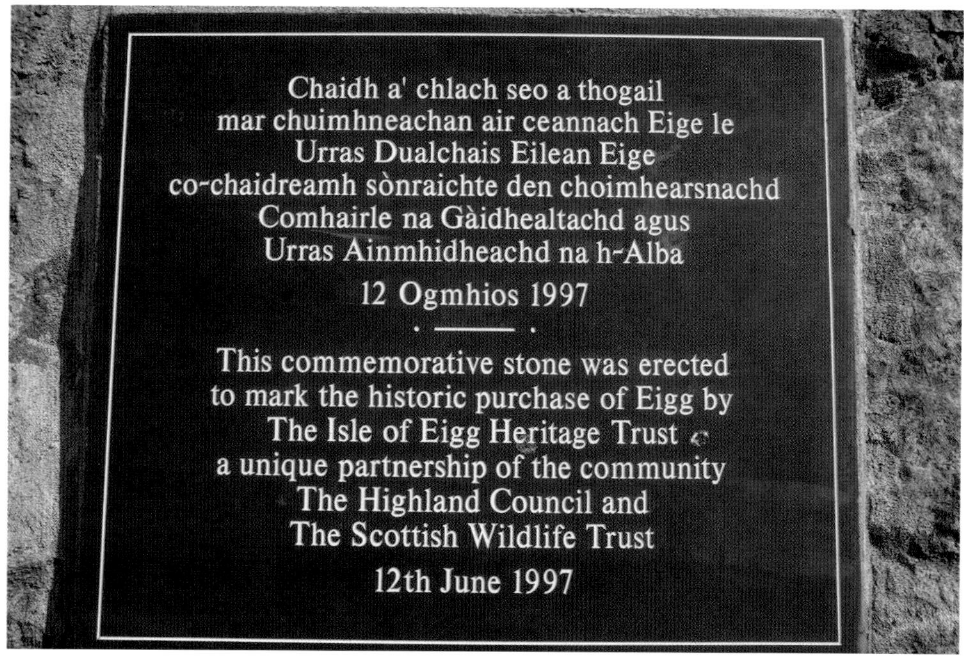

A plaque above Eigg pier commemorates the historic purchase of the island by the Isle of Eigg Heritage Trust 12 June 1997.

Despite their relatively close proximity being some 12km apart, it would be difficult to find a greater contrast between two islands than that between Skye and Eigg. Skye, often busy with summer tourists, over 120km long much of it being barren moorland broken only by its high cliffs and peaks and with a population of almost 9000; Eigg, intimate, about 8 x 5km, fertile, part wooded with an outstanding variety of scenery including three beautiful sandy beaches, but a population of only 80. Add to this that Skye is considered by some not to be an island any more due to its bridge and yet Eigg is accessible by passenger ferry only – no visitors' cars being allowed, which thus limits its tourism potential – then the difference between the two islands is profound. Skye is still owned by numerous landlords and individuals; Eigg since 1997 is owned by the population themselves under the aegis of the Isle of Eigg Heritage Trust in conjunction with the Highland Council and the Scottish Wildlife Trust.

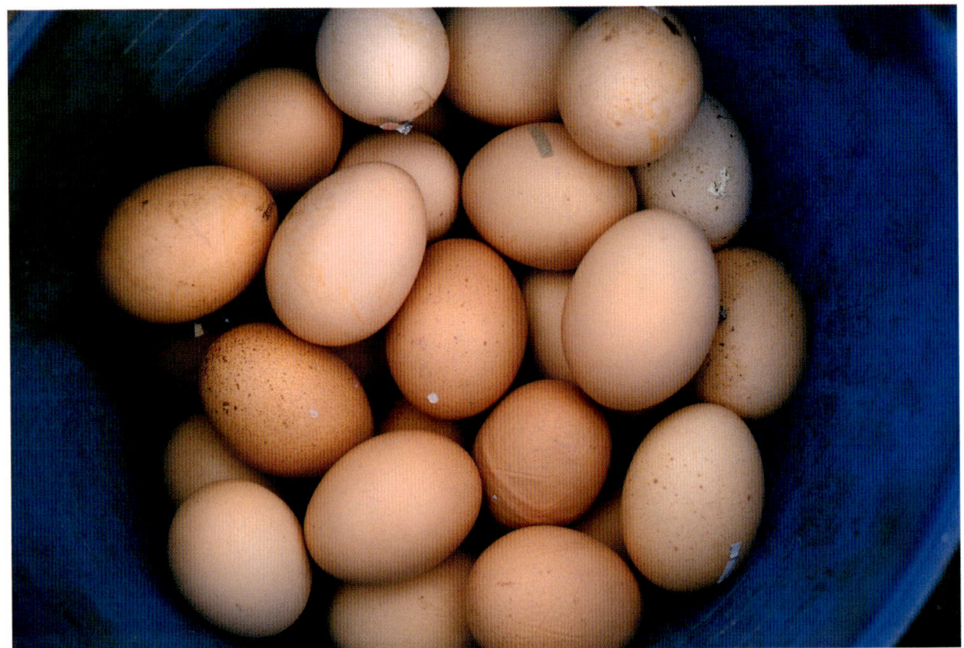

Eigg Eggs! The name Eigg is derived from the Gaelic word meaning 'the notch' and describes the lower moorland interior set between the two highest points as seen from an approaching vessel. Eigg in many ways is an island of colour and light. When the sun shines the colours are more reminiscent of the Mediterranean rather than Scotland, with often deep blue skies due to the total lack of industrial pollution. The island can sometimes be found basking in a mini heat wave whilst the mainland can be seen only 20km away shrouded under a blanket of dark rain-filled cloud. It is considered by many to be one of the most beautiful, fertile islands in all the Hebrides and few can equal it for its variety of plant and bird life. The first car only arrived in 1921 and the island's road system totalling some 10km was not properly surfaced until the late 1950s. Yet satellite television is everywhere, computers abound and a new wind-powered island electrification system has recently been completed. Eigg is now well and truly into the twenty-first century.

Immediately after the purchase of the island by the Trust, it was clear that a vast amount of work was necessary to bring much of Eigg's housing, buildings, land and fencing etc. back from the state of neglect it had suffered over many years under previous laird ownership. Suddenly a new enthusiasm had been injected into the community and in the first year alone a new pier centre was built accommodating a general shop plus tea and craft shops, offices and waiting facilities. This together with later improvement works to much of the housing, community centres and school have been carried out mostly using island labour. Sheep and cattle are once more in abundance with many signs of land re-use and considerable new fencing. Now, eleven years on from that historic purchase this inspired, vibrant, proud community is an example to us all.

An Sgurr from Galmisdale. If there is one particular distinguishing feature of Eigg, it has to be the highest peak, The Sgurr. The 393m craggy pitchstone lava monolith not only dominates the island but seen from afar is one of the region's most distinctive silhouettes. Despite its dramatic form and fearsome cliffs, it is easily climbed from the west, the views from the summit being some of the finest in the entire Hebrides. Eigg is another geologist's paradise and the creation of The Sgurr, the multitude of rock forms found, together with the 300m cliffs that surround much of the island attract many interested visitors and study groups. This classic view with Galmisdale House (once the island's Inn) in the foreground and The Sgurr enveloped in low cloud gives the impression of the peak seemingly being far higher than it really is.

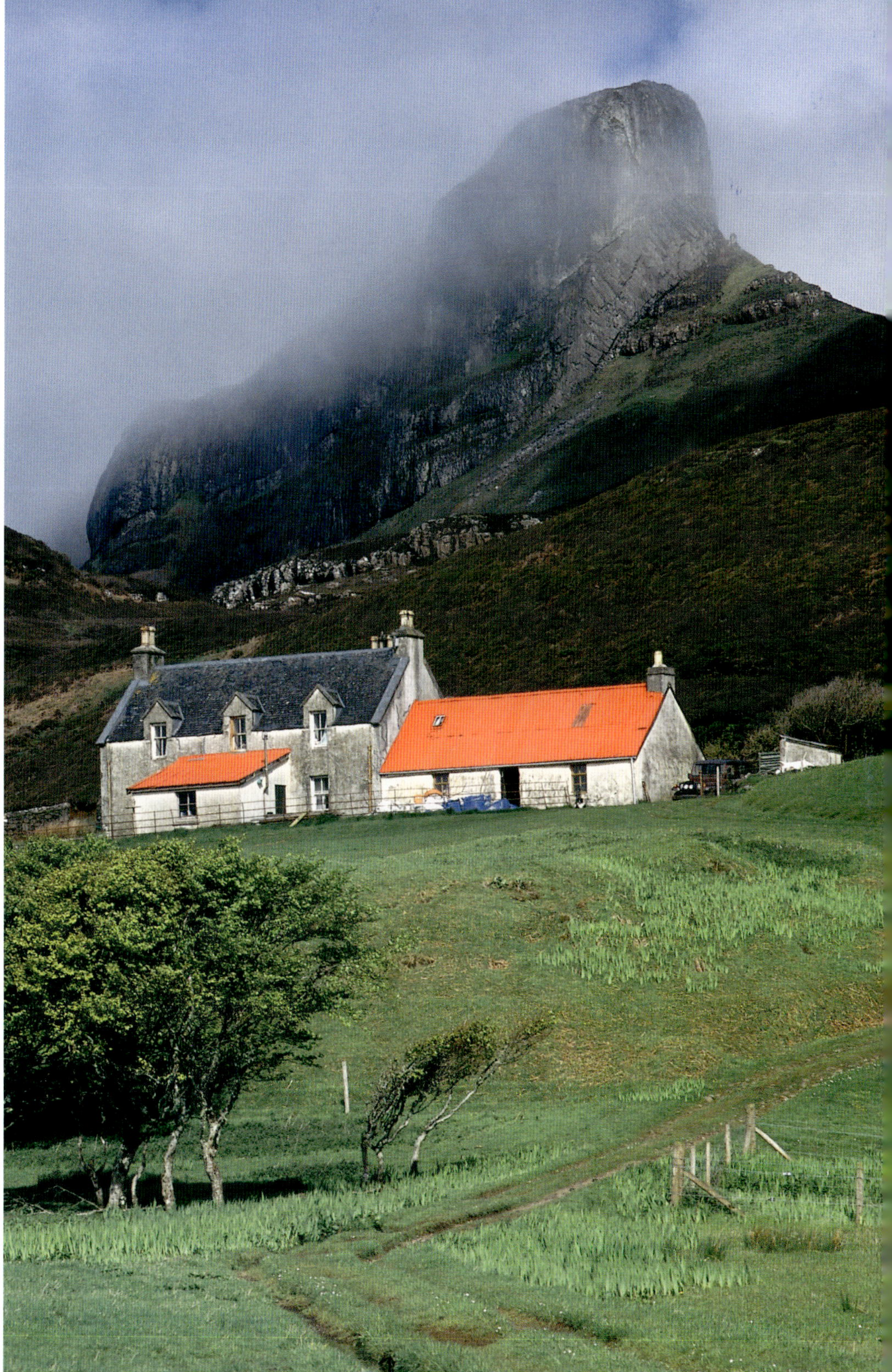

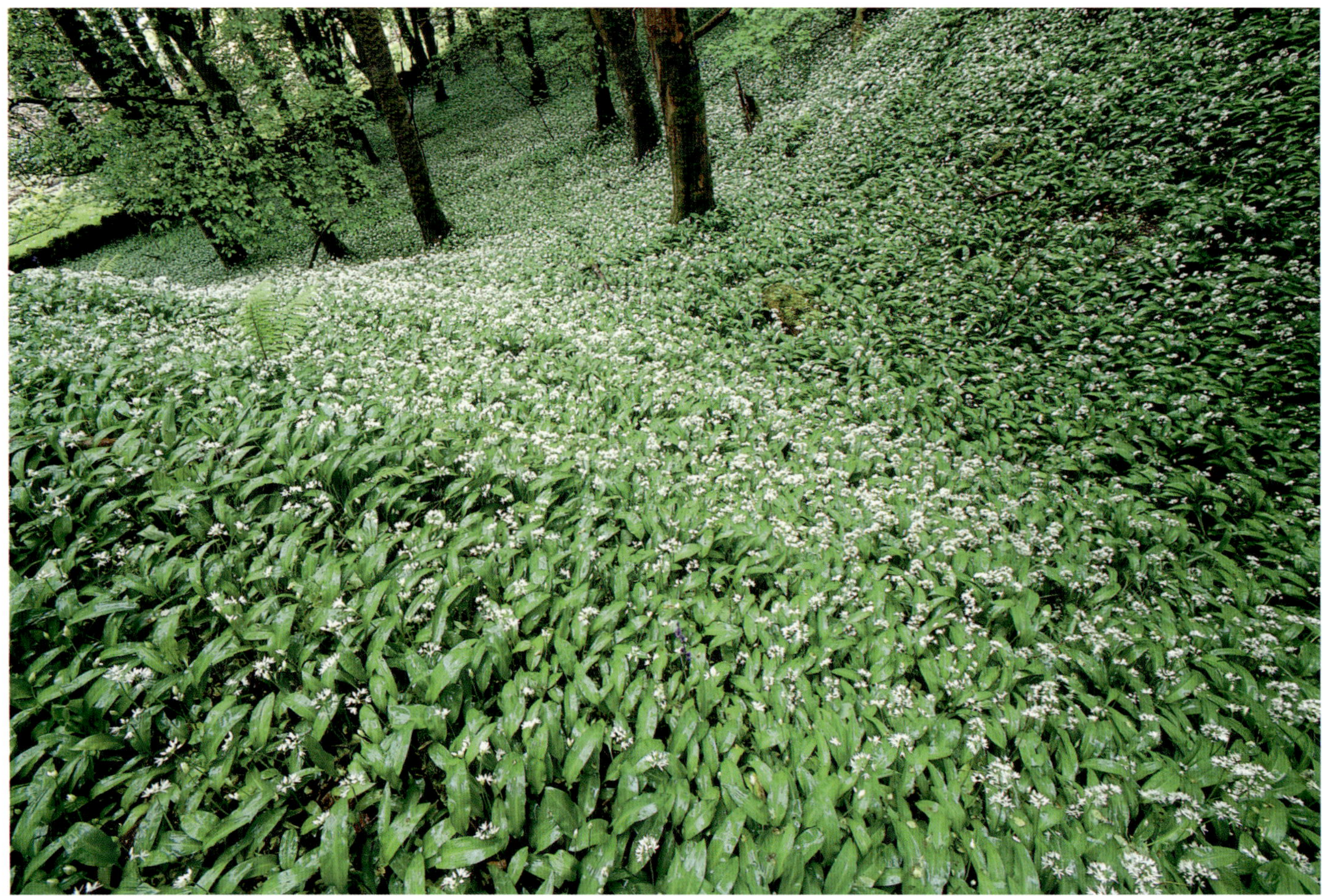

Another feature of Eigg is the beautiful, mainly deciduous woodland that rises from the harbour shoreline up to bare hilltops. Much of it planted around the traditional laird's home 'The Lodge' was originally intended to act as a windbreak but with the later addition of palms, bamboo and several other exotic species over the years parts of the woodland have now taken on a semi-tropical nature. In the spring the banks, slopes and folds of the woodland floor are often carpeted with bluebell and wild ramson as shown here.

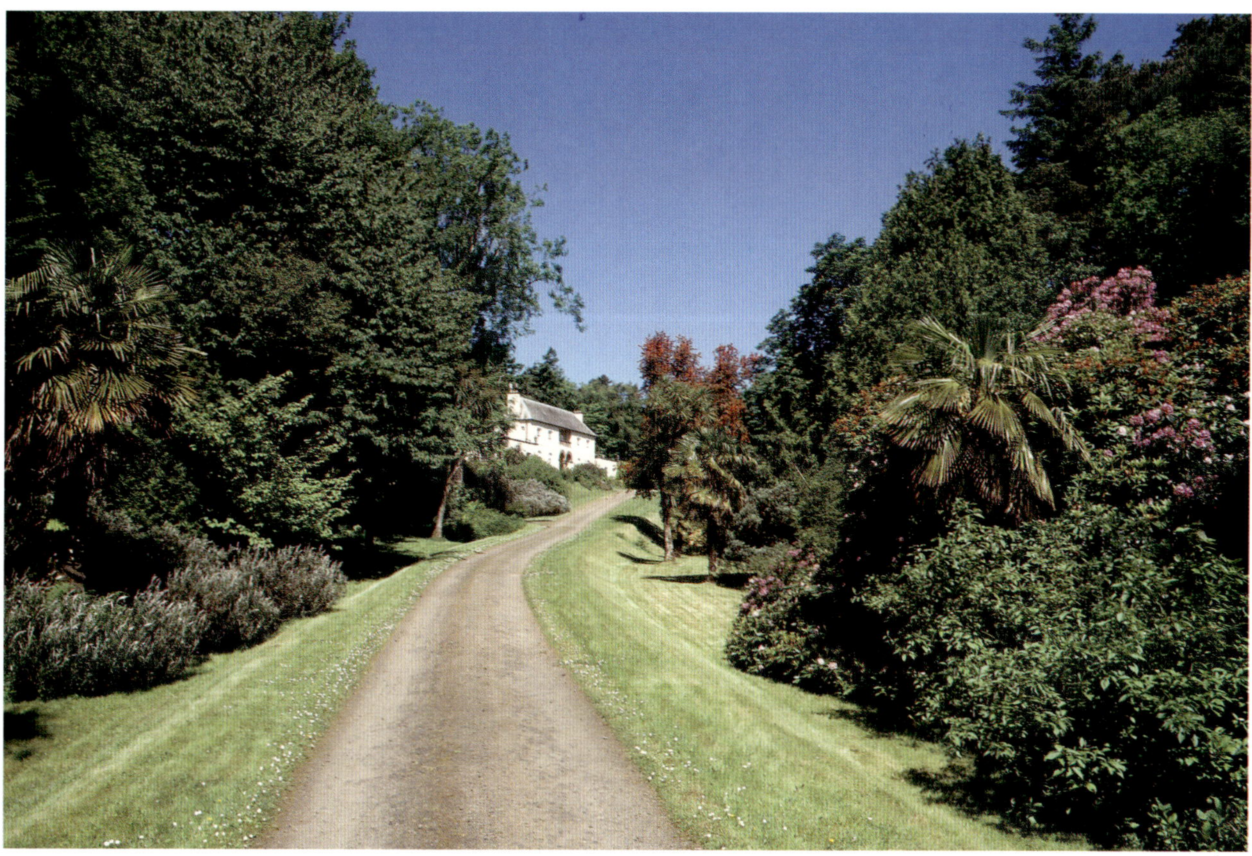

The Lodge. In an almost colonial setting amongst the woods, the present building dates back to 1927 completed for the then laird Sir Walter Runciman after previous buildings had been destroyed by fire. The garden design was influenced by that at Inverewe and with its lush surrounding woodland featuring such unusual species as Chilean flame trees, Strawberry trees and Magnolias, the entire complex in some respects is more akin to the South of France than the Hebrides. With the purchase of the island by the Trust, the ten-bedroomed Italianate lodge remained empty for a number of years until 2004 when it was purchased privately. It is intended that the building, once refurbished and renovated, will act not just as a home but as a centre for sustainable living to educate and advise on greener lifestyles.

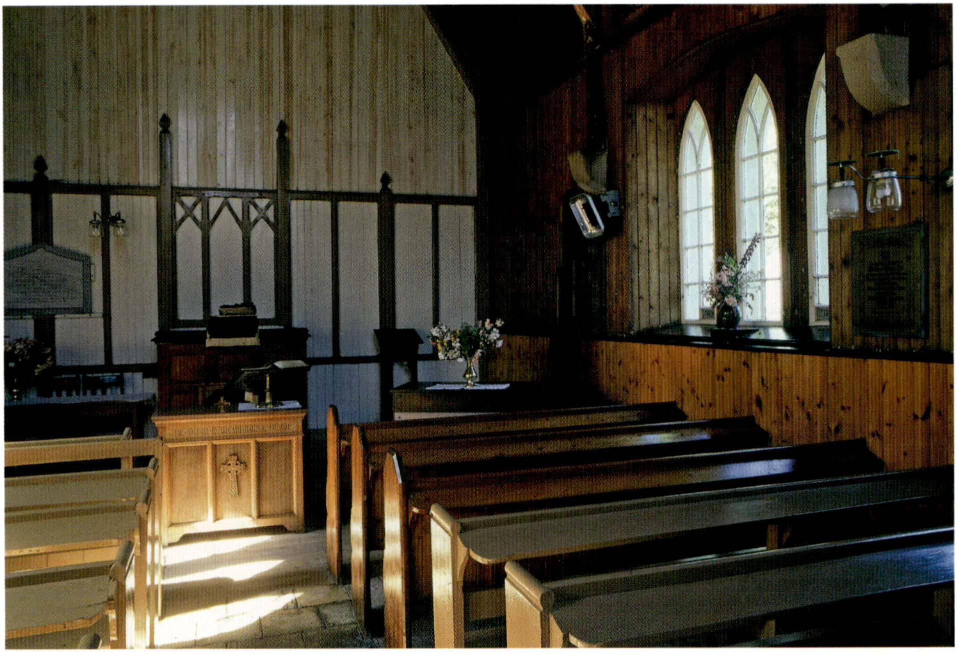

The sunlit interior of the nineteenth-century Church of Scotland building. Services are held here regularly throughout the summer months and in wintertime as weather permits.

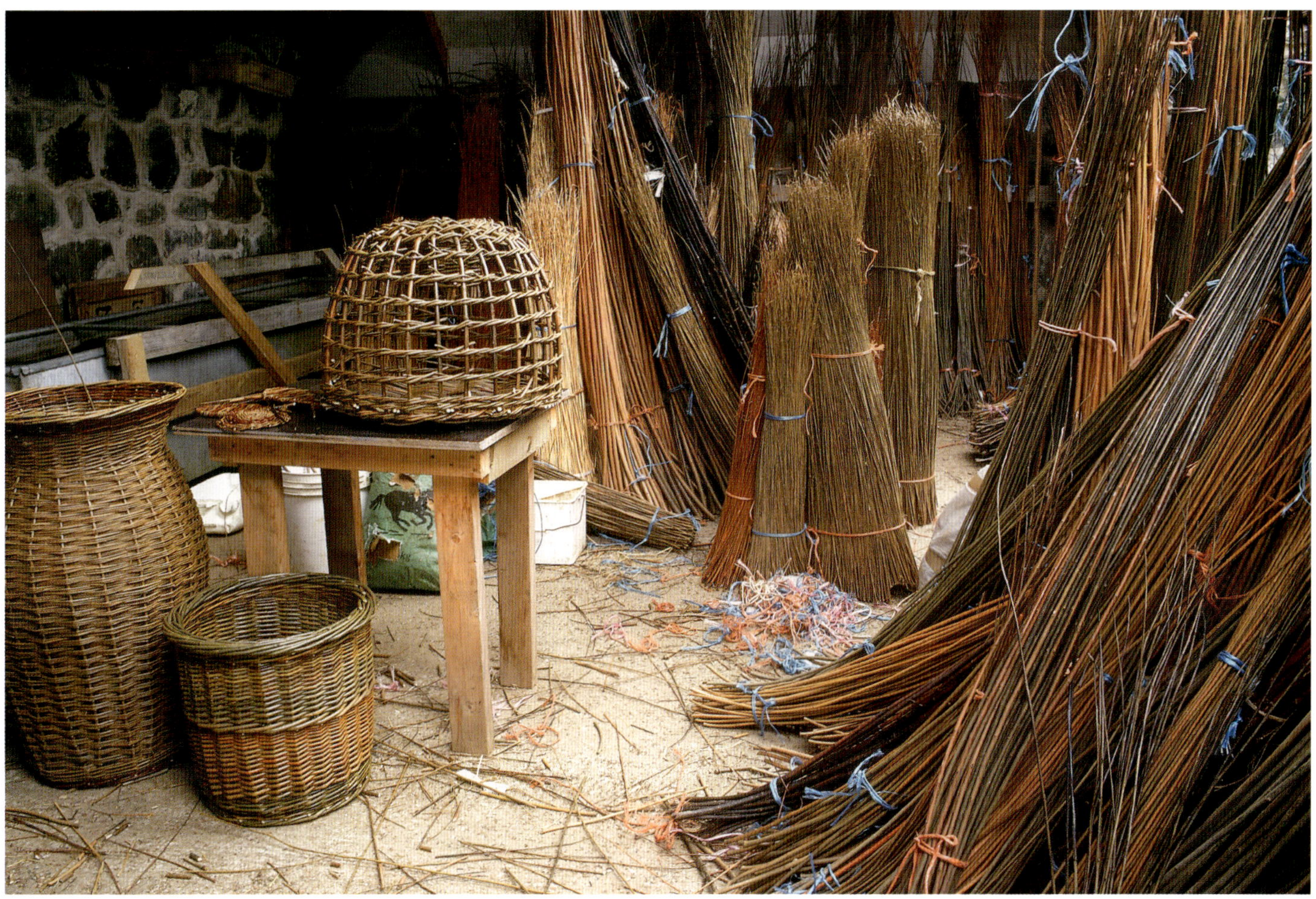

Basket makers' workshop. The baskets and other decorative wares are made using twenty varieties of willow organically grown in the surrounding garden. Each variety has a different colour and degree of strength and depending on the size and shape of the article being produced, the willow is chosen accordingly.

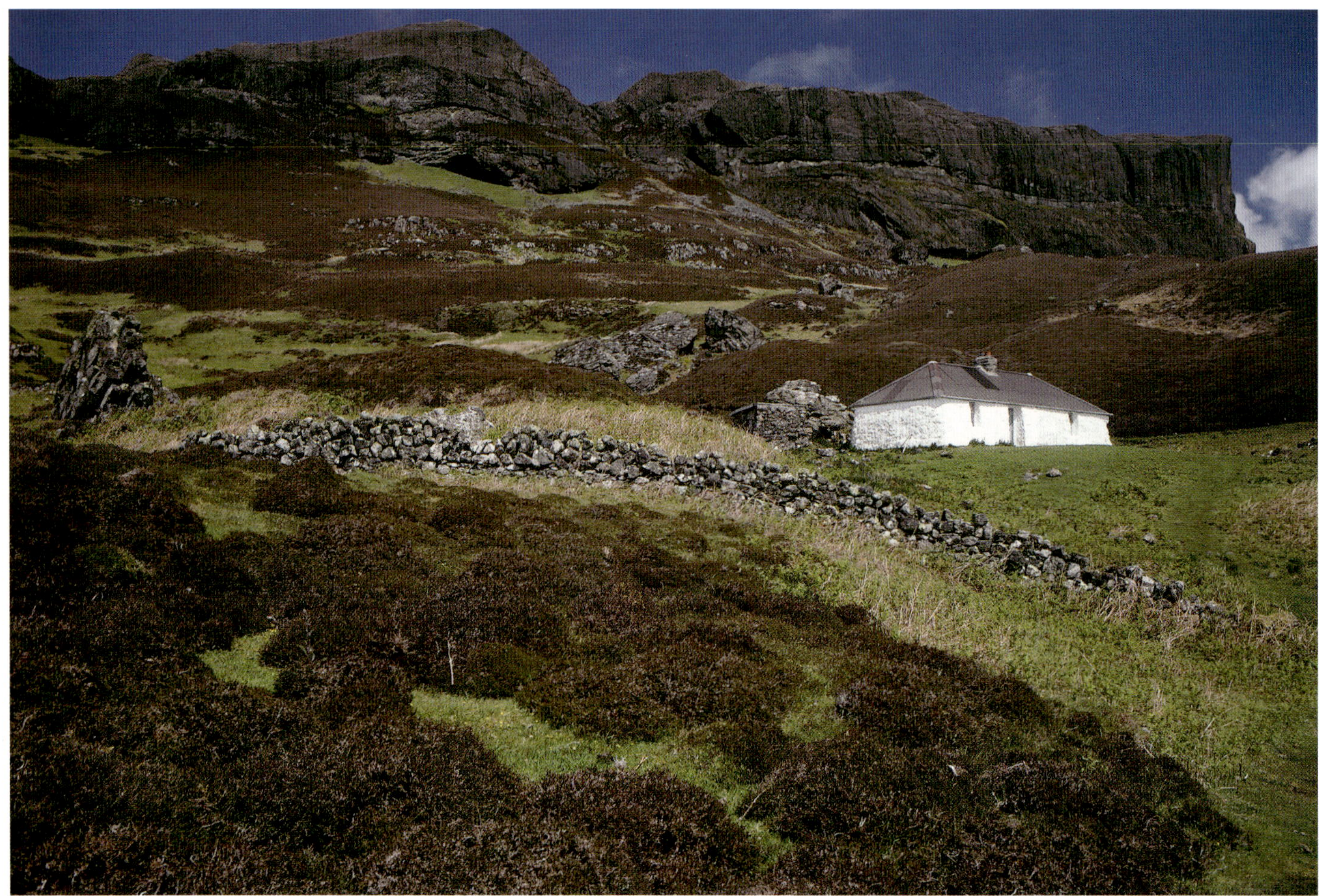

Shepherds bothy, Upper Grulin. On the southern coast of Eigg above low cliffs and with the steep flank of An Sgurr behind lie the remains of the two crofting townships of Upper and Lower Grulin. In 1853 the inhabitants of both settlements were forcibly cleared from their homes and shipped to Nova Scotia except for one family that remained as shepherds. Today apart from the bothy nothing survives other than lichen-encrusted stone walls amongst the boulders and bracken, yet more monuments to the appalling social consequences of nineteenth-century agricultural 'improvements' in Scotland. It is thought that this beautiful sloping site with its south facing aspect and long views to Mull and beyond had been settled since prehistoric times. For centuries it has been known as having some of the finest pastures on the island.

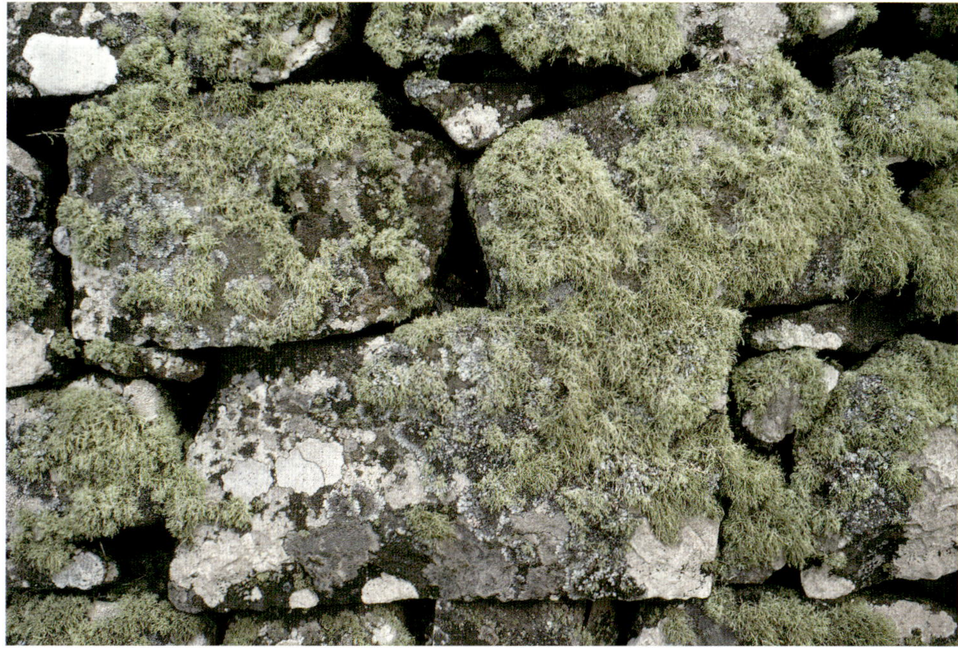

House walling, the Grulins.

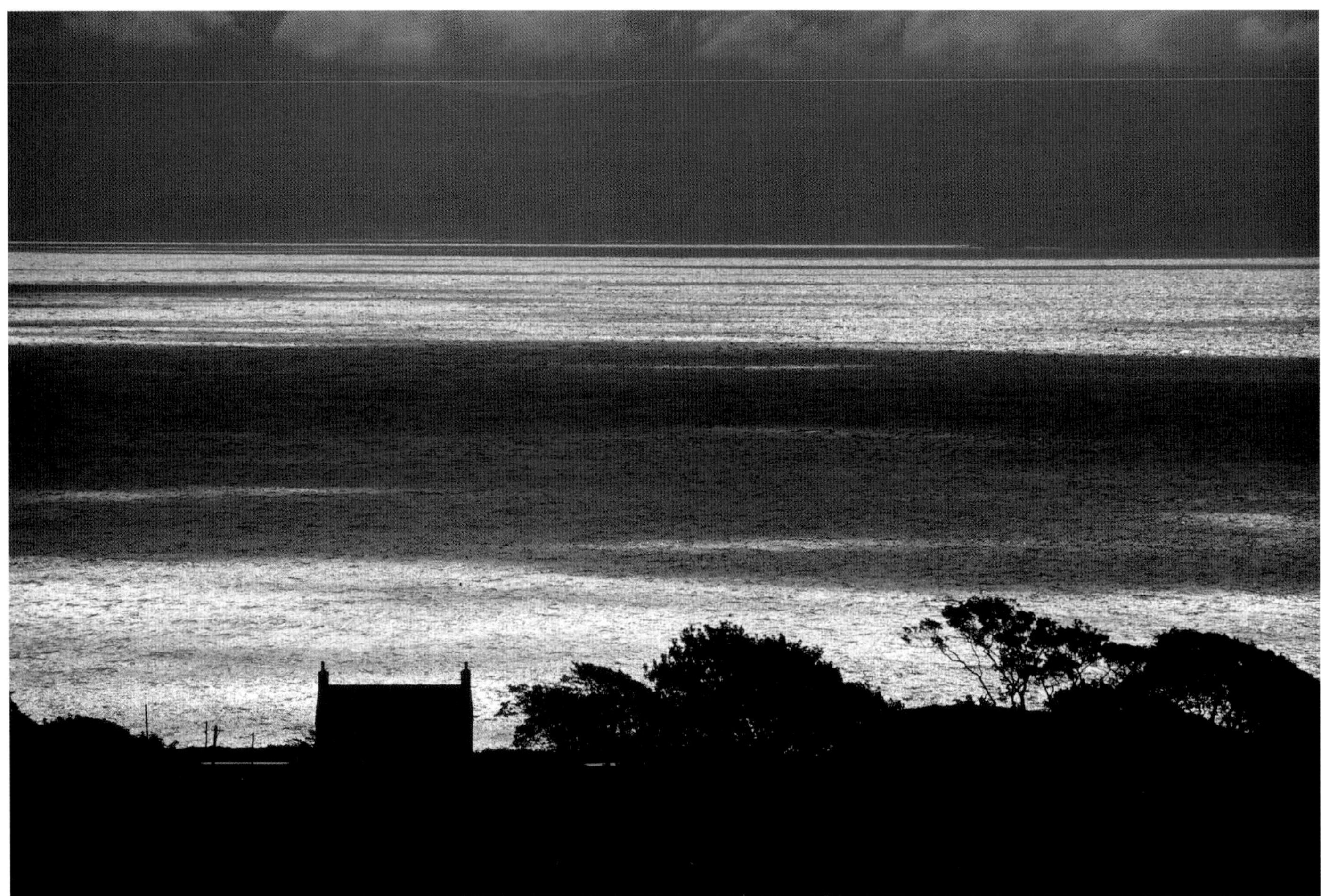

Light and shade looking east over Kildonnan Farm and open sea towards the mainland.

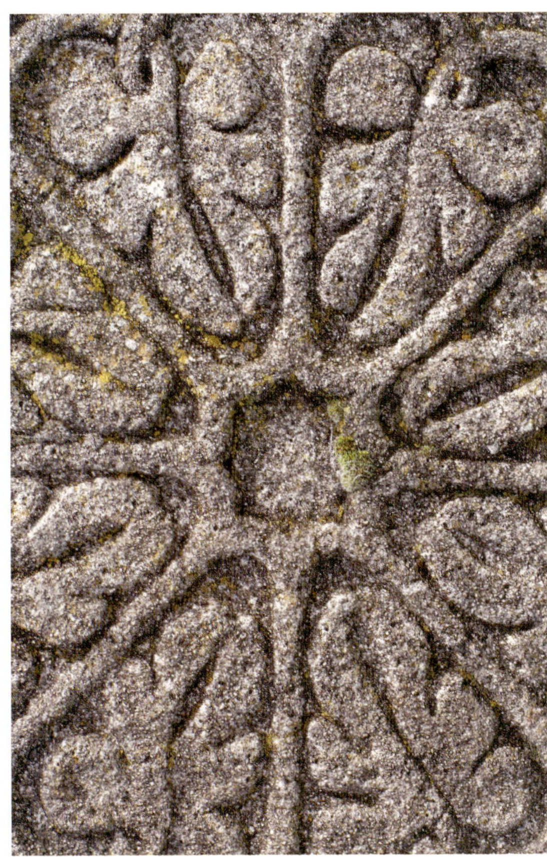

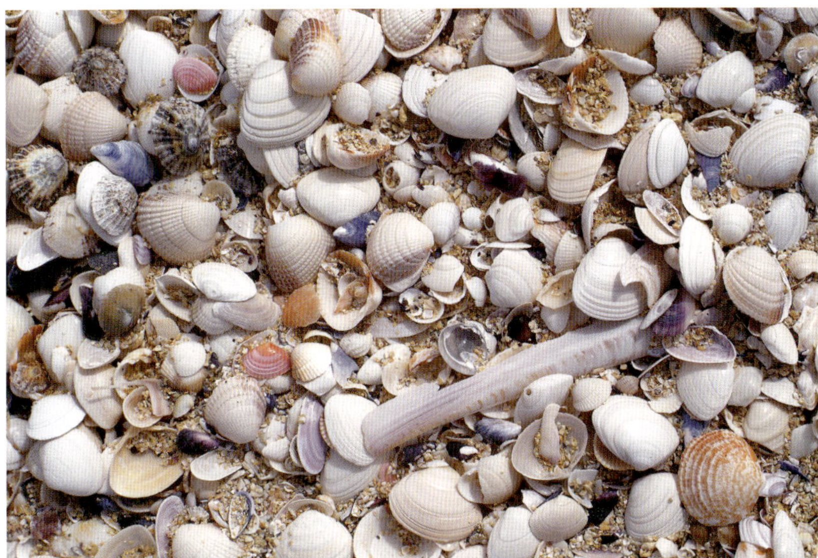

Aspects of Kildonnan. Kildonnan is named after St Donnan the island's patron saint martyred on Eigg in the seventh century. *Above:* Part of the broken Celtic cross situated in the island graveyard. *Top right:* Sea shells near Poll nam Partan. *Bottom right:* Gated footpath in woods below the cliffs.

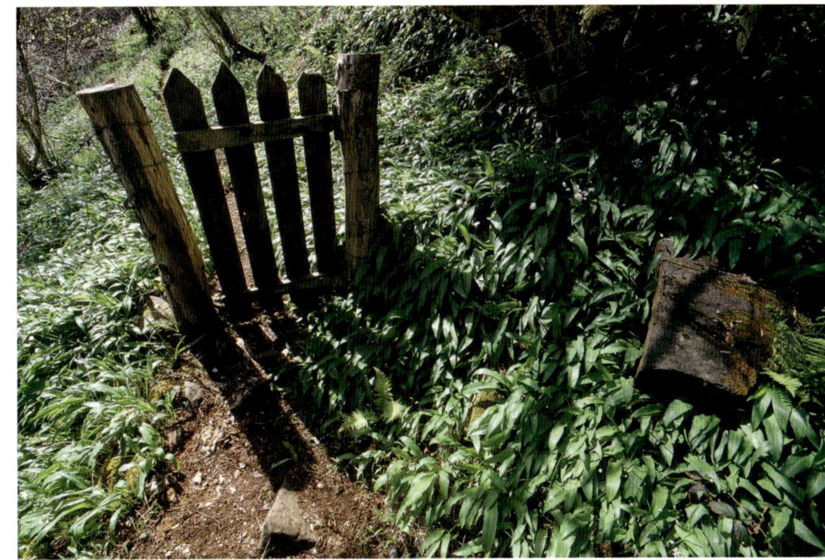

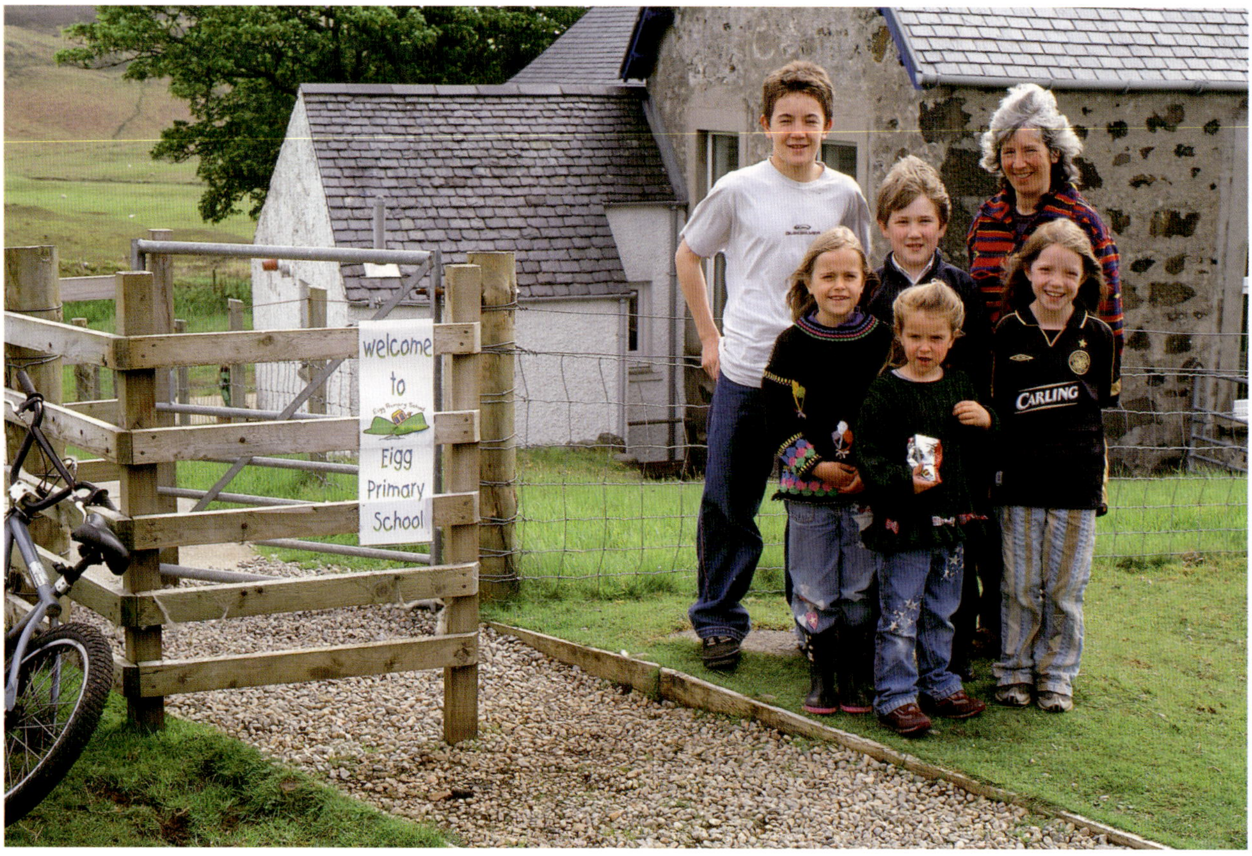

The island school. Originally built in 1829, the school now takes pupils ranging from a toddler's group up to the age of eleven when they then complete their education at secondary level at Mallaig High School. Prior to the 1930s the school would have accommodated 30-40 pupils but with the slow decline in Hebridean island populations, the numbers in later years have never exceeded ten. However, in very recent times particularly after the community buy out, the island population is again starting to grow and a new extension to the school was completed in 2007. The population of Eigg reached its peak of 546 in 1841 when almost every available piece of land was cultivated. This then halved rapidly through the period of the clearances, decreasing more slowly afterwards to a low point of just 60 in the mid 1990s.

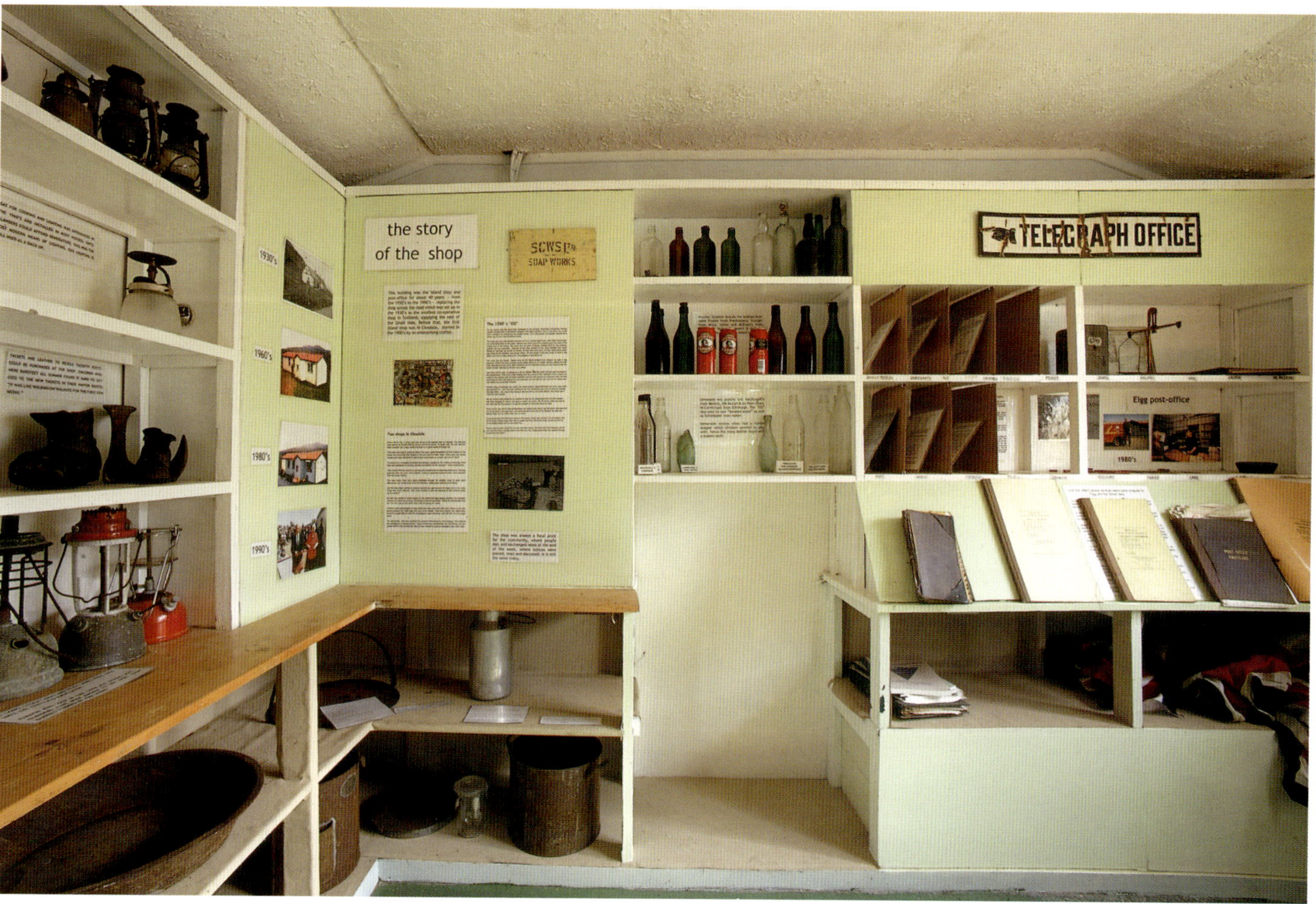

The island's old corrugated iron shop, originally opened in the early 1940s as a co-op store and post office (the smallest in the country), has now been refurbished as a small museum following the construction of the modern pier centre. The museum tells the story of Eigg in both geological and historical terms supported by numerous artefacts from around the island.

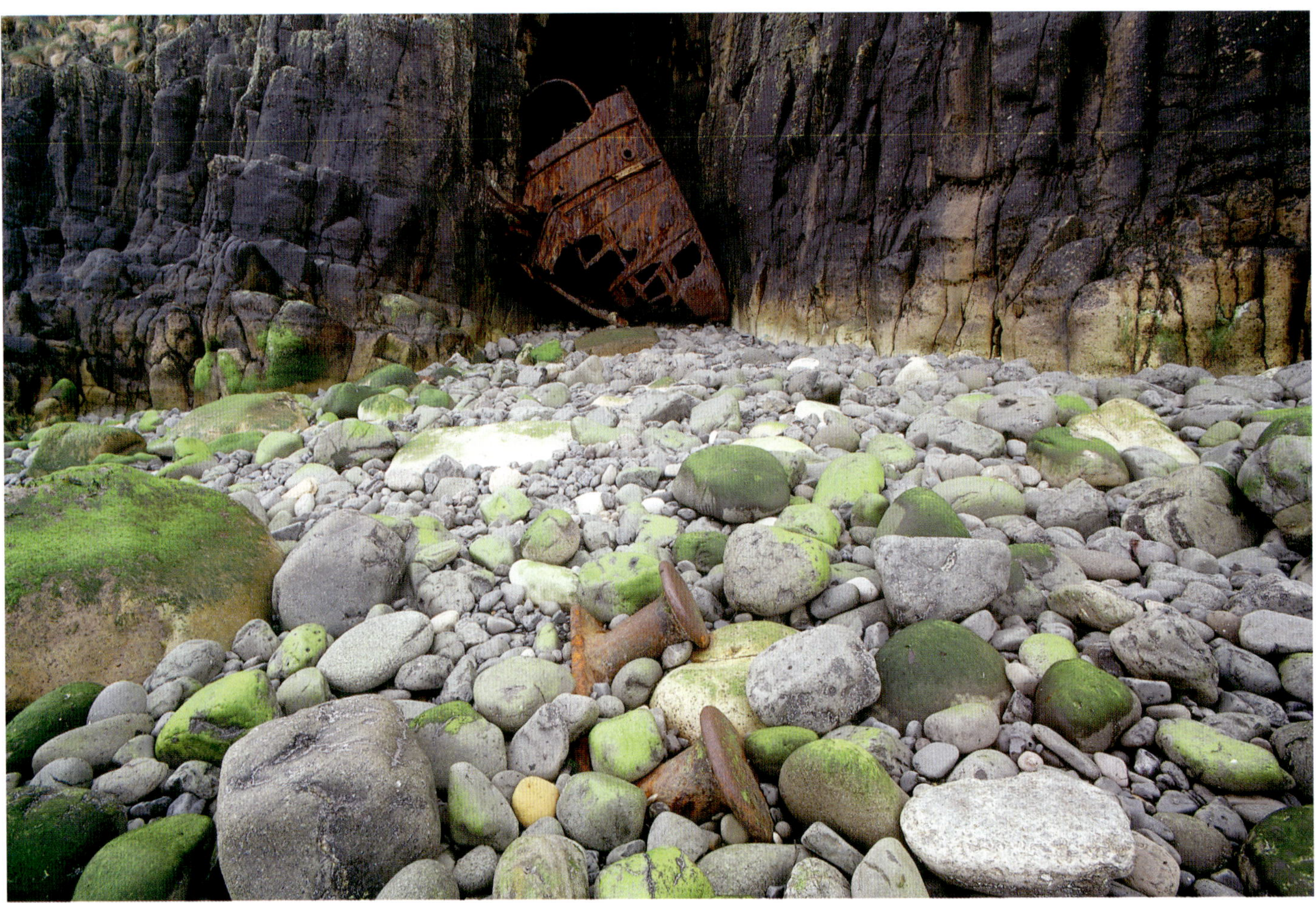

The last remains of the wreck of the puffer *The Jenny of Glasgow* smashed into a cave on the northeast corner of the island near Sgurr Sgaileach. Puffers were small coastal steamers with a flat-bottomed hull enabling them to berth on sandy beaches and were at one time very common throughout the islands. With its rocky coastline Eigg has numerous caves, most notably the infamous MacDonald massacre cave where the entire population was suffocated through fire by the MacLeods in 1577 and the nearby Cathedral cave once used for services during the persecution of the Roman Catholic church following the Reformation.

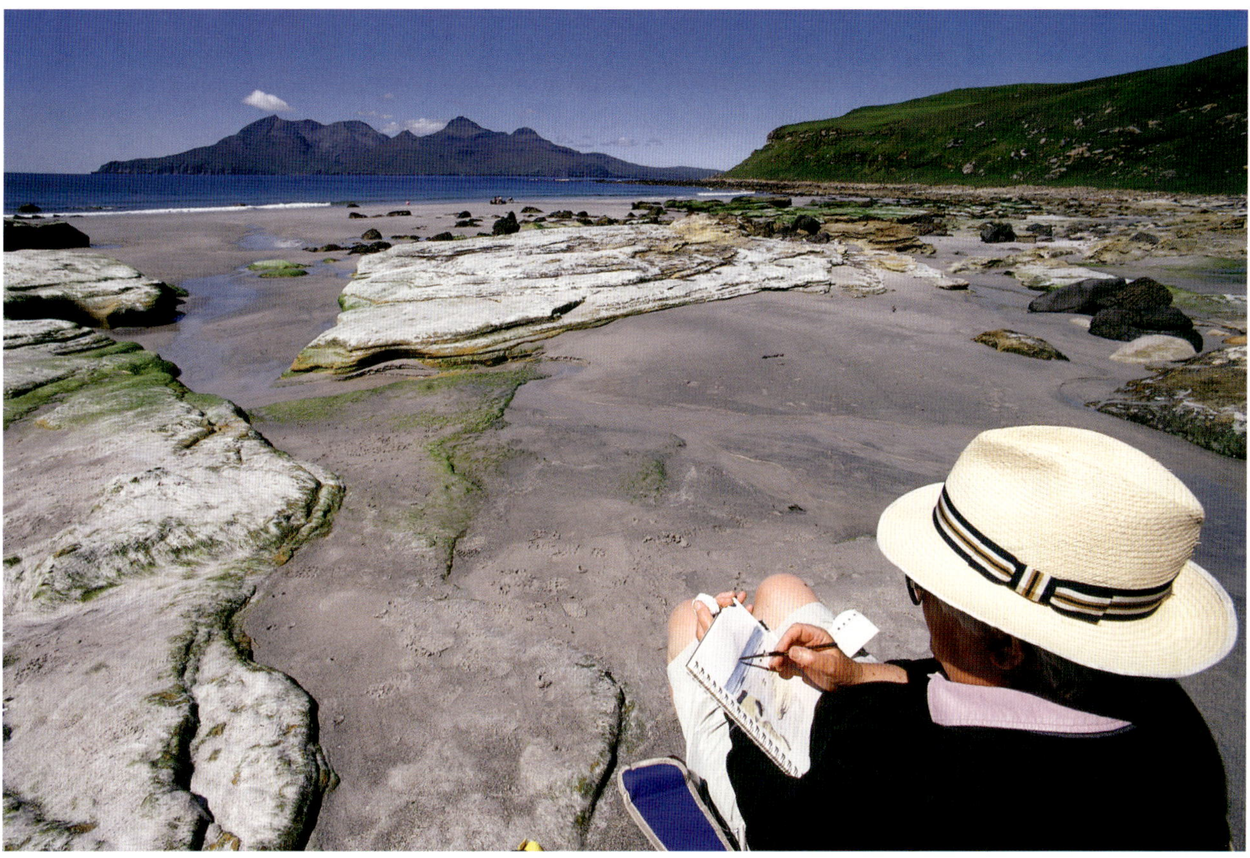

A painting session on Singing Sands beach. The sands, so called because of the shrill screech produced when trodden or scuffed in dry conditions, look out westwards to the island of Rum and are one of Eigg's most popular attractions. Much of the sand is often removed by gales and tidal action during the winter months only to be washed in again during early spring.

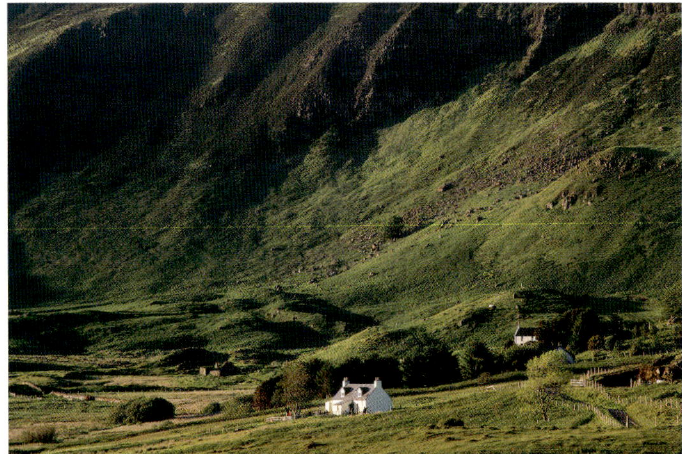

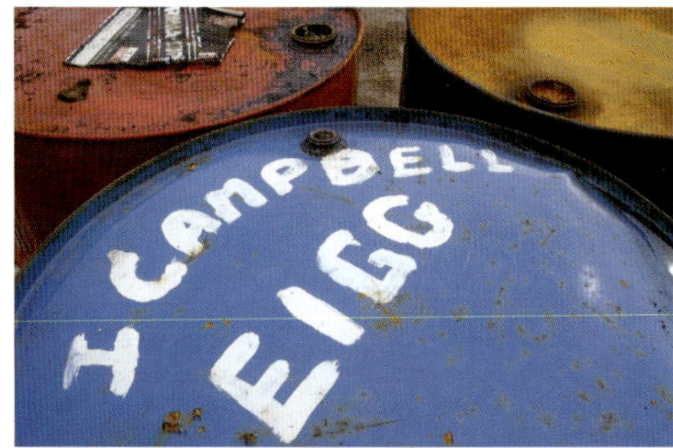

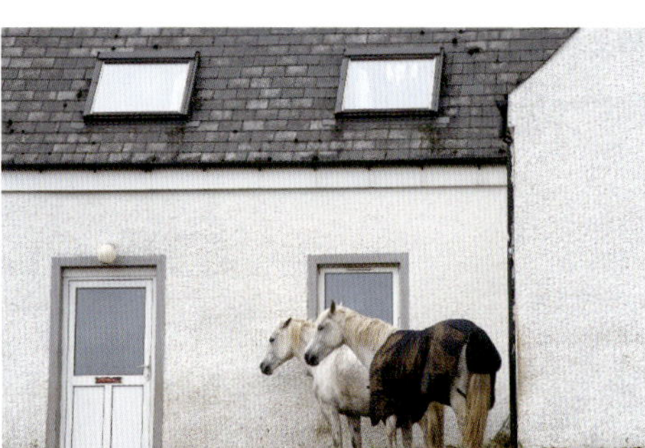

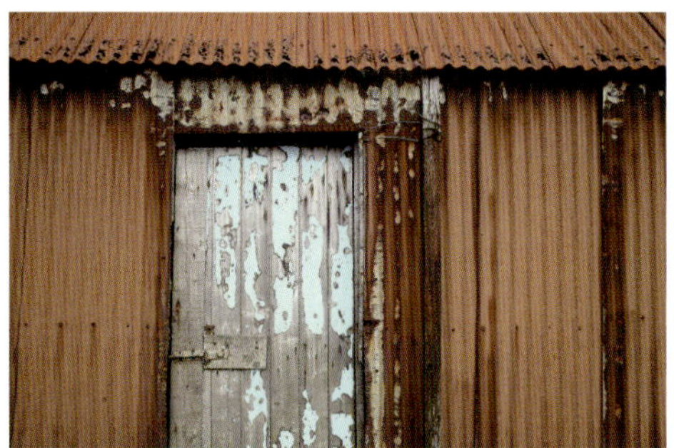

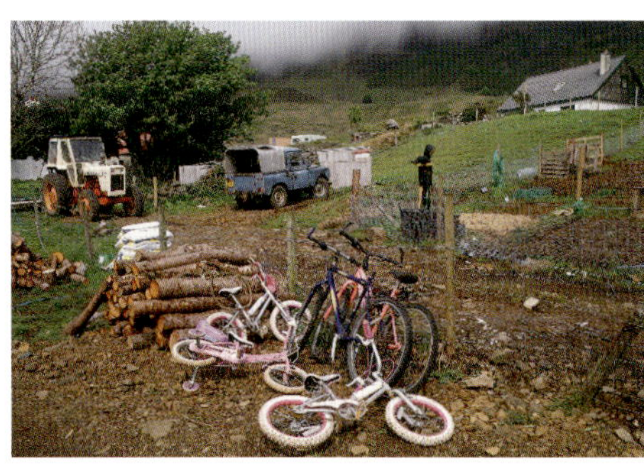

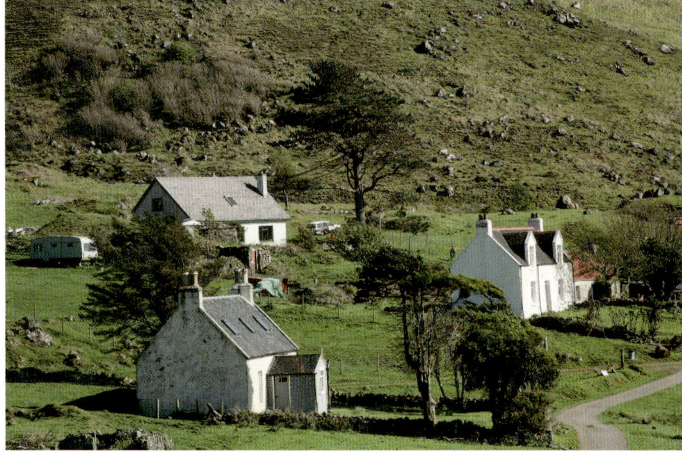

This page and opposite: Cleadale. The fertile coastal plain of Cleadale, taking in the old crofting townships of Cuagach, Five Pennies, Howlin, Illtaig and Laig, faces west sheltered in an amphitheatre of dramatic cliffs reaching up to the 336m Beinn Bhuidhe plateau. It is the main crofting area on the island and where most of the Eigg population now live.

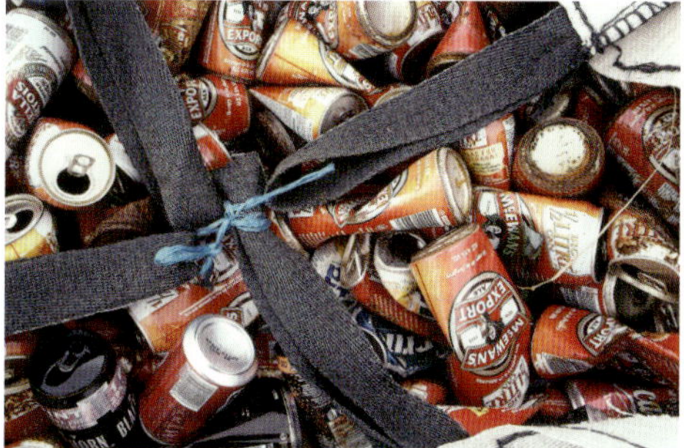

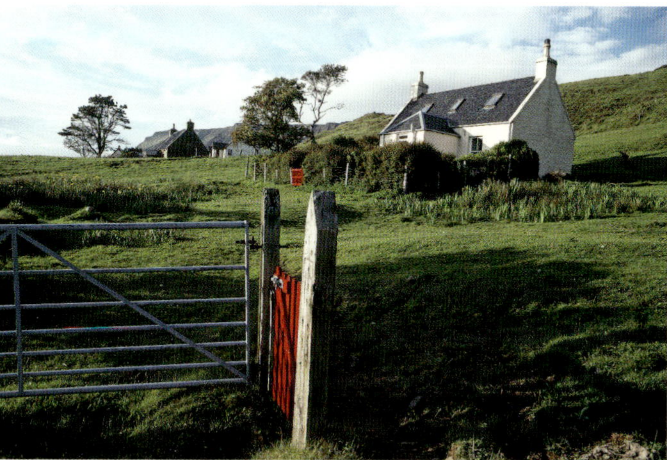

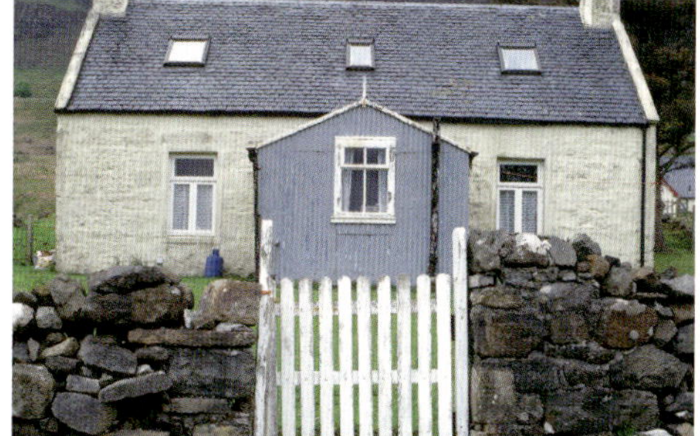

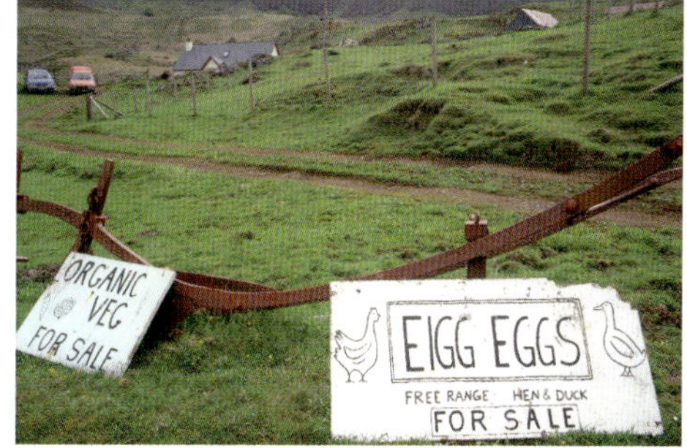

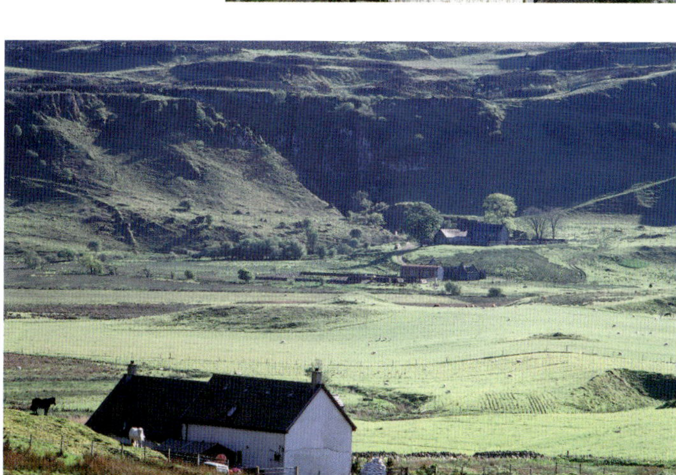

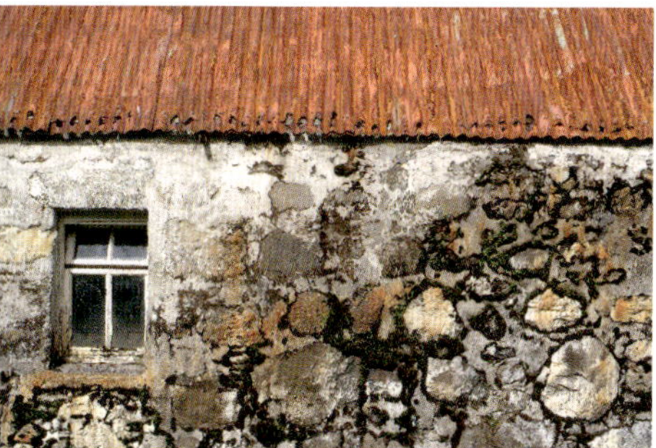

Much of the croft land stretches to the sea's edge of Laig Bay and undulates across the entire amphitheatre broken only by burns, tracks and clusters of cottages and houses. The photographs here give an impression of this fascinating area and lifestyle.

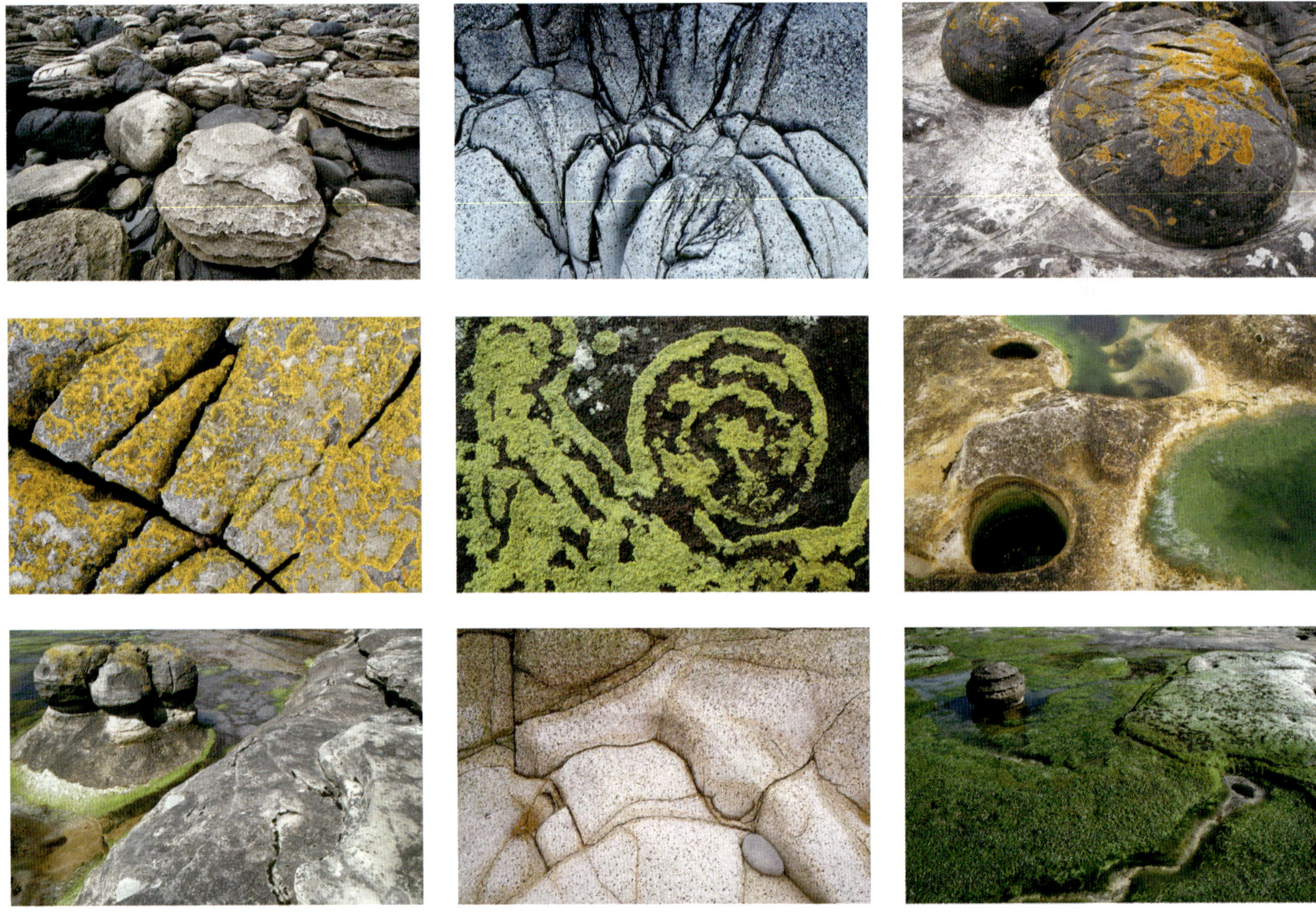

This page and opposite: On the blunt coastline between Singing Sands Bay and Laig Bay can be found the most remarkable rock formations. Sometimes spread out in wide Valtos sandstone or volcanic lava sheets and platforms, often eroded into water-filled pots, cavities or fissures or sometimes formed into rounded concretions, mushroom-shaped protrusions, dramatic cliff overhangs, narrow passageways or natural arches, the area provides an outstanding wealth of interest for the geologist and naturalist. Secret waterfalls can be heard, burns tumble to the sea in a vast natural rock garden broken by numerous basaltic dykes angling their way to Rum whilst orchids and yellow iris can be found in profusion on the grassy banks behind. The famous Scottish geologist Hugh Miller arrived on Eigg in the 1840s to discover not only the bones of a Plesiosaur together with other fish and reptilian remains but to determine the age and history of this amazing place. *Opposite:* Looking from the southern end of the rocks abutting Laig Bay towards Rum on a stormy day.

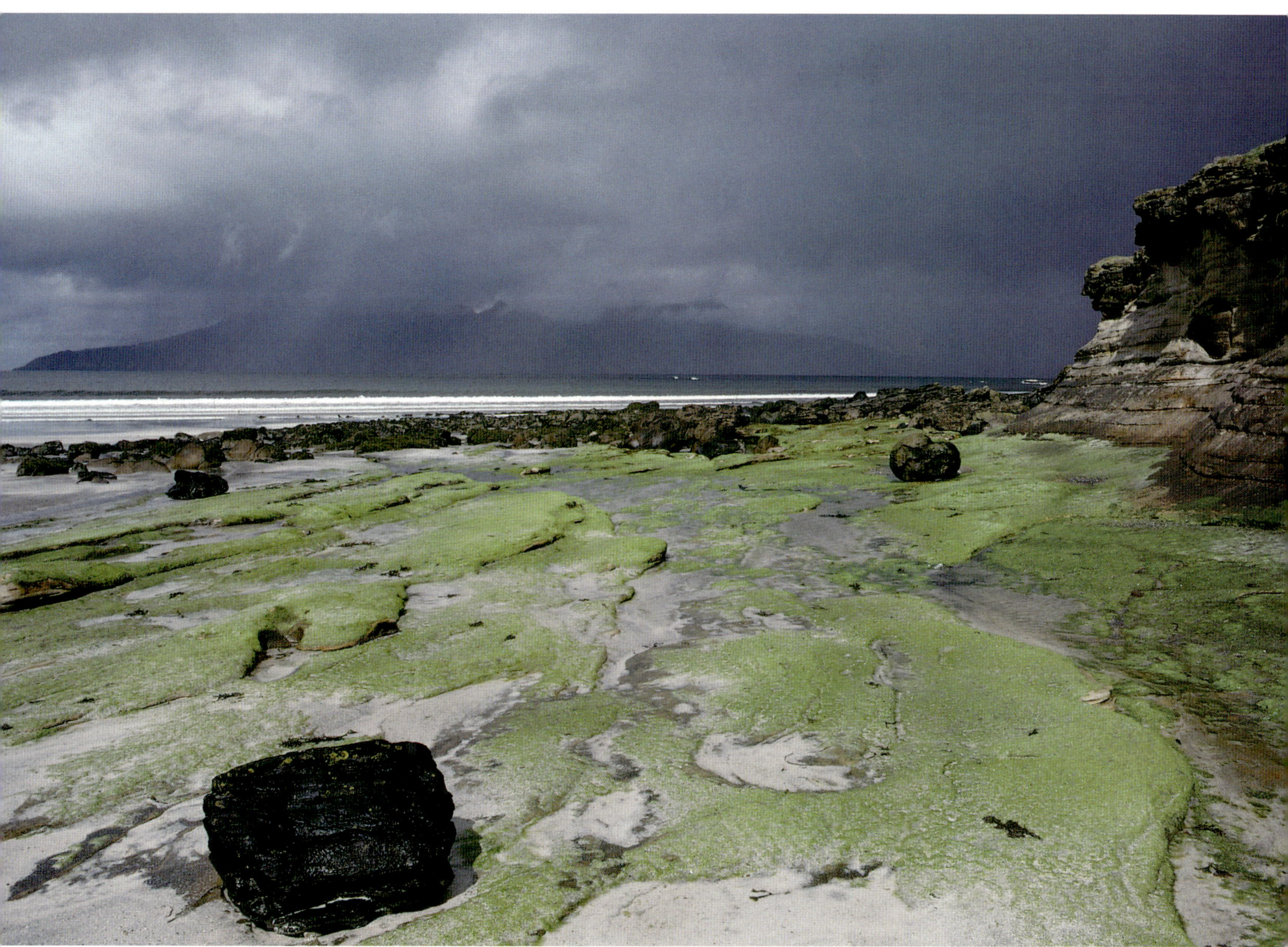

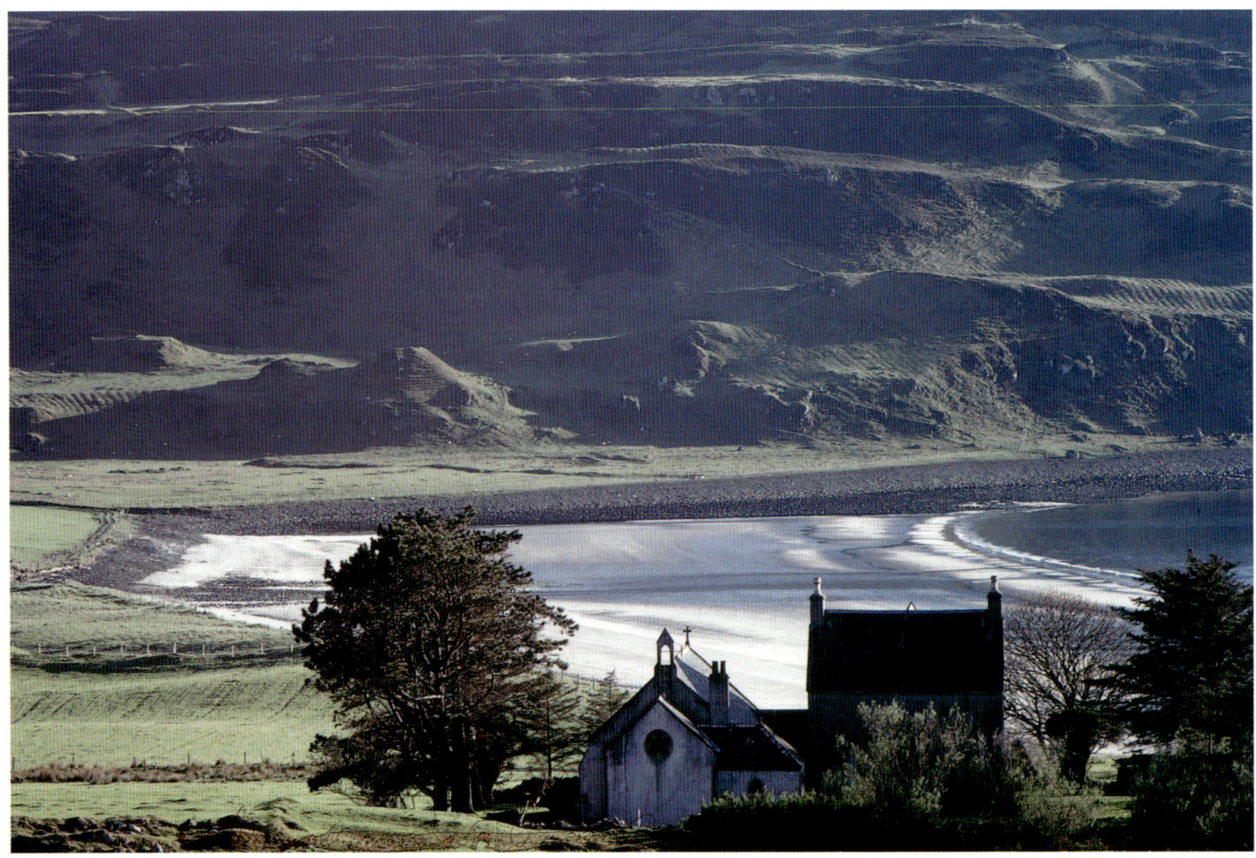

The Roman Catholic Chapel of St Donnan at the back of Laig Bay was completed in 1910 incorporating an adjacent Priest's House. In recent years much needed repair work has been carried out although the house is now a forlorn ruin. The chapel's years of exposure to the southwest gales and rain make it an extremely vulnerable building requiring almost constant maintenance but despite this services have still been held regularly. When the distant sounds of the sea breaking on Laig Bay together with cries of gulls intermingle with the congregation's singing then a sense of peace pervades all.

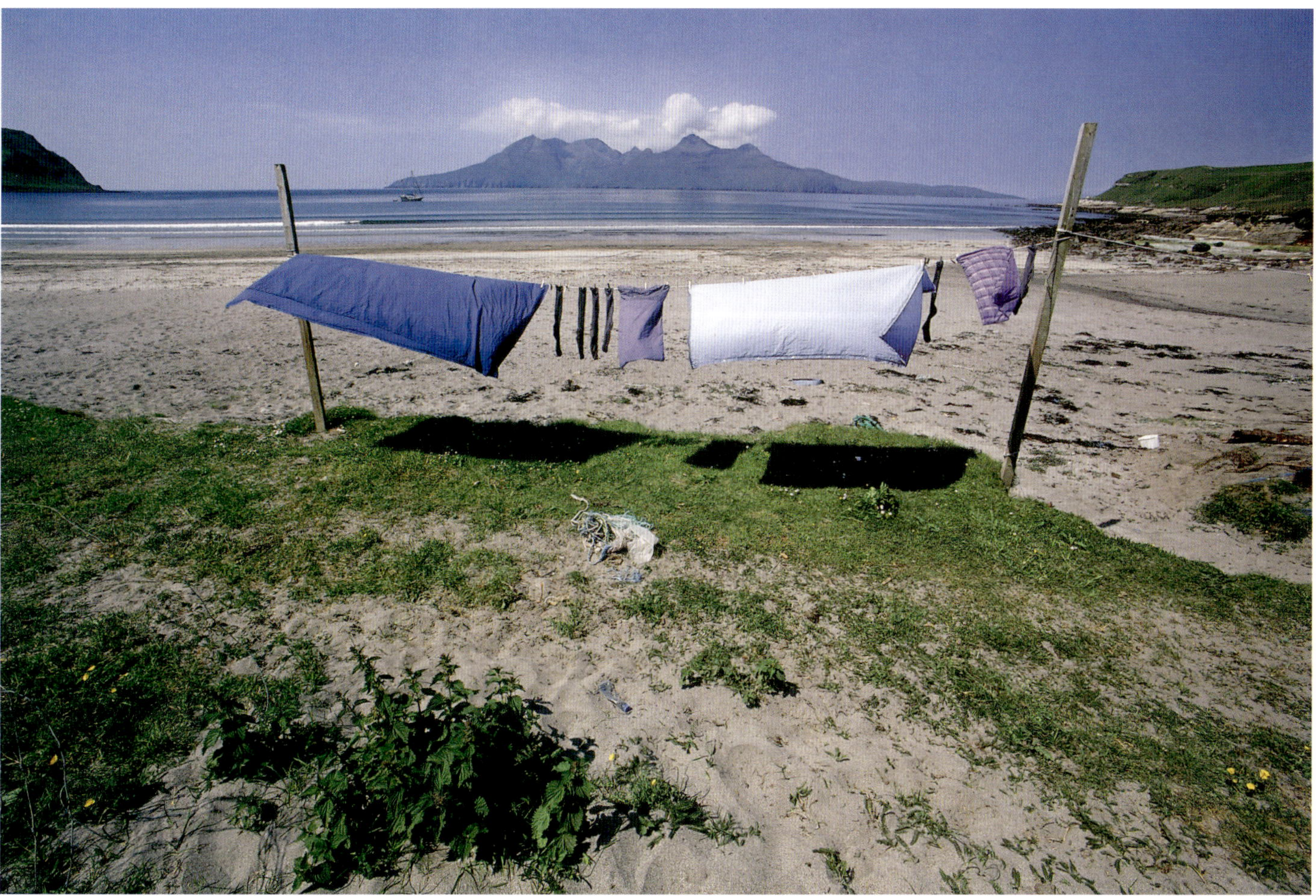

Washday at Laig. Laig Bay with its views west to Rum is one of the great sights of the Hebrides and possibly one of the finest seascape locations in Great Britain. Rum's dominating classic peaked outline some 10km away together with the constantly changing weather, light and mood make this a marvellous place to paint, sketch, photograph or simply lie on the beach and savour the bay's sheer perfection. The photographs on the remaining pages of this chapter illustrate just a few aspects of this spectacular scene.

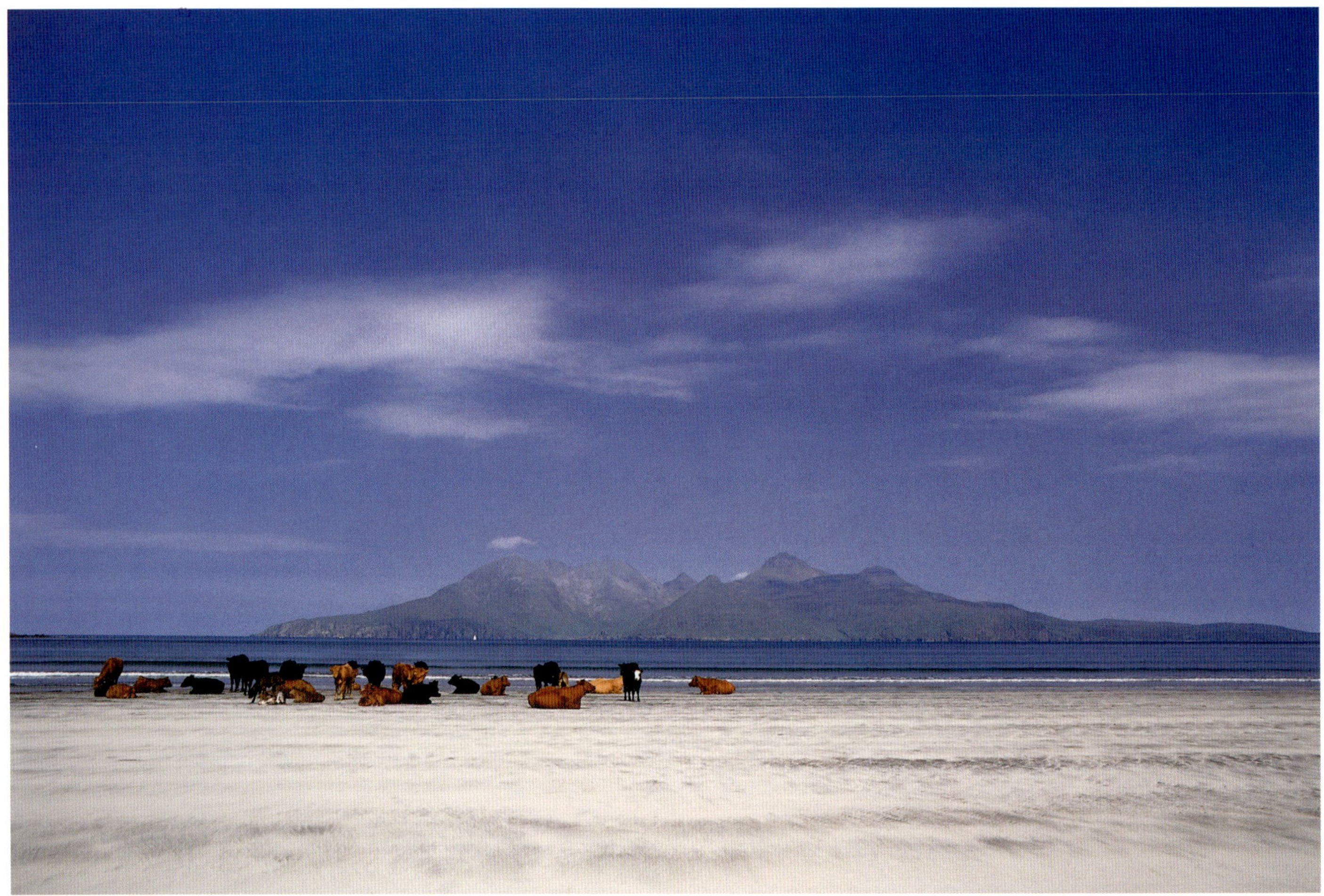

An idyllic summer's day when even the cattle seem to appreciate their magnificent surroundings.

Colour at Laig.

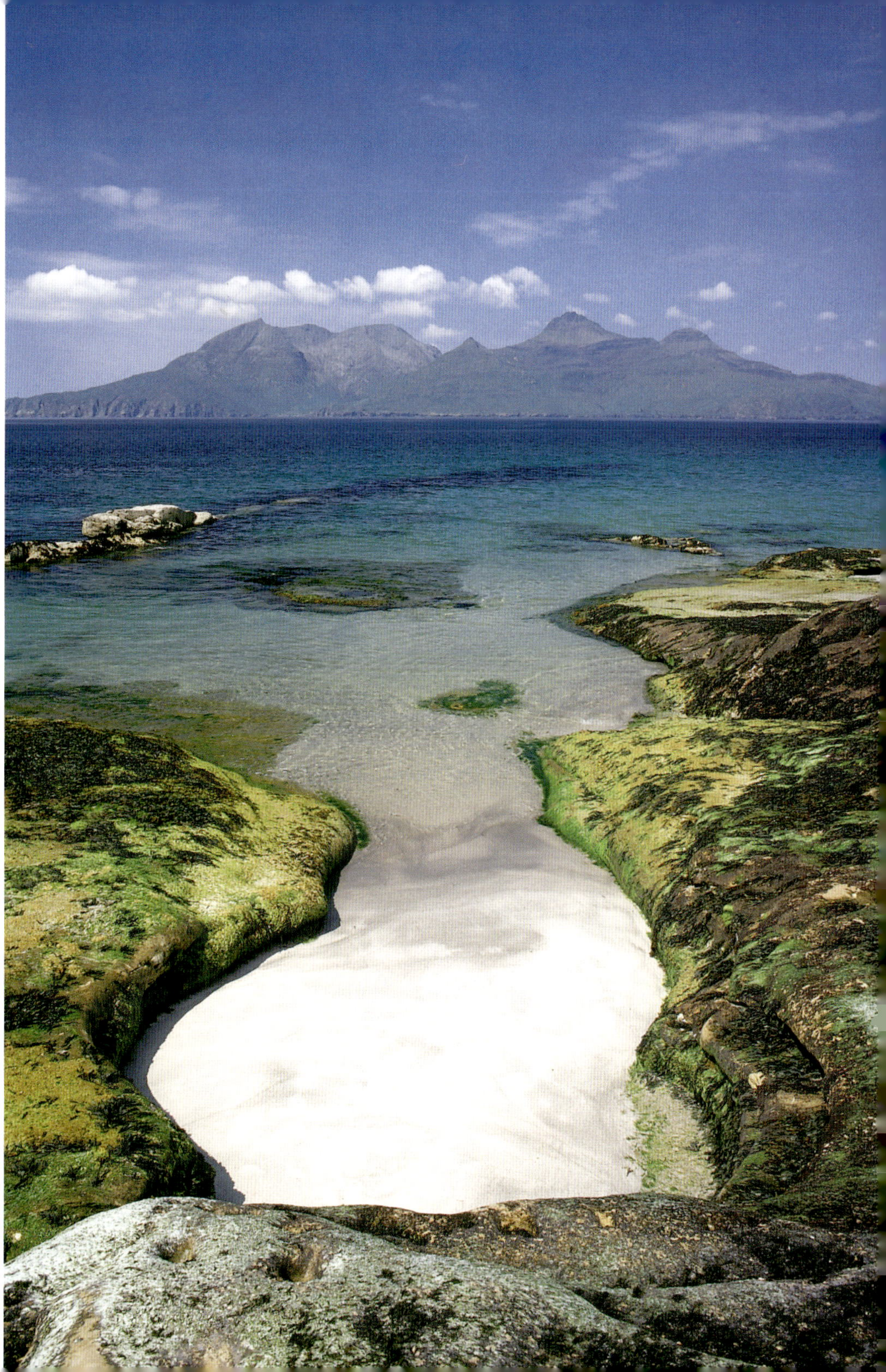

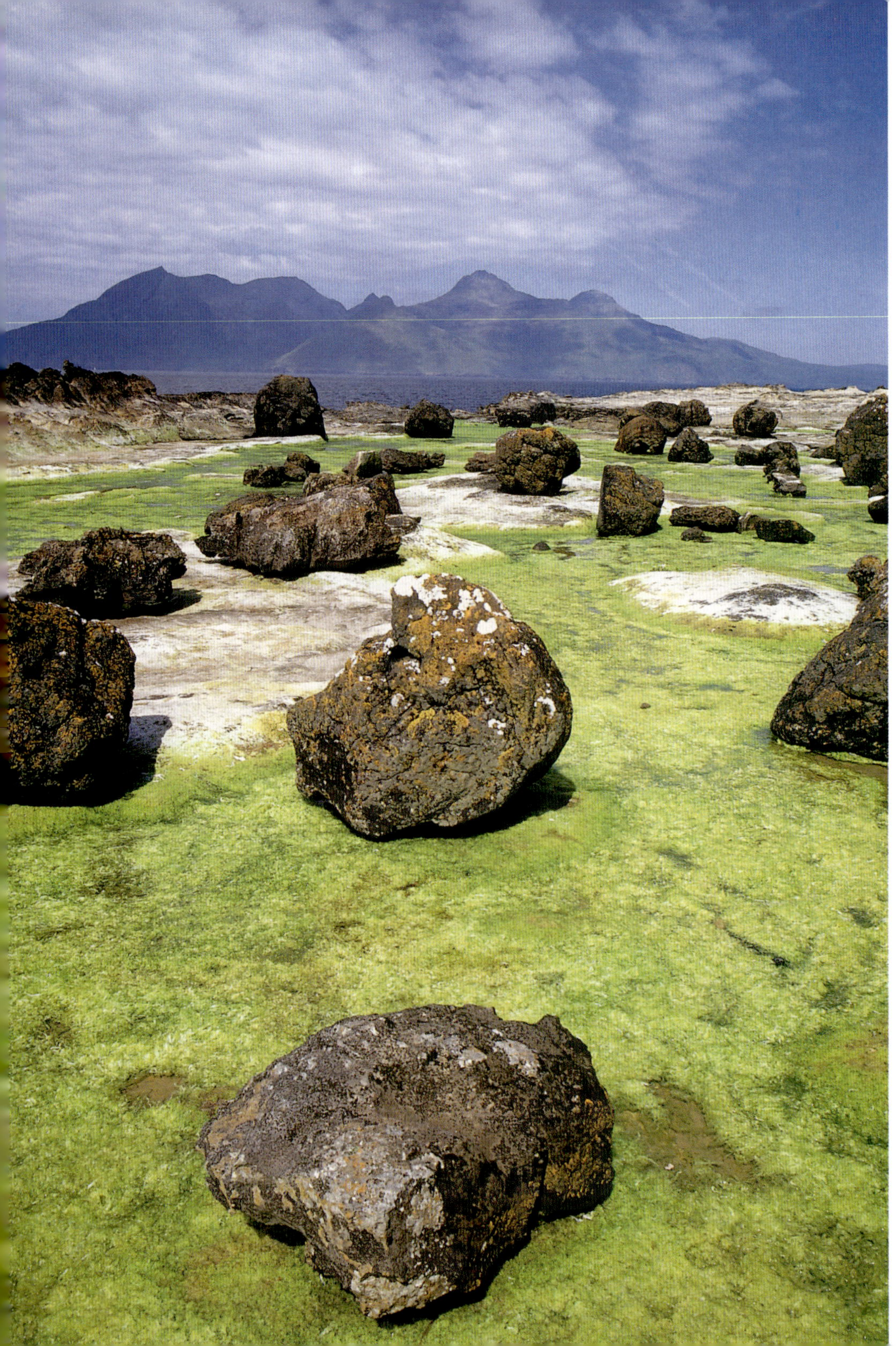

The scattered boulders in the foreground act as a reminder of the period when Rum was an active volcano. The boulders would have been hurled out during eruptions to land on the Eigg foreshore, cool and in many cases crack open. To walk here during a slight sea mist evokes an utterly timeless, eerie scene.

> 'Every rock is a tablet of hieroglyphics, with an ascertained alphabet; every rolled pebble a casket, with old pictorial records locked up within.'
>
> Hugh Miller, *Cruise of the Betsy, 1858.*

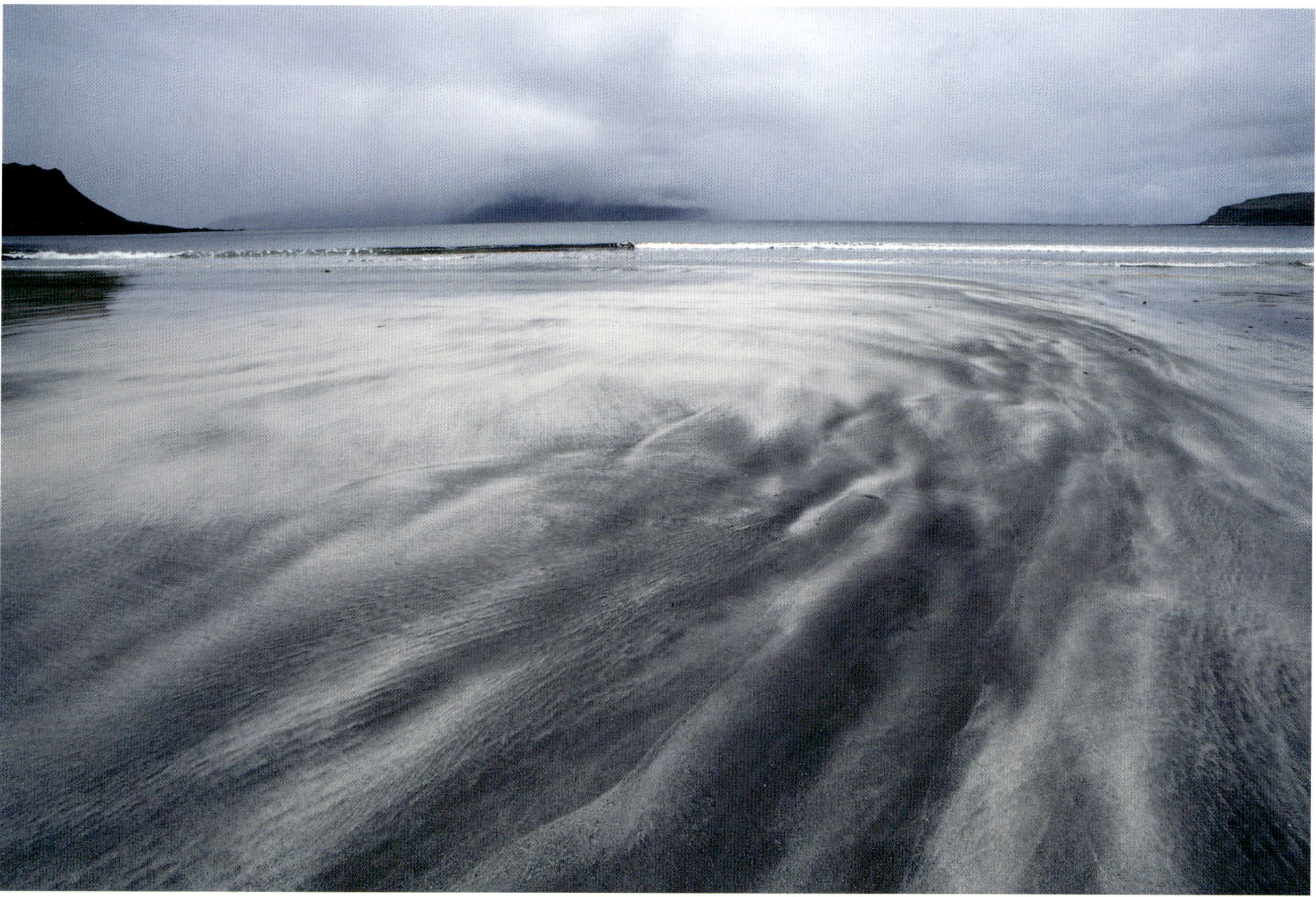

A grey day when low cloud covers Rum's peaks. There are times when the island entirely disappears as if being towed away in the mist and yet on other days, when the light seems to sparkle, Rum appears close enough to touch. The foreground sand patterns change constantly with every tide to produce a myriad of shapes and designs.

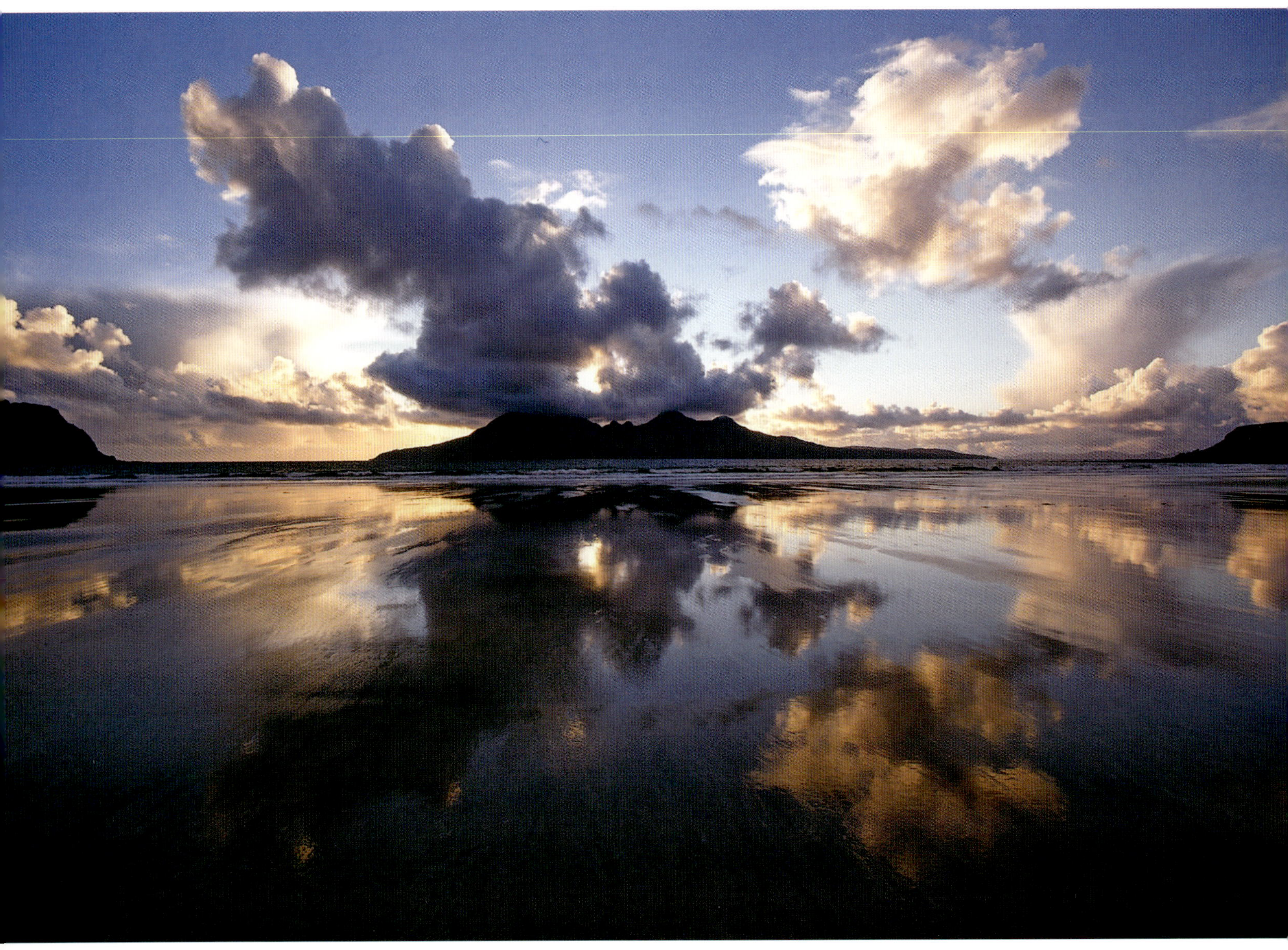

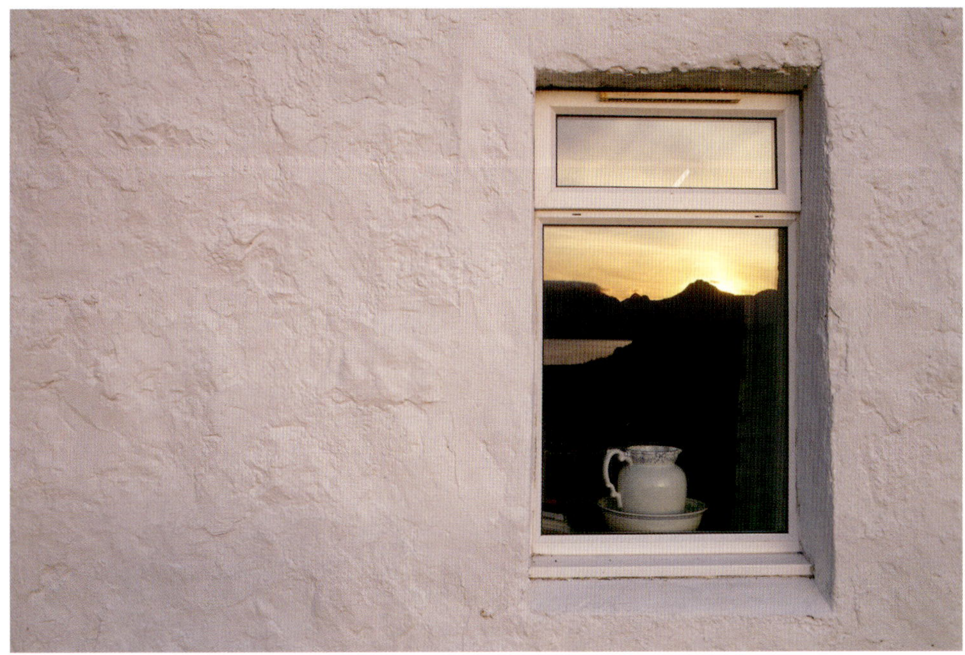

Evening reflections, Laig.

Opposite: Late afternoon on a falling tide when the wet sand acts as a mirror to this wonderful scene.

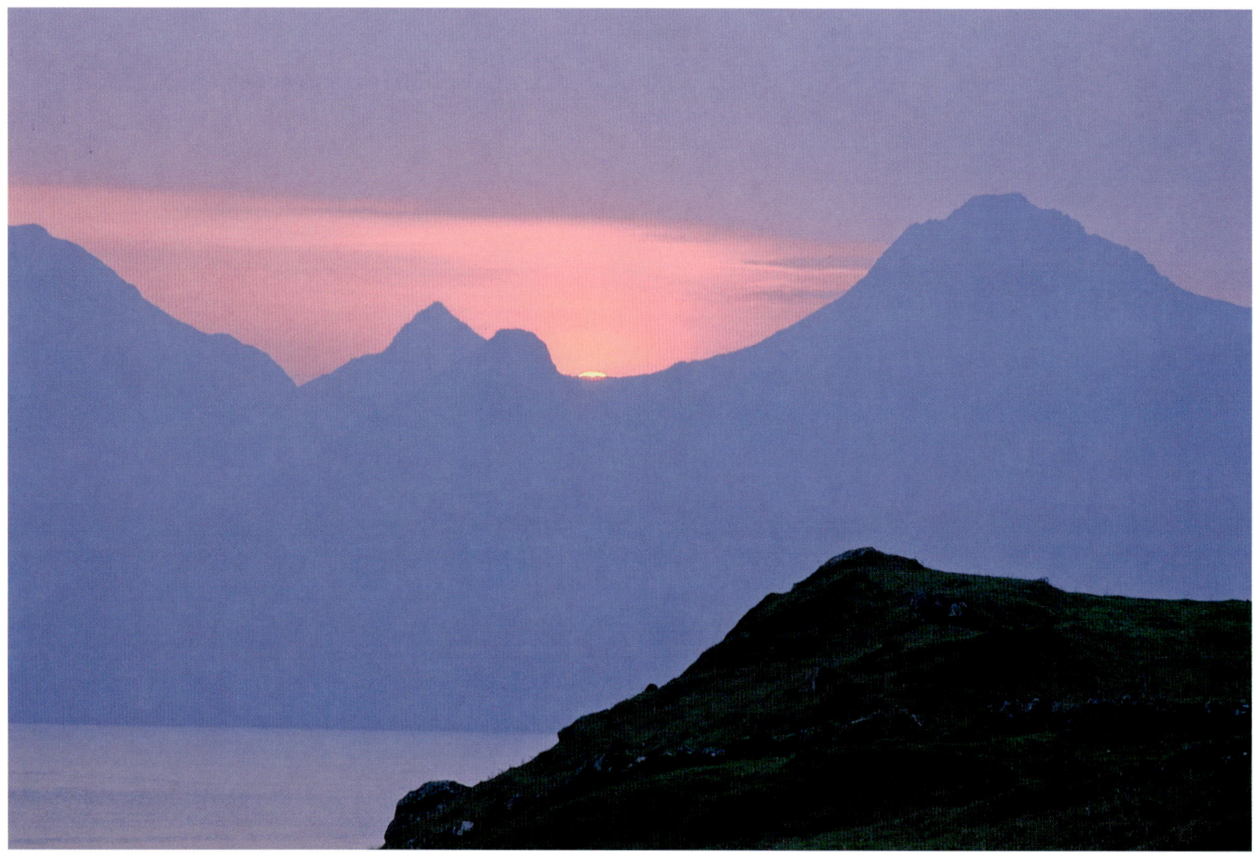

A foreground hill echoes the shape of Rum's peaks with a last glimpse of the setting sun as it sinks slowly behind the island.

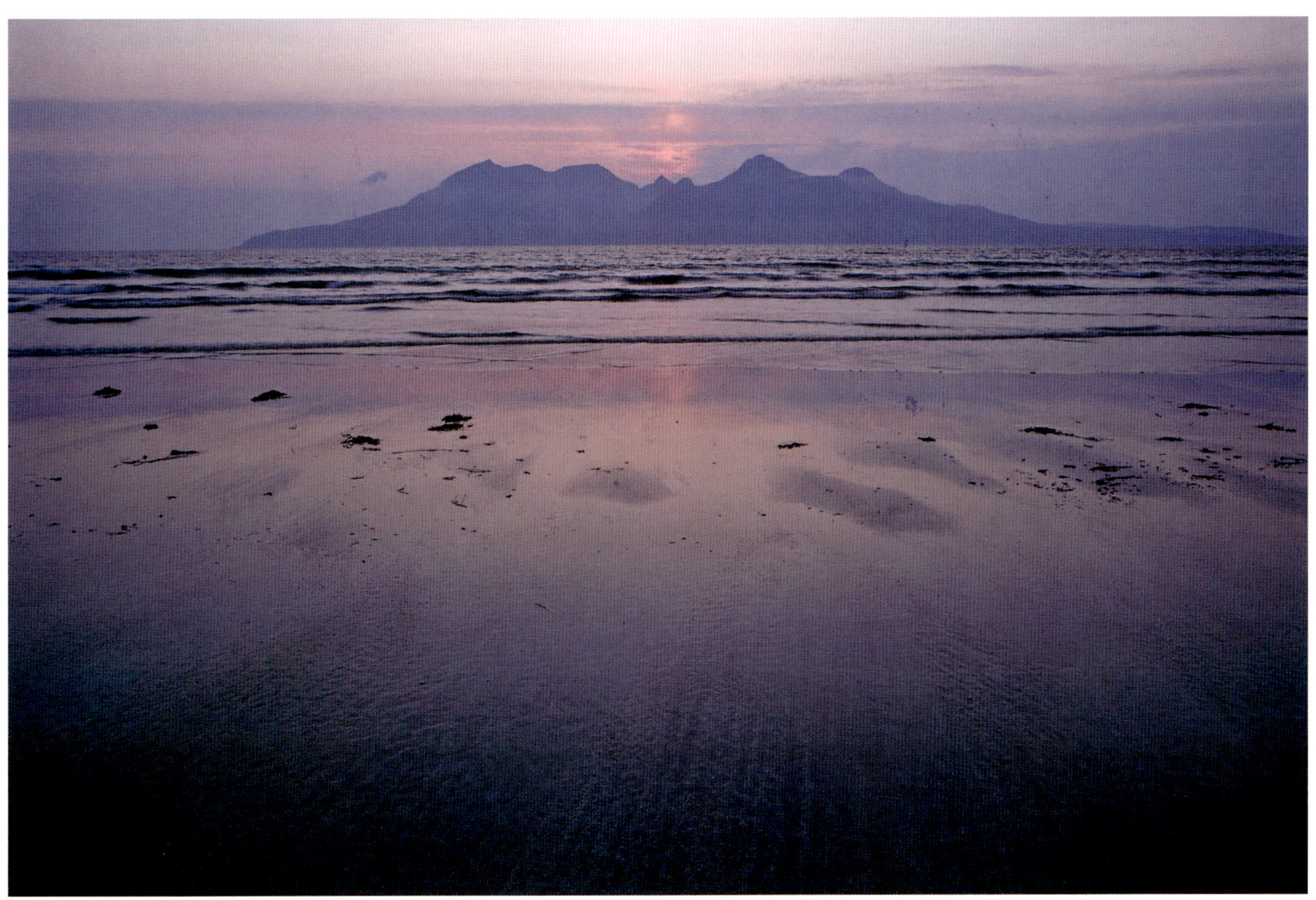

A perfect end, a perfect day, a perfect place.

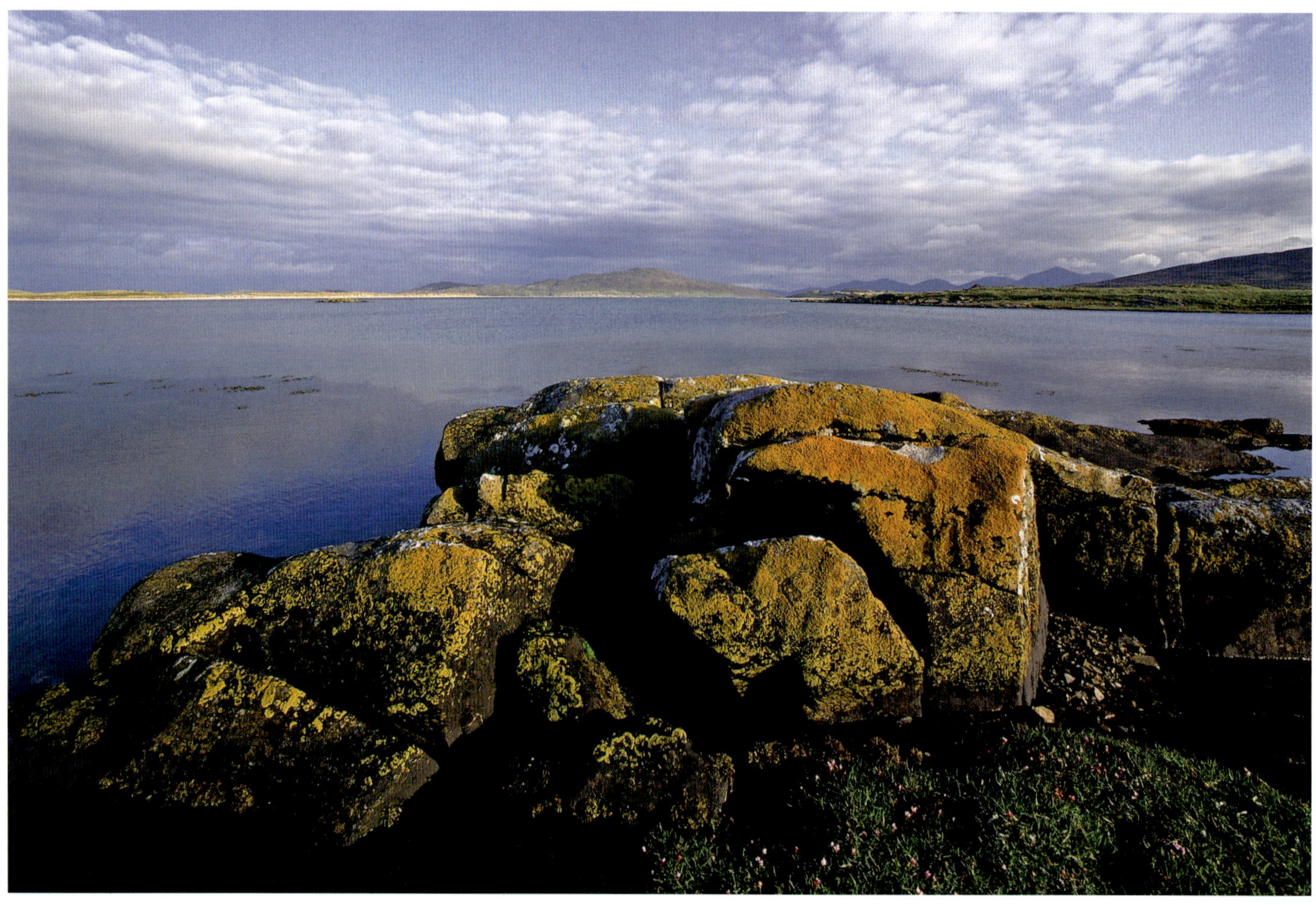

Early morning calm at Seilebost on the west coast of Harris overlooking Tràigh Losgaintir (Luskentyre) with the island of Taransay in the background and the North Harris Hills in the far distance. Waters flood into the estuarine bay at each tide through winding, sinuous channels producing a myriad of colour variations, shapes and patterns depending on light, skies, wind and depth of water at any one point, a mecca for any artist or photographer.

Sea, Sand and Showers
HARRIS

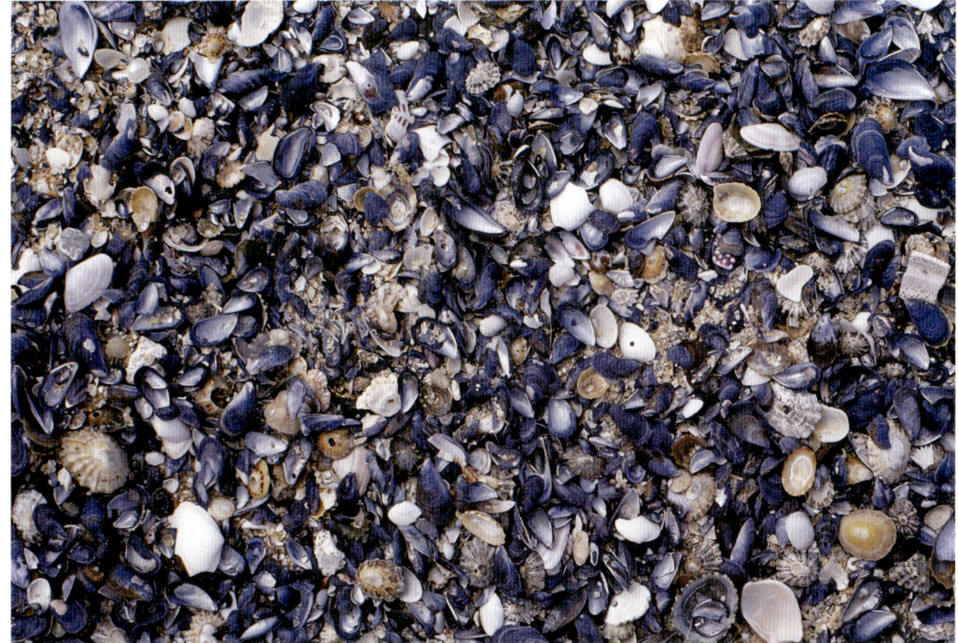

A carpet of sea shells at Horgabost.

For many, to dream of the Hebrides evokes a scene of empty white or golden sand beaches backed by lush machair and marram grass, sparkling blue waters and with the outline of distant islands or mountains beyond. Perhaps a crystal clear sunny day is intertwined with these thoughts or alternatively a soft grey blanket of low cloud or mist when water and sky combine. More than any other Hebridean island these visions seem to say Harris. For here, despite being linked by the same wild land mass to its much larger and bleaker Outer Hebridean neighbour of Lewis, Harris and in particular South Harris features some of the most colourful and memorable coastal views in Britain. Long, curving, often deeply scalloped, deserted shell sand bays form almost the entire west coast and much of the south. Yet, in utter contrast the east coast and hinterland, together with mountainous North Harris abutting the Lewis boundary, is a lunar landscape of treeless, undulating, naked rock broken only by small lochans and occasional peat workings. It is this variation of character, the change between the colours, the milder, gentler atmosphere, almost a softness of the beach scenes contrasting with the stark, desert like, protruding Gneiss rock with its lack of soil that provides much of the fascination of Harris.

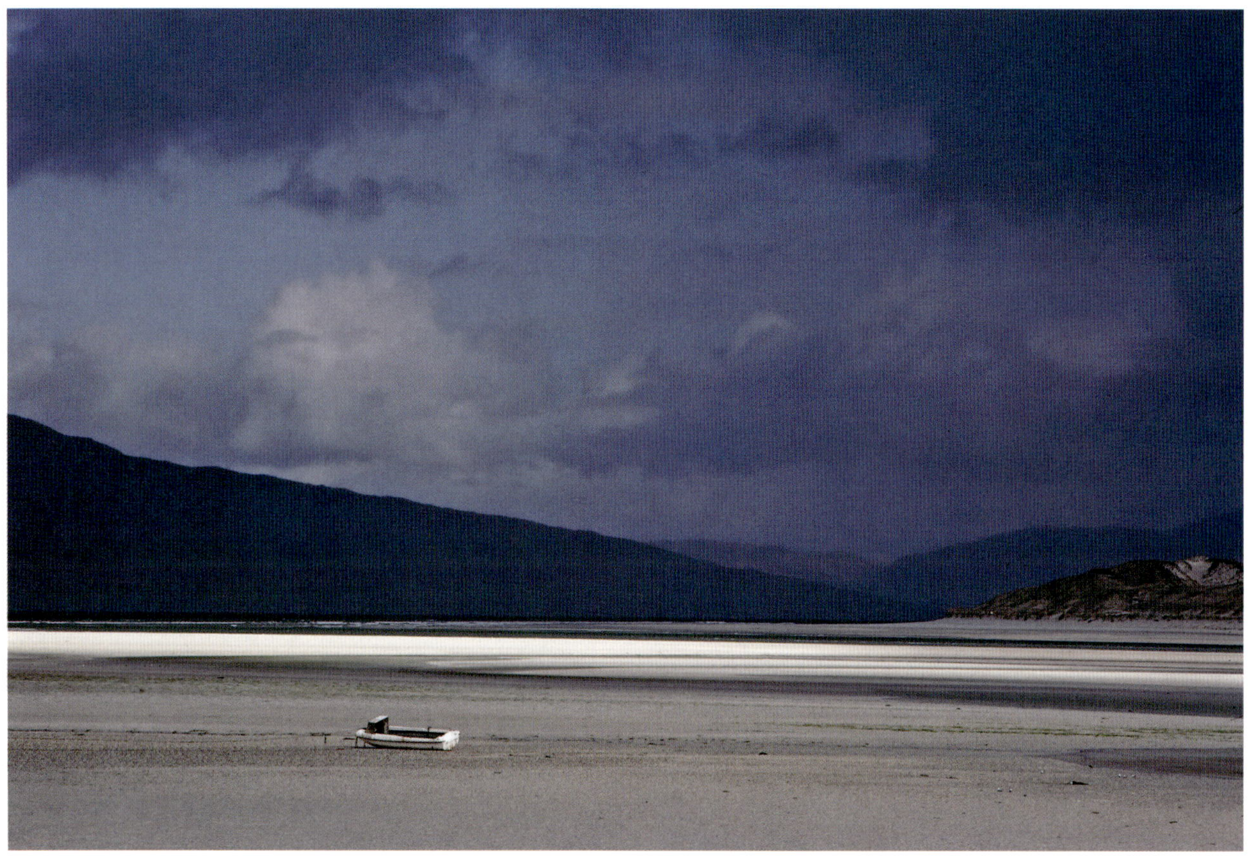

Looking towards Taransay (on the left) and the high dunes of Luskentyre across the bay in stormy conditions from Seilebost.

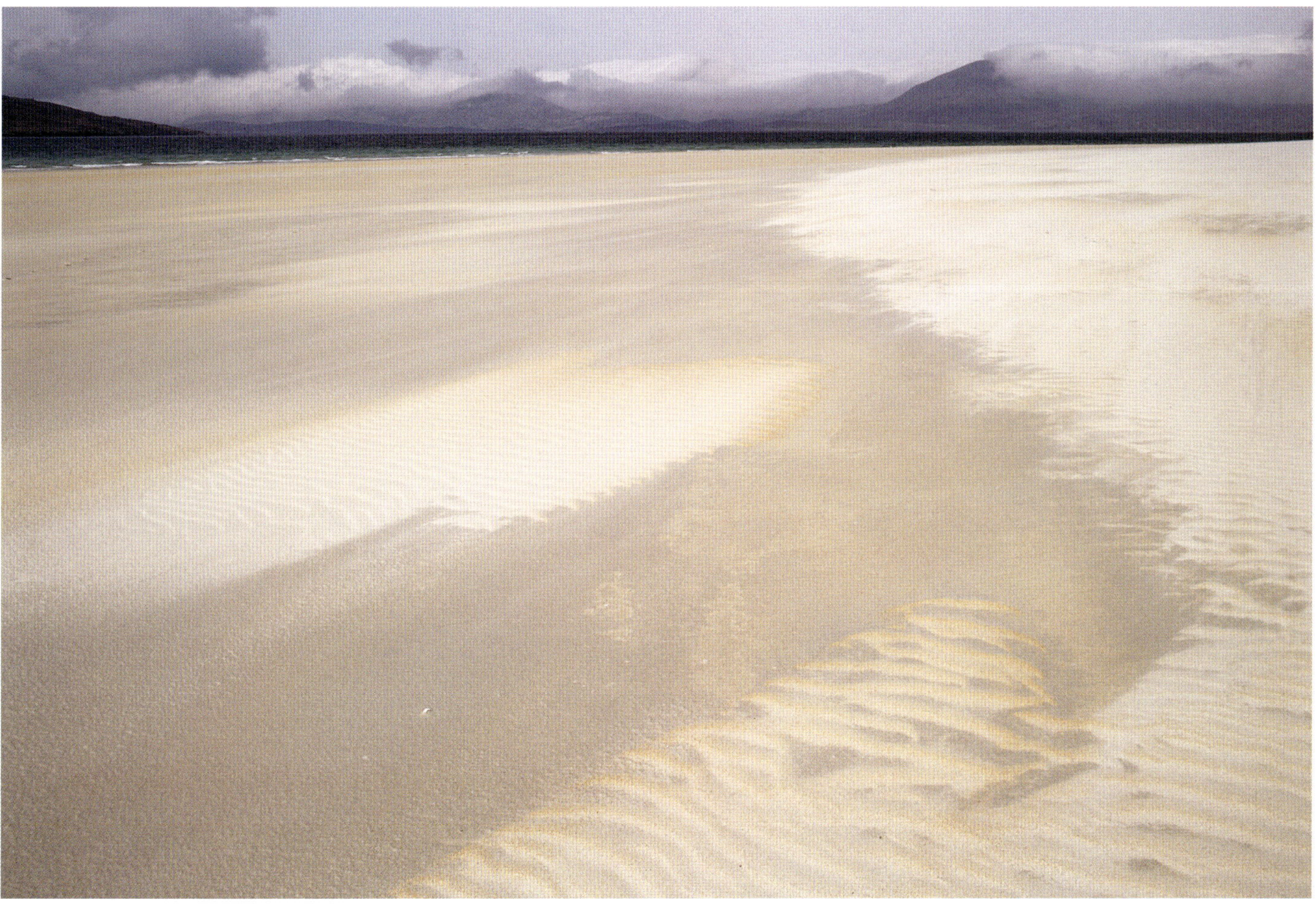

Wind-blown sand sweeps across Tràigh Rosamol near Luskentyre with the cloud-enveloped North Harris Hills in the distance. It is only the much-maligned and unpredictable Hebridean weather that allows such glorious beaches as these to remain almost devoid of human activity throughout the year. This is not a place for beach barbecues, sun umbrellas or amusement parks.

The view south along Tràigh Rosamol to the distant 339m Toe Head on the southwest corner of Harris. It only needs a few palm trees on days such as this for one to be transported in imagination to the islands of the Caribbean or Indian Ocean. The intense blue and clarity of the skies is a simple indicator of the total lack of industrial pollution.

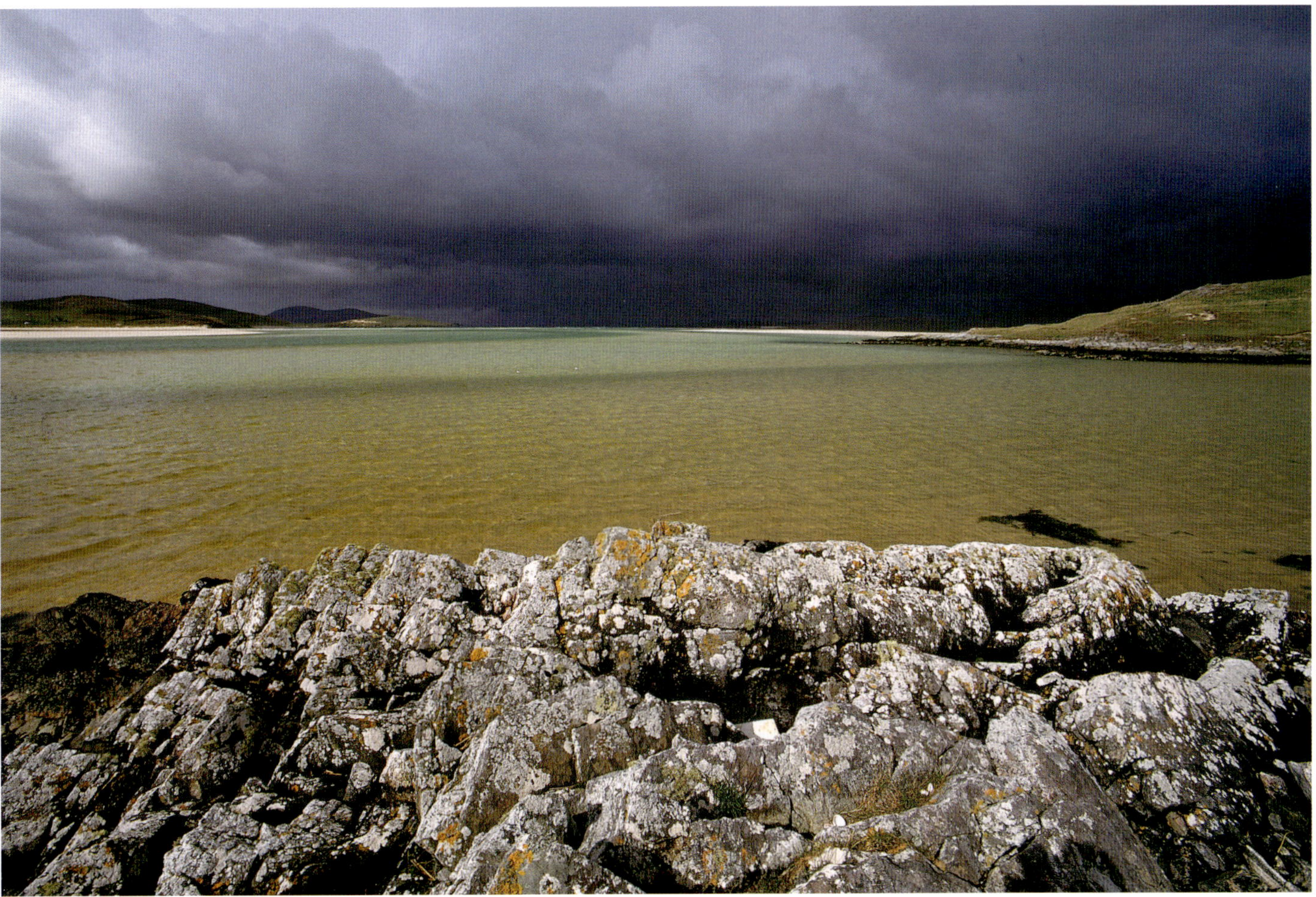

Approaching storm over sandy Tràigh Losgaintir as the last of the sunshine illuminates the incoming tide. During the late spring and early summer the saltings at the head of the bay are coloured by sheets of sea pinks whilst the crofts of Luskentyre itself are richer in their land than any other part of Harris, fertilised by the wind blown shell sand.

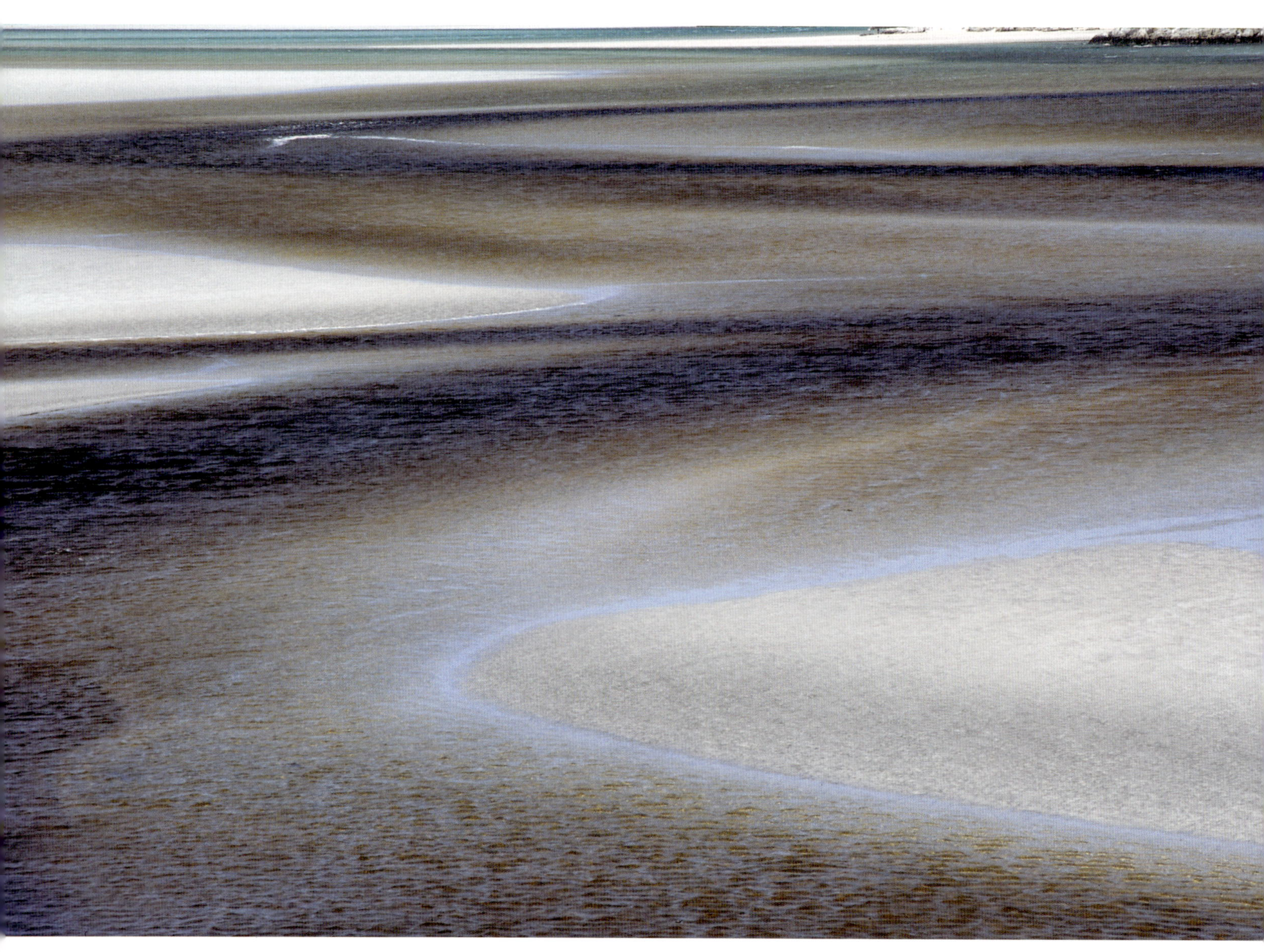

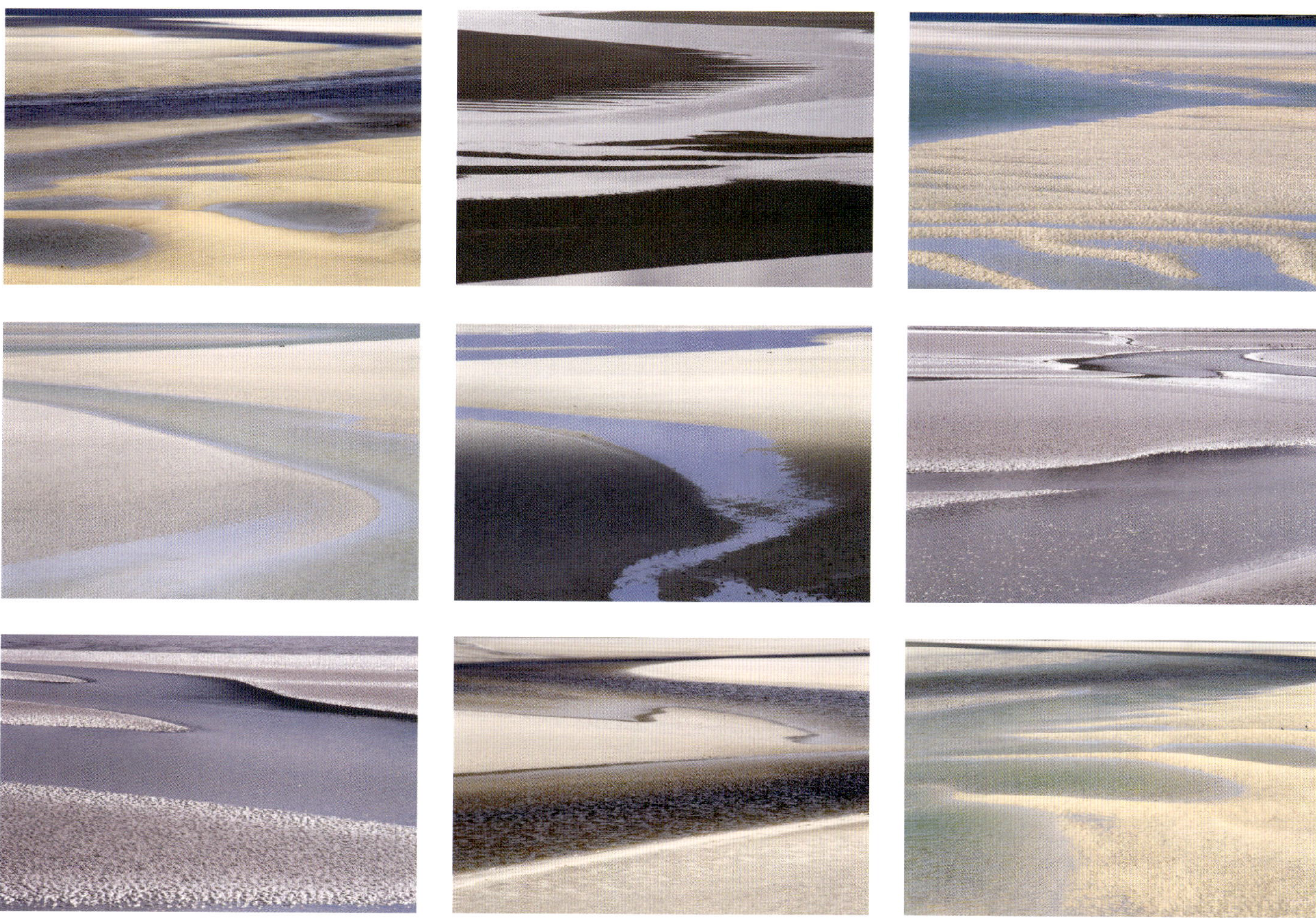

This page and opposite: Tidal patterns at Tràigh Losgaintir. The variations in tidal flow and colours in this bay are truly remarkable changing every second of the day as the waters race in or recede across the almost flat sand. As the depth of water changes in the meandering channels so do the shapes and tones ranging from the most intense hues to the most delicate of shades. To sit on the grassy flower-strewn machair overlooking these scenes is an antidote to all the stresses of modern day living.

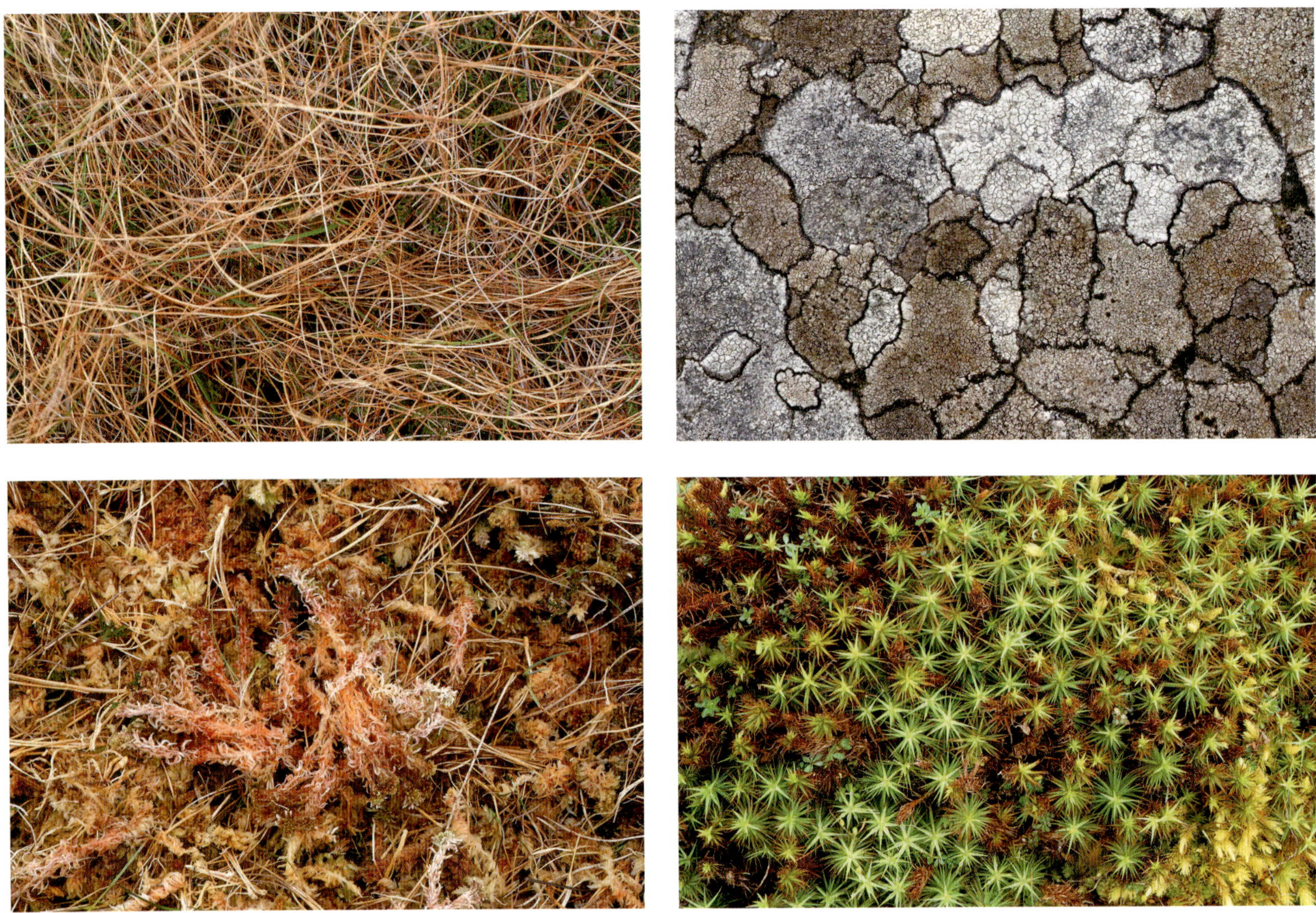

To some, the word Harris is indelibly linked to Harris Tweed. It is from the colours of the surrounding landscape and its changing seasons and the colours of the mosses, grasses, lichens and plants that much of the magical qualities of the cloth are derived and inspired.

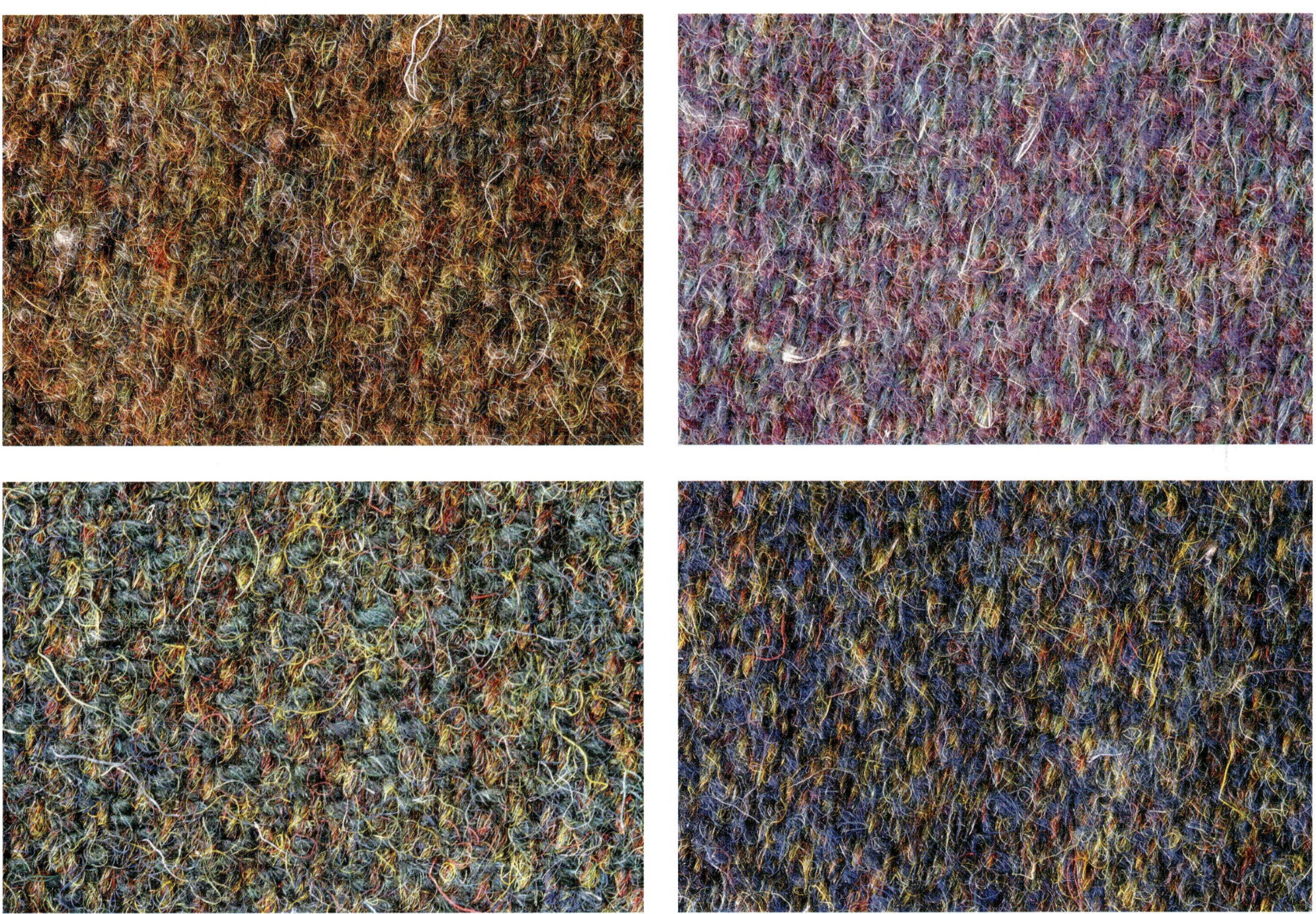

Until the Second World War eight out of ten people on Harris wove tweed for their own needs with any surplus fabric being sold to help the family economy. The entire family would be involved, from raising the sheep to making the finished product. Recipes for dyes were often a closely guarded secret and a common sight at one time would be the colourful fleeces being hung over fences to dry after being dyed in pots. As demand for the tweed declined over a series of years and fashions changed, an increasing number of weavers stopped working, the looms falling silent and the old weaving sheds emptied of their history. Now, in Harris there are just a few dedicated workers still producing this fascinating cloth, these examples being woven by Donald John MacKay.

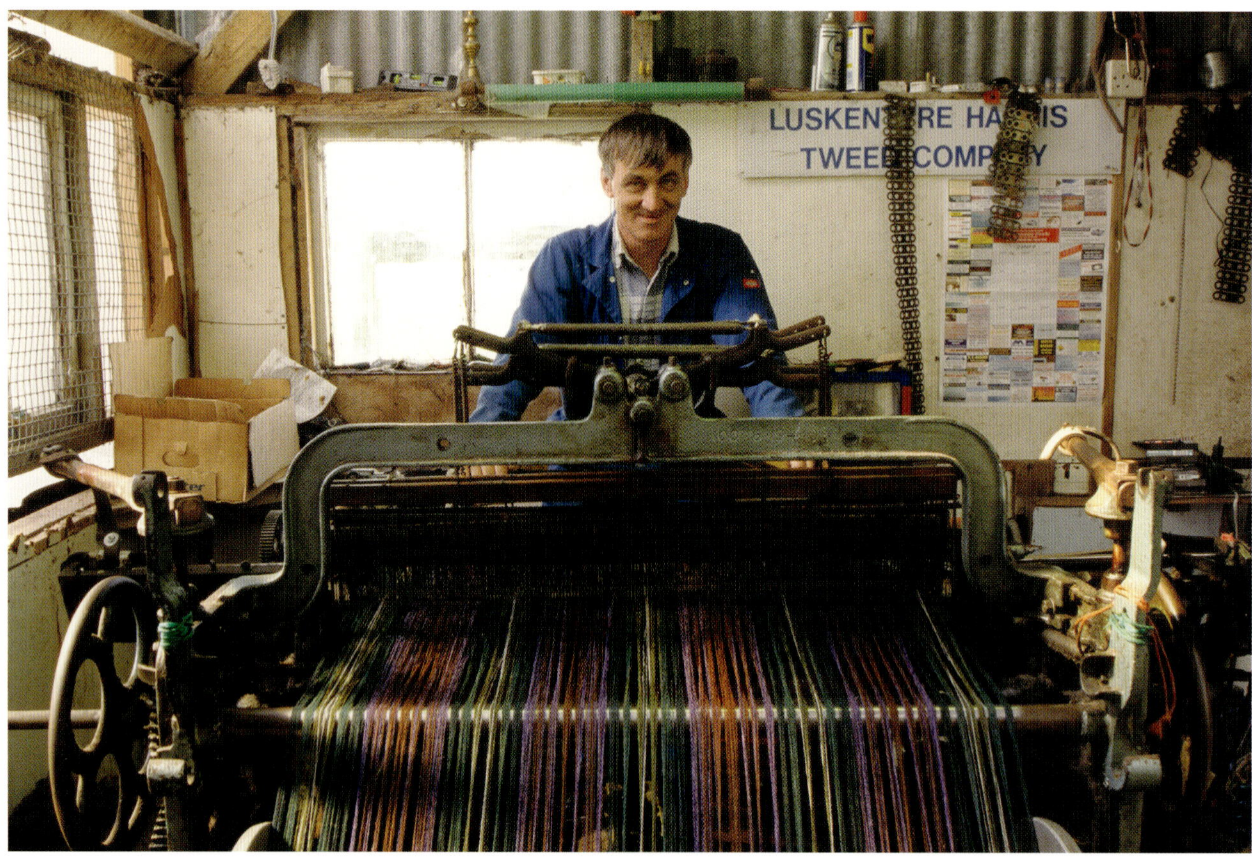

Donald John MacKay, weaver, Luskentyre. Donald John was born on Harris, both his father and paternal grandmother also being weavers and as a young boy he simply ate, slept and breathed weaving. As his skills developed, he and his wife established the Luskentyre Tweed Company in 1991 where he works in a weaving shed in the grounds of his home using a large Hattersley cast iron single width loom of the type still favoured by many of the surviving hand weavers today. As the industry's fortunes have fluctuated over the years he is now the only full time weaver remaining on West Harris. However at the present time demand for his hand woven cloth has never been higher with orders worldwide and particularly in recent years from the sports equipment manufacturer Nike. He still works a twelve hour day, six days a week with the loom producing some 5m of cloth each hour.

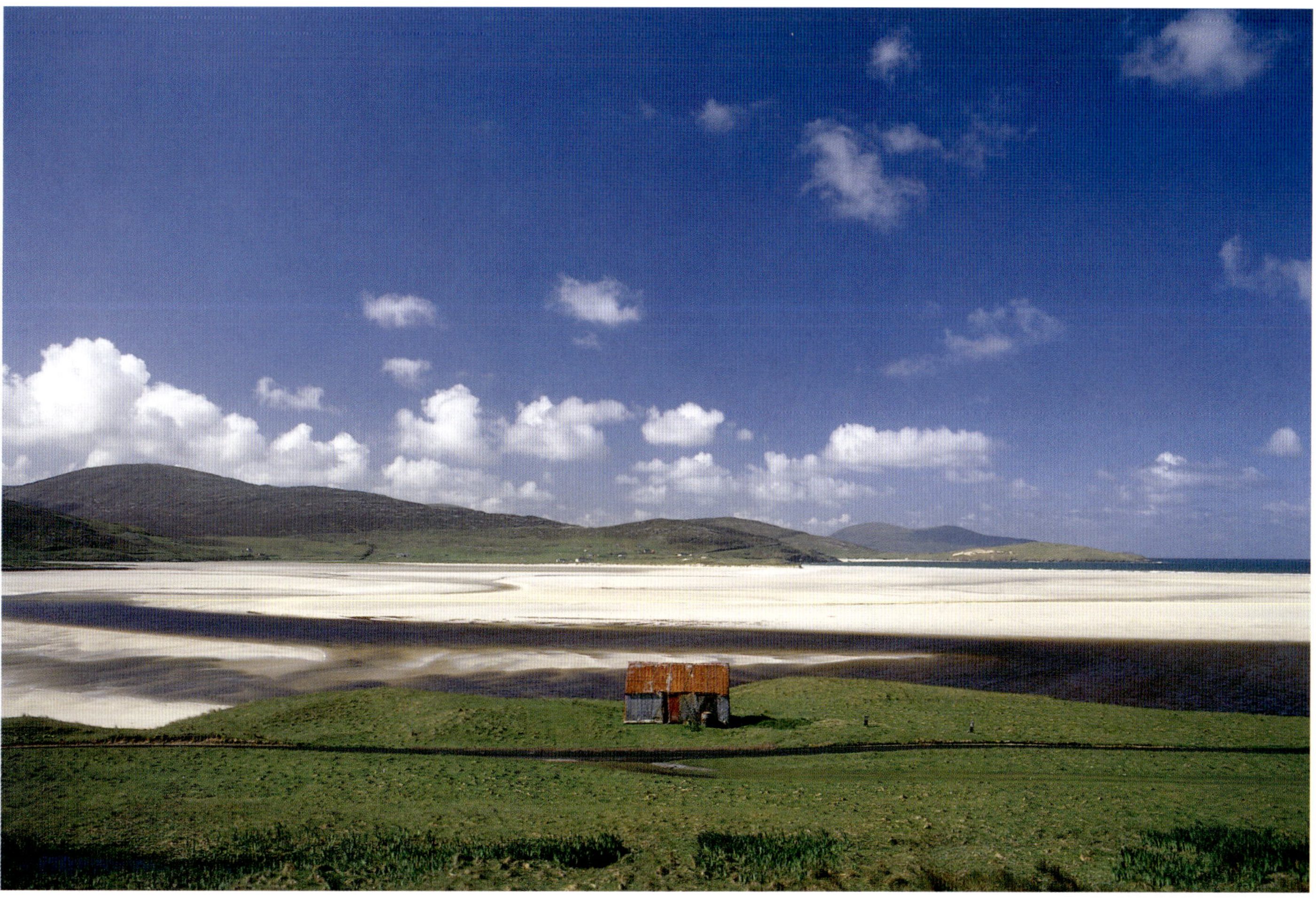

A wider view looking south from Luskentyre on a glorious late spring day towards distant Toe Head. The small corrugated iron shed in the centre foreground would probably at one time have housed a primitive loom or perhaps the later improved foot driven 'fly-shuttle' loom once so commonly found on Harris. Today the rhythmical 'clack clack' of the looms, so synonymous with the island, is almost a sound of the past.

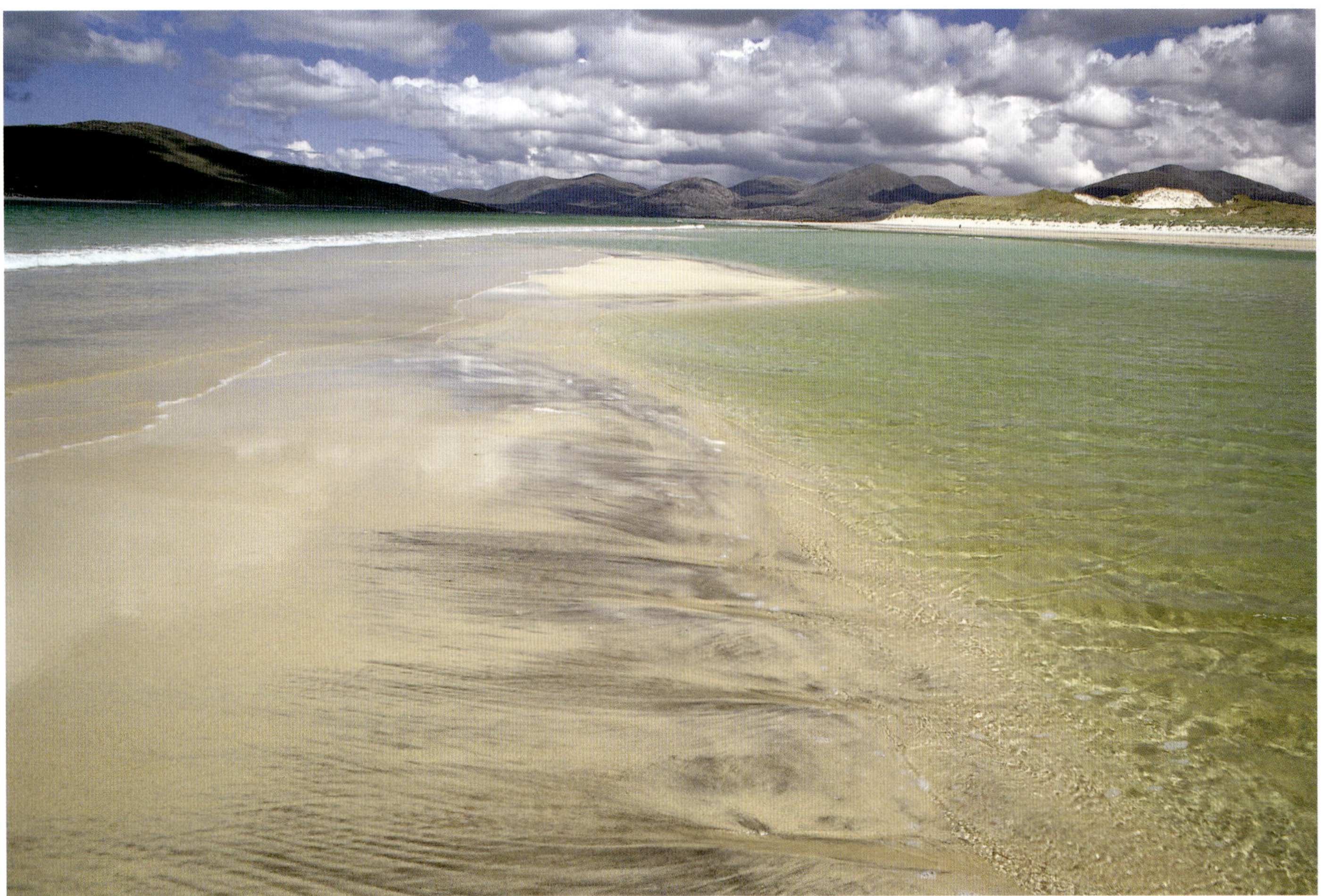

Waters flood in over the last of the exposed sand at the tip of Tràigh Seilebost in tones of green and serpentine whilst cloud shadows skim over the Luskentyre dunes and distant hills.

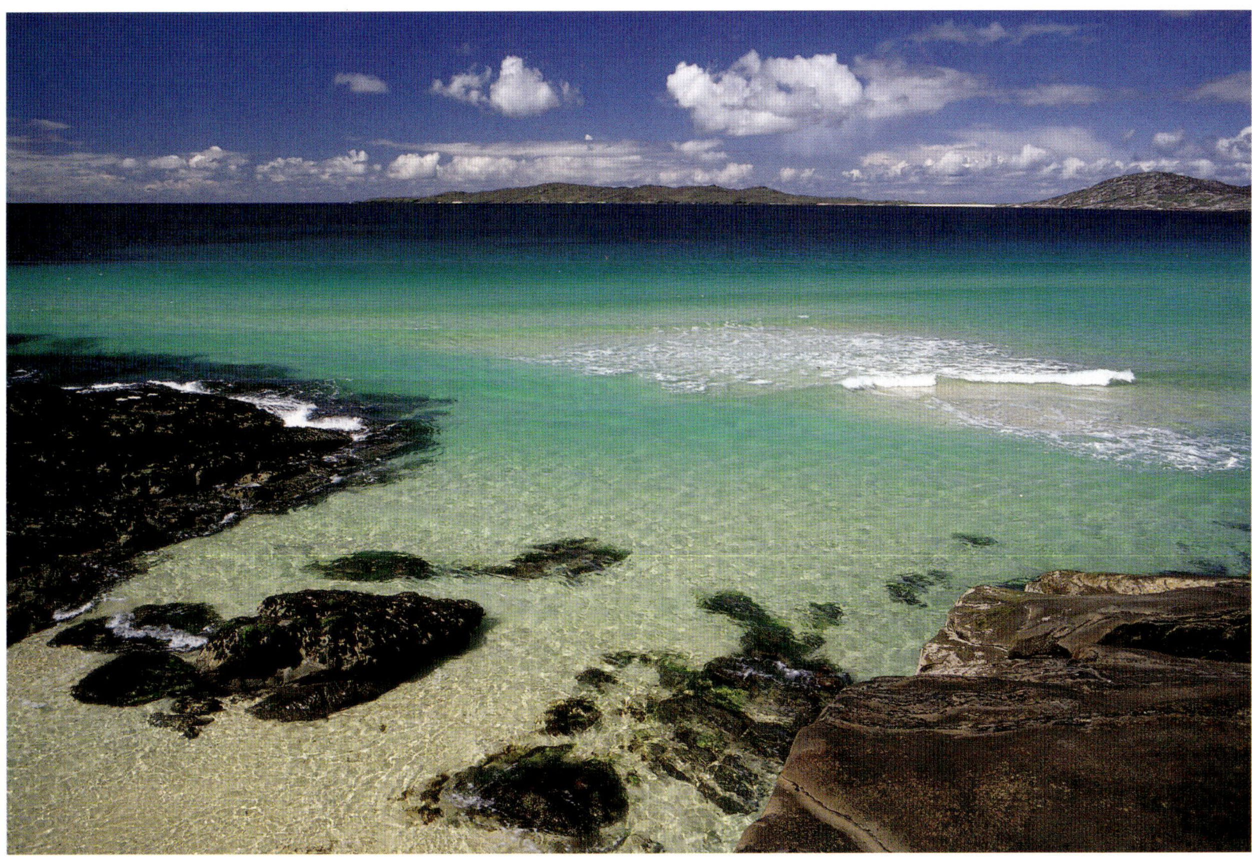

Exceptional sea colouration at Tràigh Iar near Horgabost as the tide lies over the warm sands alive with colour and light.

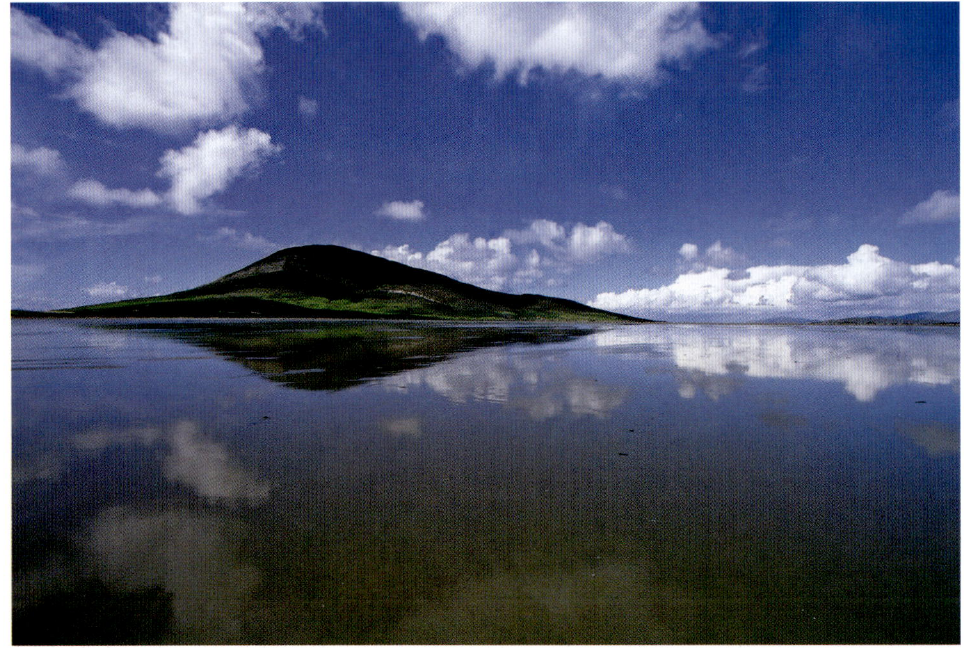

Near Northton, below Toe Head, the sandy beach known as Tràigh an Taoibh Thuath floods to a shallow depth at high tide where on a calm day such as this, mirror images can be found of the Head in the still, clear water. From the summit of Toe Head the islands of the distant St Kilda archipelago can be seen on a clear day some 80km to the west.

Opposite: From the same beach looking north towards the now distant Luskentyre and far off Harris Hills, the exposed wind blown sand at low tide takes on an almost desert-like appearance enhanced by the vivid blue skies.

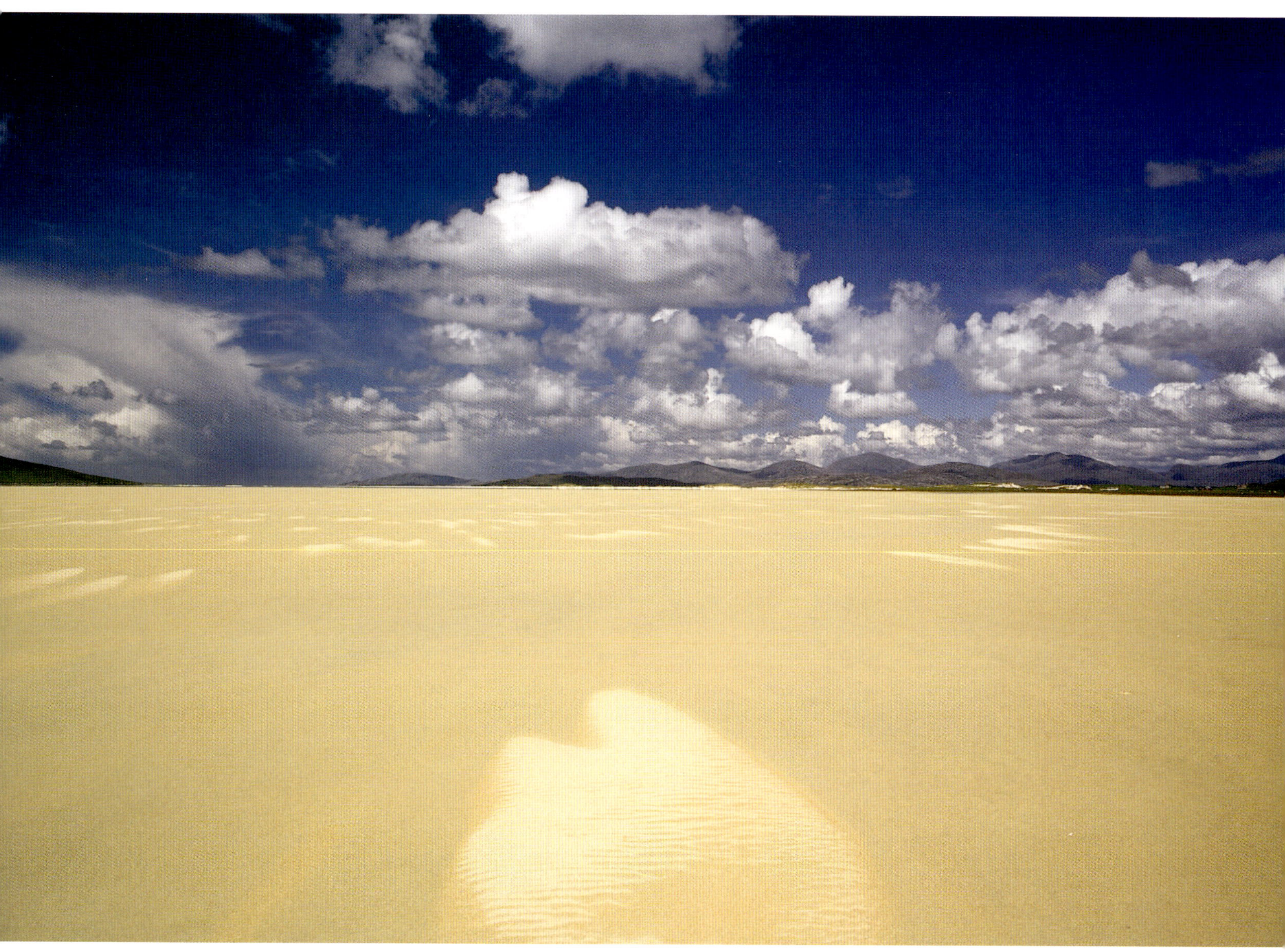

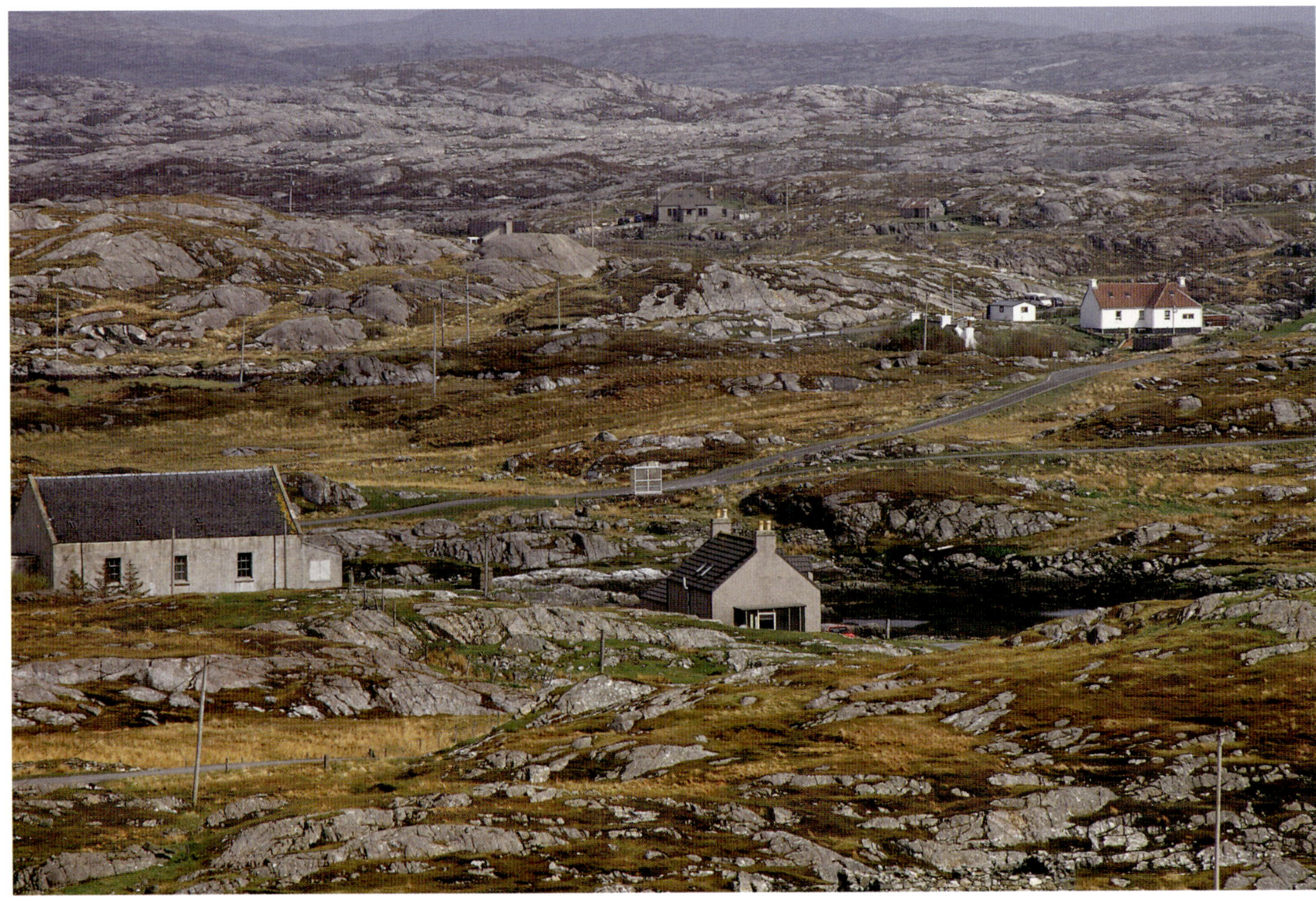

A view from near Finsbay looking over typical eastern Harris landscape of near naked rock. This desolate terrain is almost totally devoid of trees and vegetation and is a stark comparison to the lush beaches described earlier. It was to this land however that most of the crofters from the fertile west coast were forcibly removed during the Highland Clearances and where many of the Harris residents still live in the numerous small villages and townships. Known as Bays after the general profile of the coastline there is little natural soil and coffins once had to be carried across the island to be buried in the west. The bays themselves provide sheltered anchorage for small fishing boats and this, combined with the construction of 'lazybeds' in the rock hollows, trout fishing in the numerous lochans and spinning and weaving, sustained the population. To this day the sight of the landscape and its hardships still command deep respect.

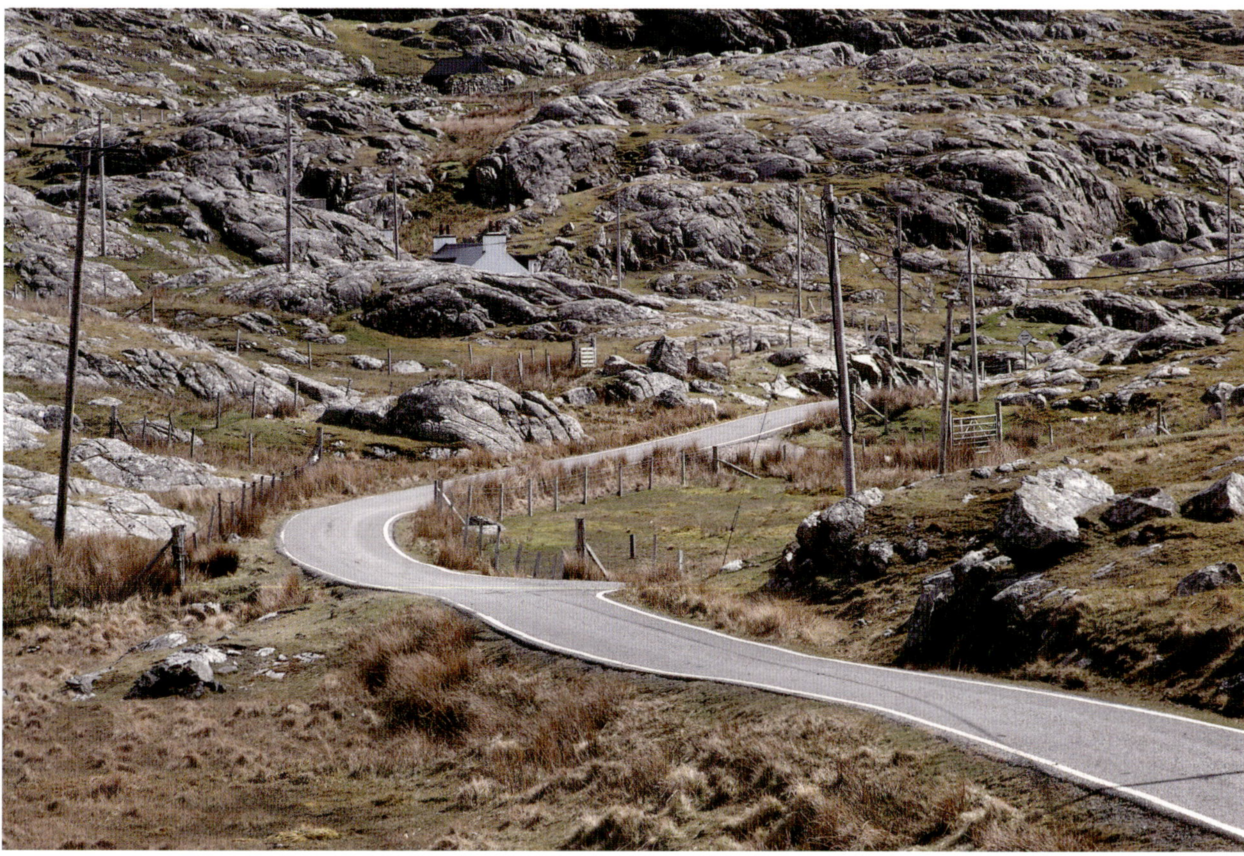

Most of the Bays district is linked by winding narrow roads undulating through a maze of lochans and ribs of rock with the coast road being known as the 'Golden Road' due to its cost of construction. Croft cottages are often tucked against rock faces, poles carrying electrical and telephone services abound and many of the old weaving sheds still survive the onslaught of the wind and winter rains. In a few places weaving is still continued but in more recent years small art galleries and studios have brightened the scene. This view shows the 'Golden Road' near Cliuthar.

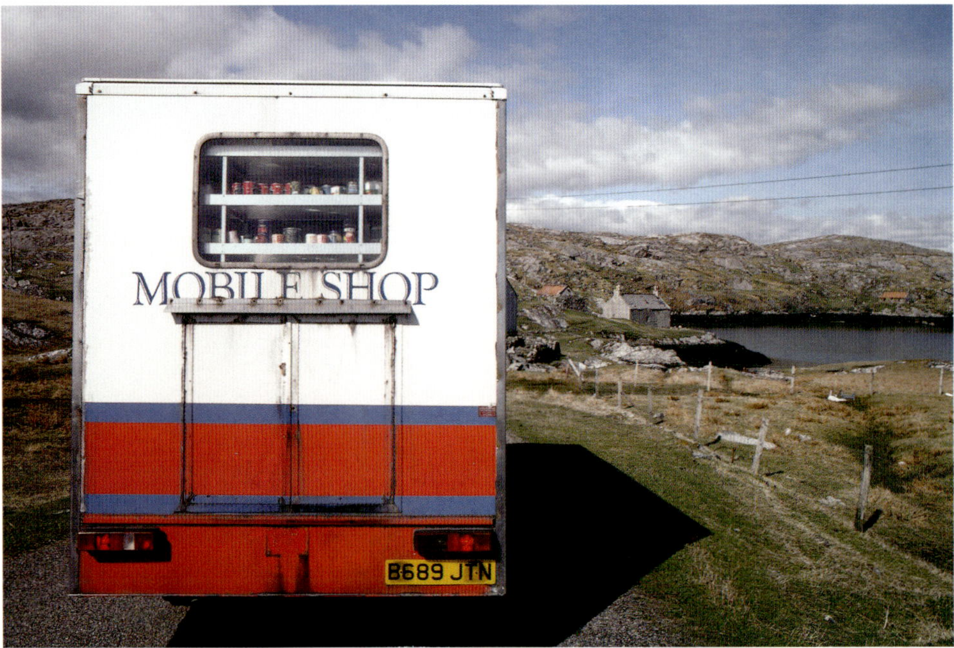

For many of the older residents in these eastern districts the mobile shop services provided by several companies act as a lifeline. Not only do they supply general groceries but mobile banks and libraries together with post buses offer valuable links and considerable help to these sometimes isolated communities.

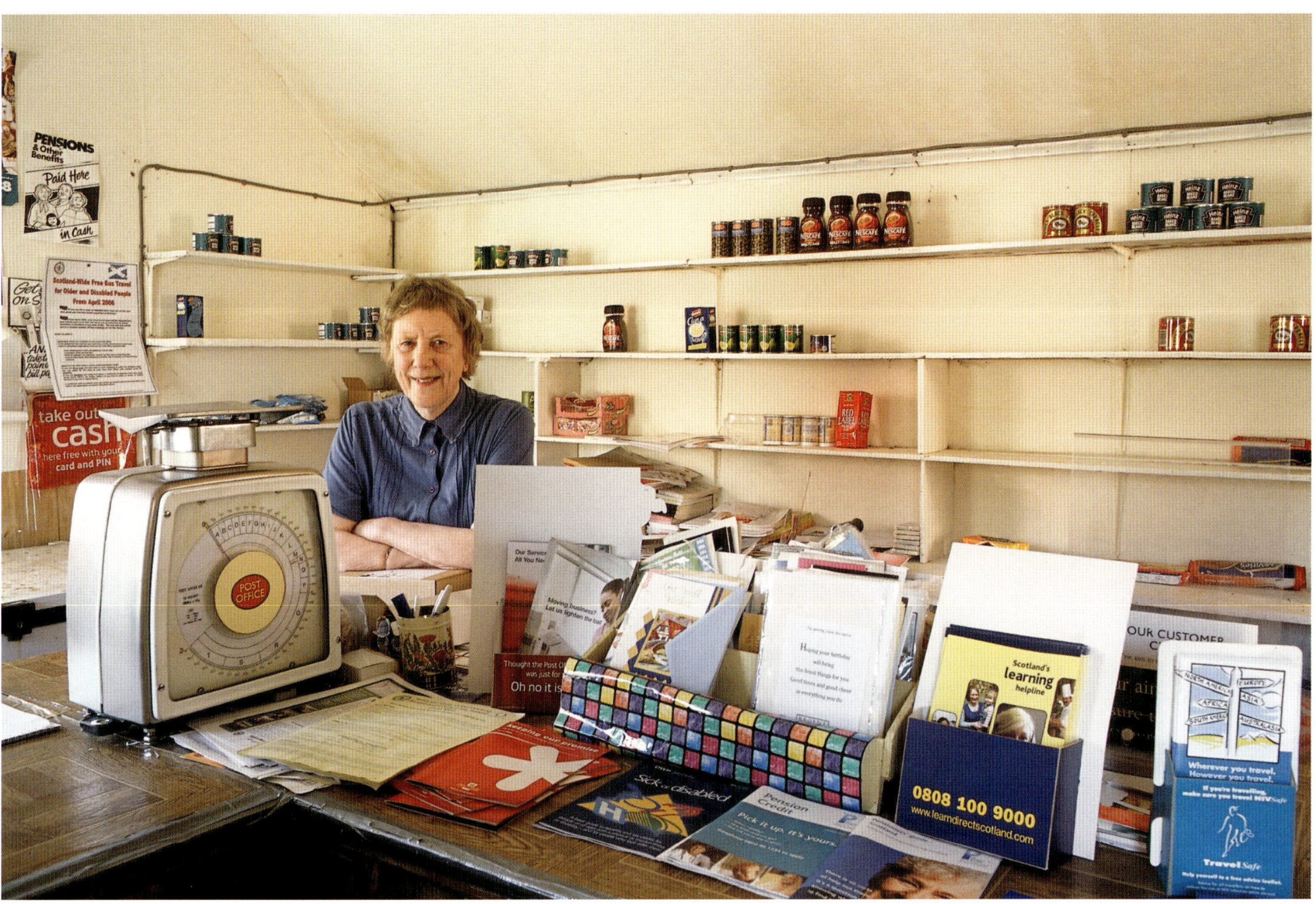

In a few of the small townships tiny post offices and general stores still survive and are often the very heart of the community. This is the interior of Amhuinnsuidhe post office on the Hushinish road where its services are sadly and gradually being cut back in line with more modern and regrettable trends.

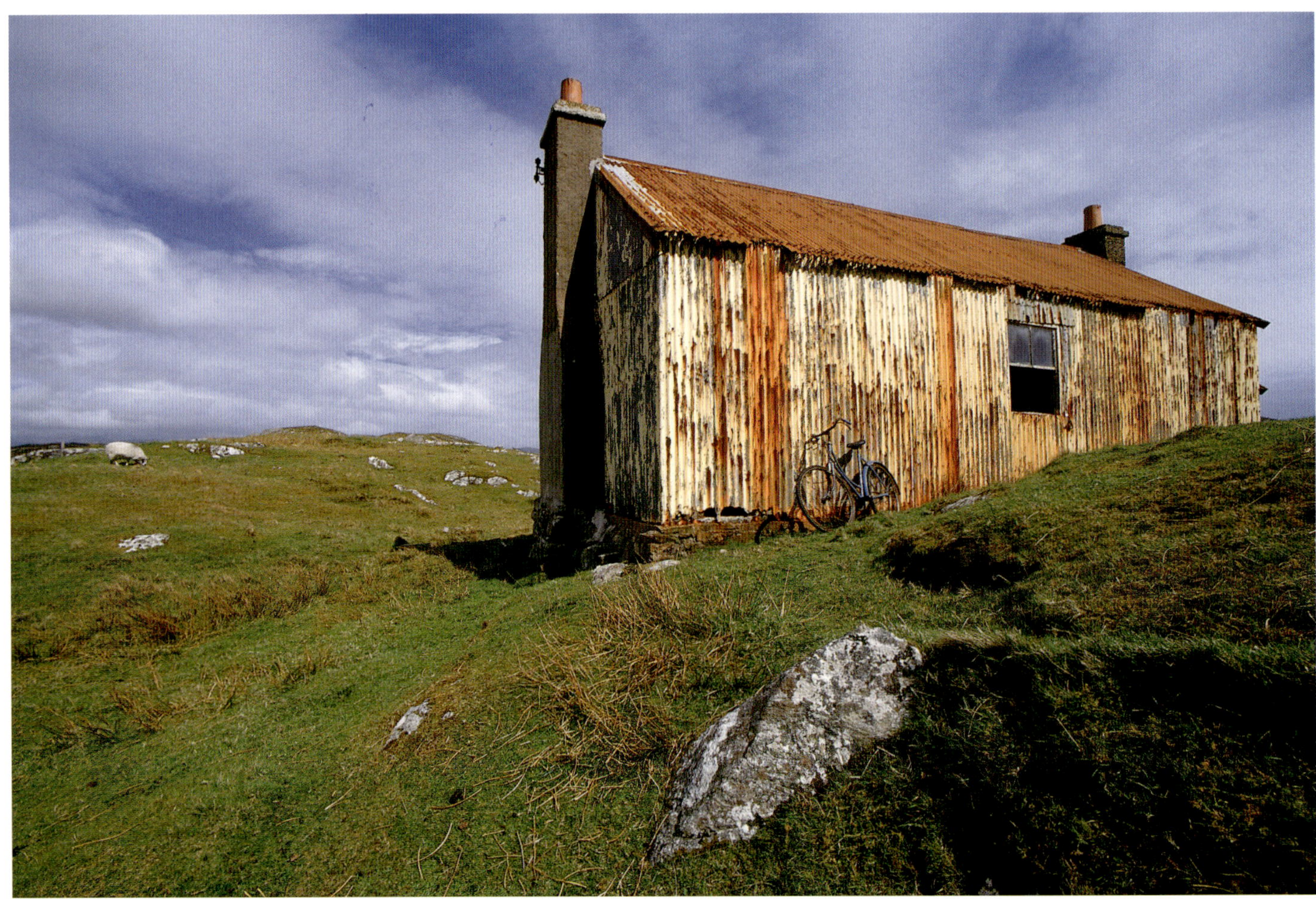

This page and opposite: With the continuing hardships of living in such inhospitable landscapes as the eastern areas of Harris, many of the older cottages slowly fall into disuse and decay as their former residents either die or move away and for which the buildings then have no further use. In the case of those constructed cheaply using wood and corrugated iron, decline and dereliction in these climates can be swift as shown by this series of details of abandoned and empty homes.

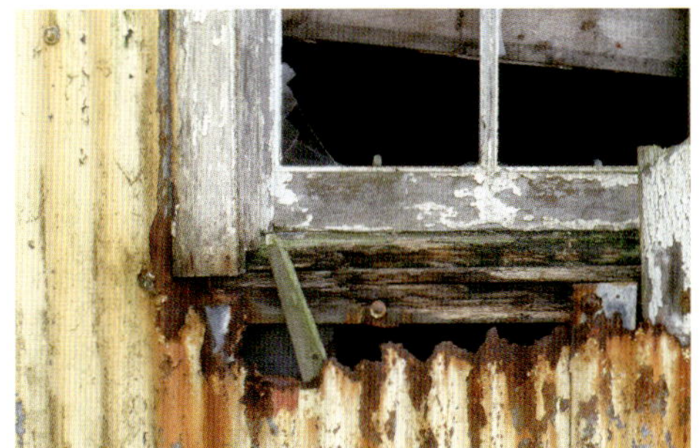

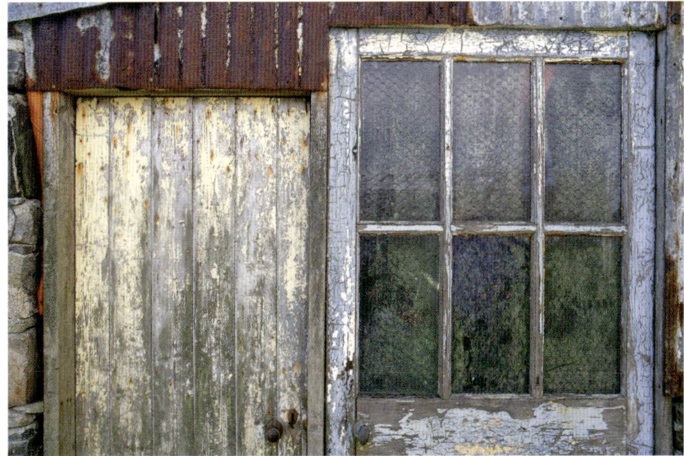

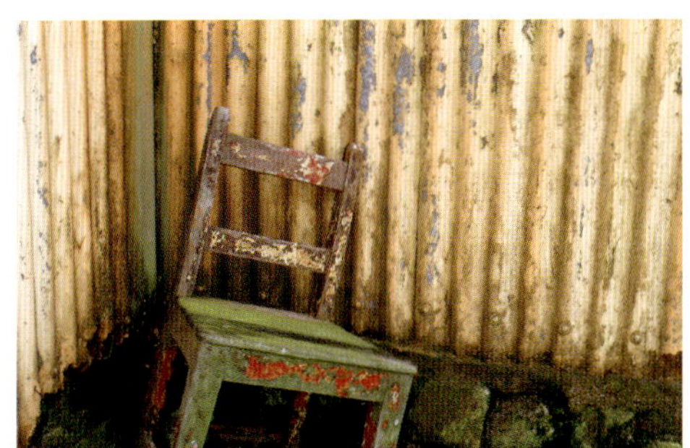

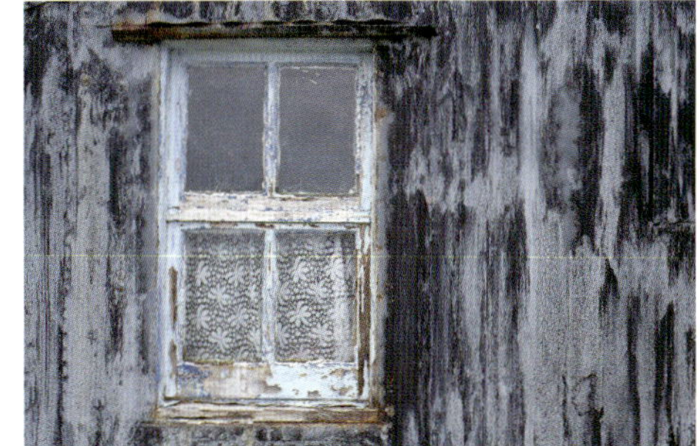

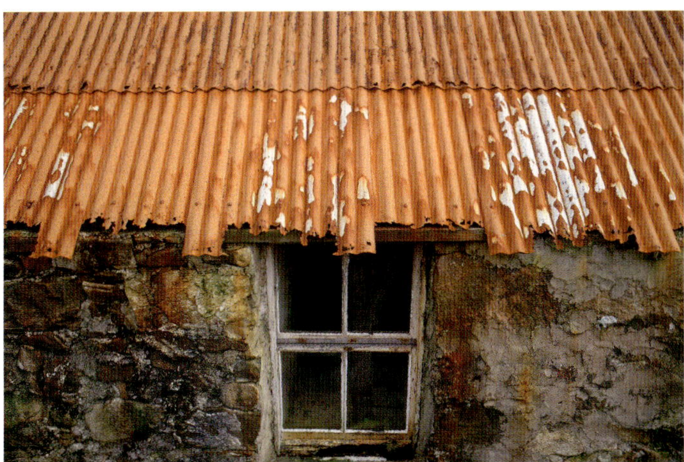

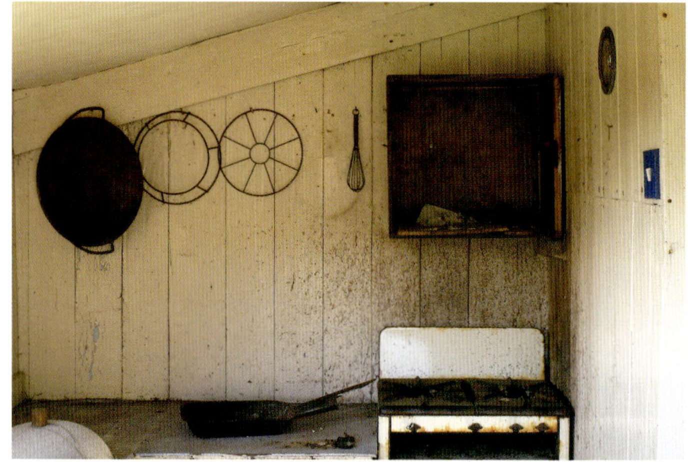

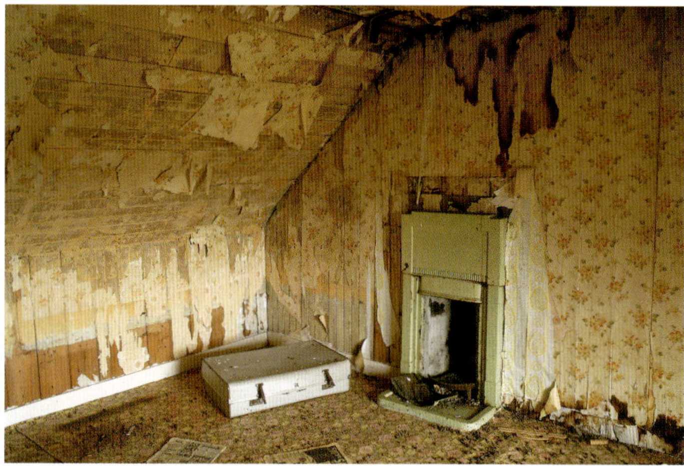

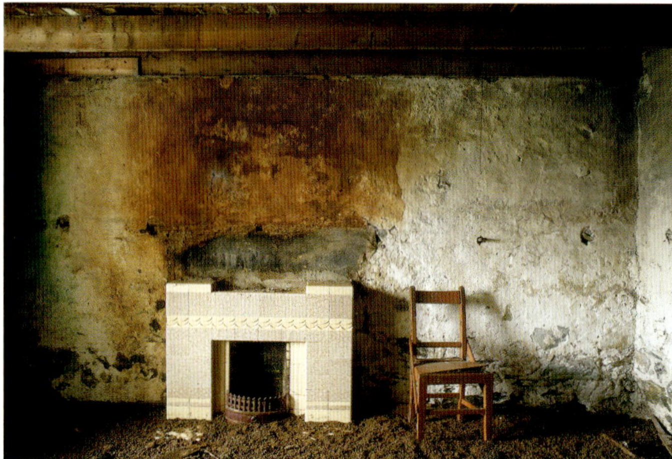

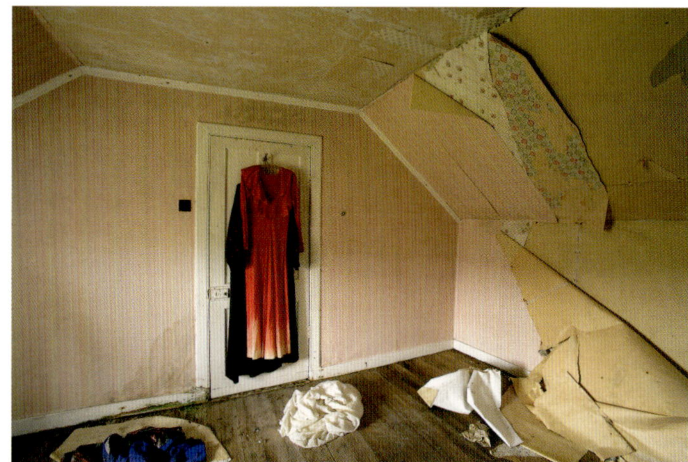

This page and opposite: In many instances the doors of the empty buildings are left open, the sheep move in for shelter and the few items of furniture, household possessions and clothing still remaining act as a pathetic and sad reminder of happier times.

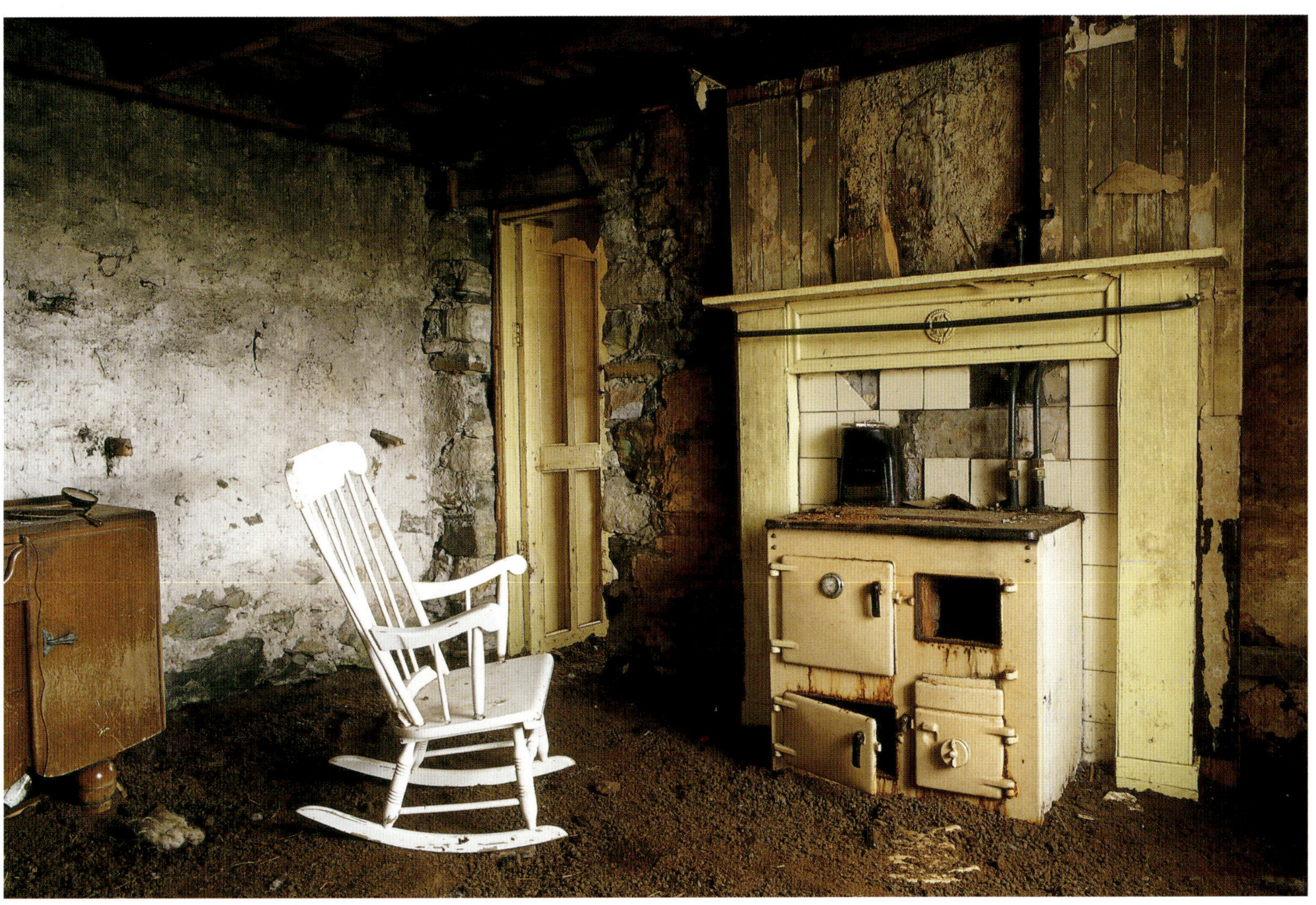

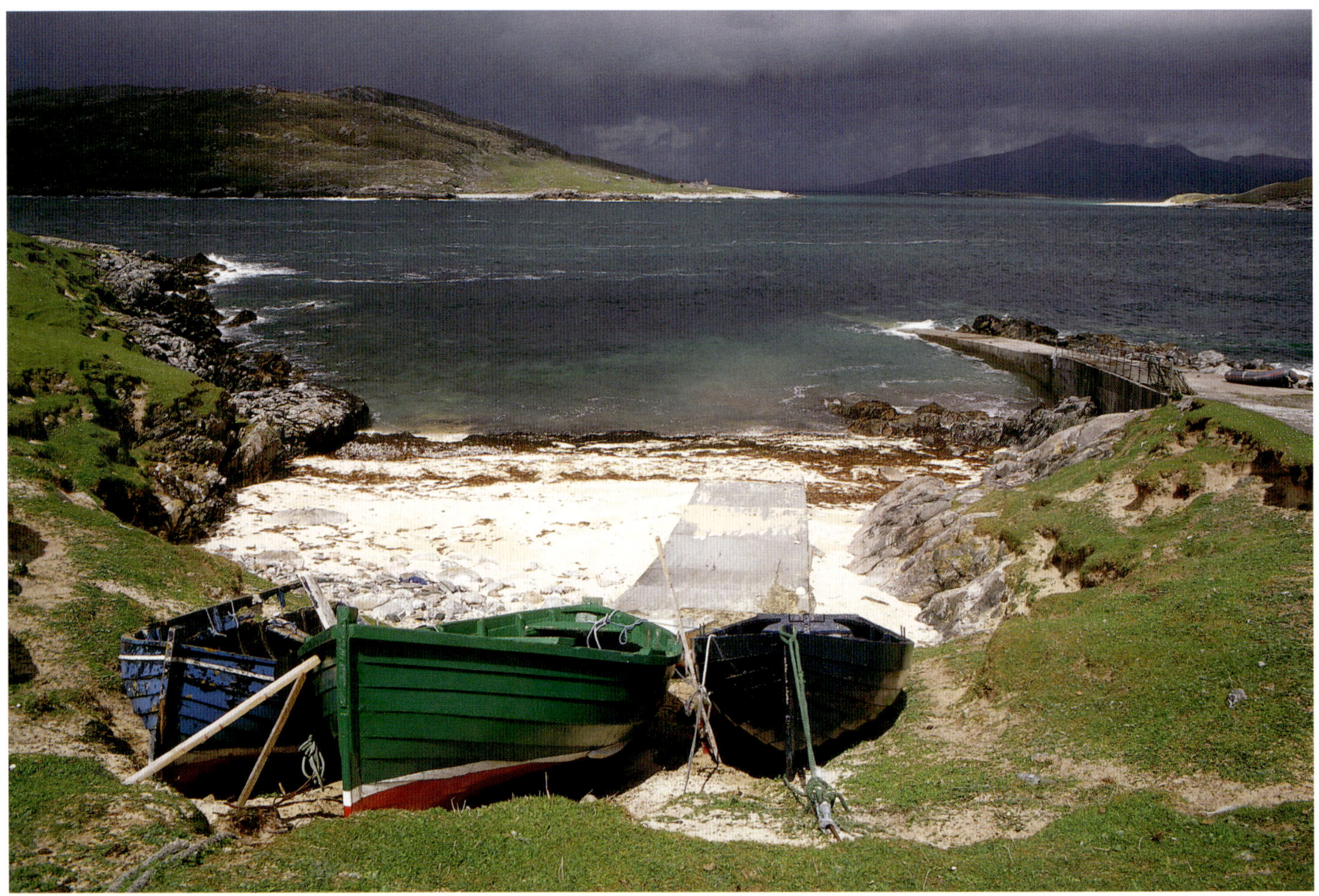

Under the rampart of the North Harris Hills dividing Harris from Lewis, a long meandering switchback road runs to Hushinish the most westerly point of Harris. Here a small group of cottages stand on a windswept peninsula with bays to both north and south. A jetty on the north bay faces the now deserted island of Scarp where the remains of old homes can be seen in this view under stormy conditions. Scarp was briefly famous in the 1930s as the location where experiments with rocket powered mail delivery were carried out but later abandoned.

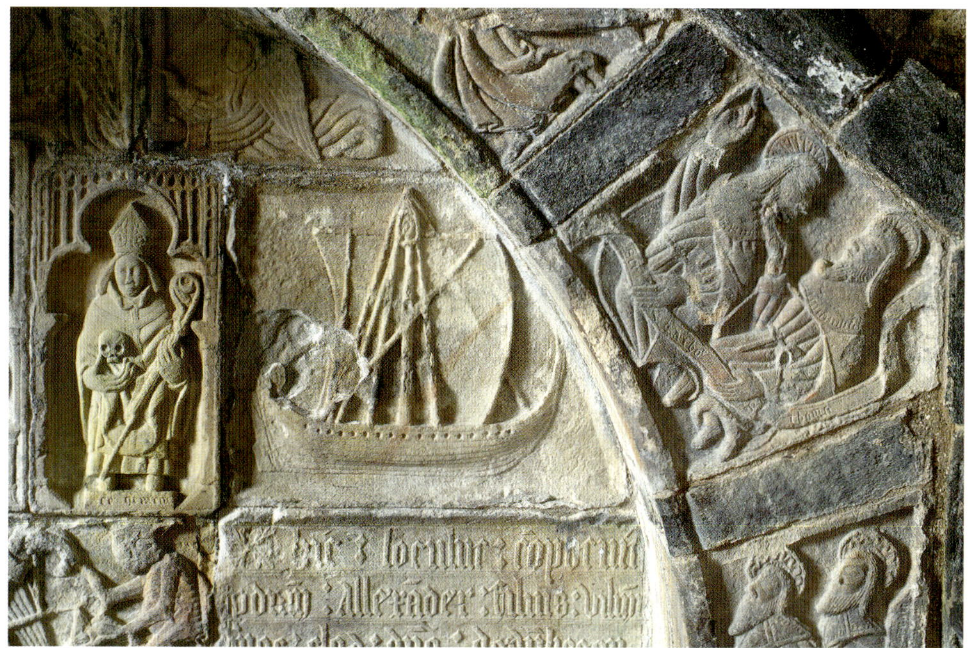

The cruciform church of St Clement at Rodel on the southeast tip of Harris is one of the very few surviving ancient buildings in the entire Hebrides. It is thought to have been built about 1500 probably by Alasdair Crotach the 8th MacLeod chief of Dunvegan using in places sandstone imported from the island of Mull. Its solid rectangular tower is a unique feature in the Western Isles. In the nave the tomb of Alasdair is set into an arched recess highly decorated with carved scenes and figures to both arch and inner wall and now regarded as one of the finest of its type in Scotland. A detail of the tomb is shown here.

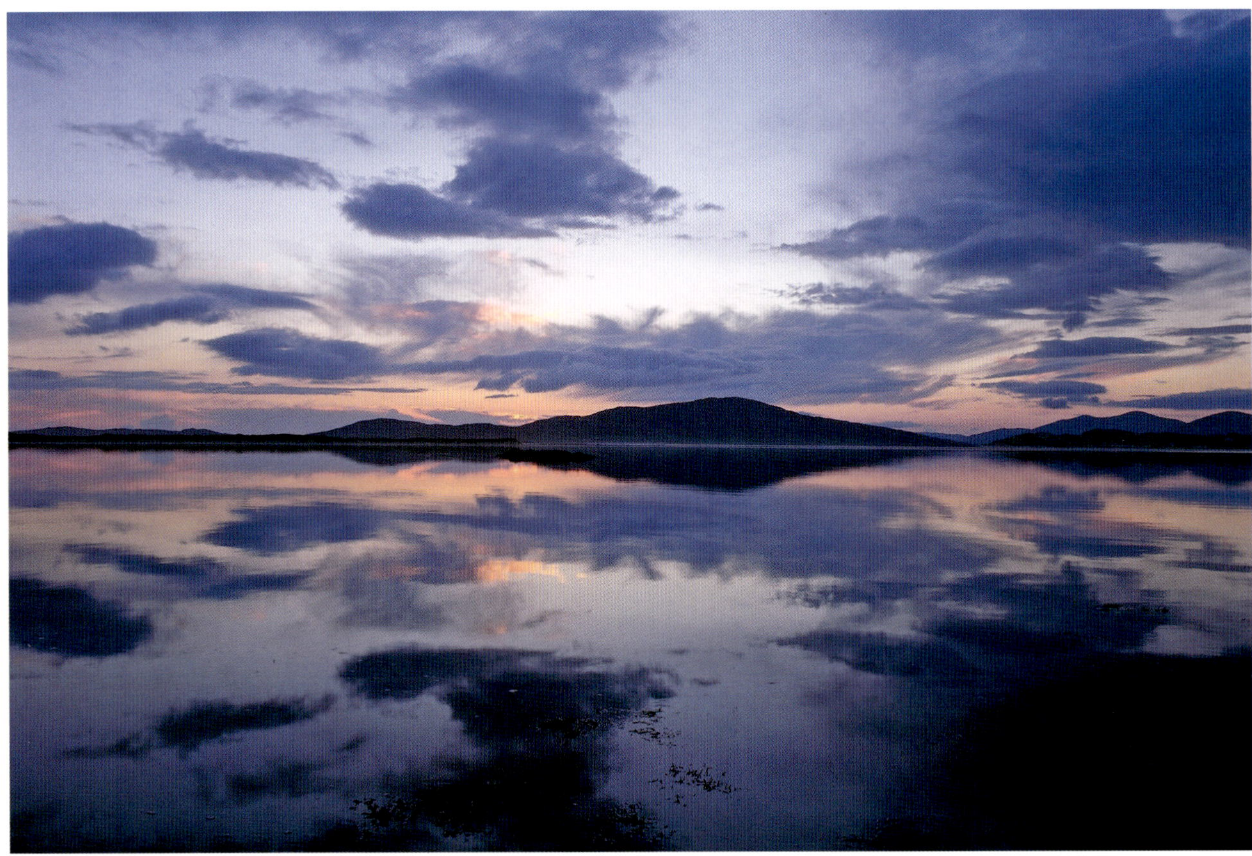

The sunsets on the west coast of Harris can often be glorious, particularly in the area of Tràigh Losgaintir where at high tide on a calm, still evening the colours are reflected as if in a mirror. This view from Seilebost looks west towards Taransay silhouetted in the centre of the image.

Opposite: Another sunset viewed from Seilebost looking towards Luskentyre itself and the North Harris Hills.

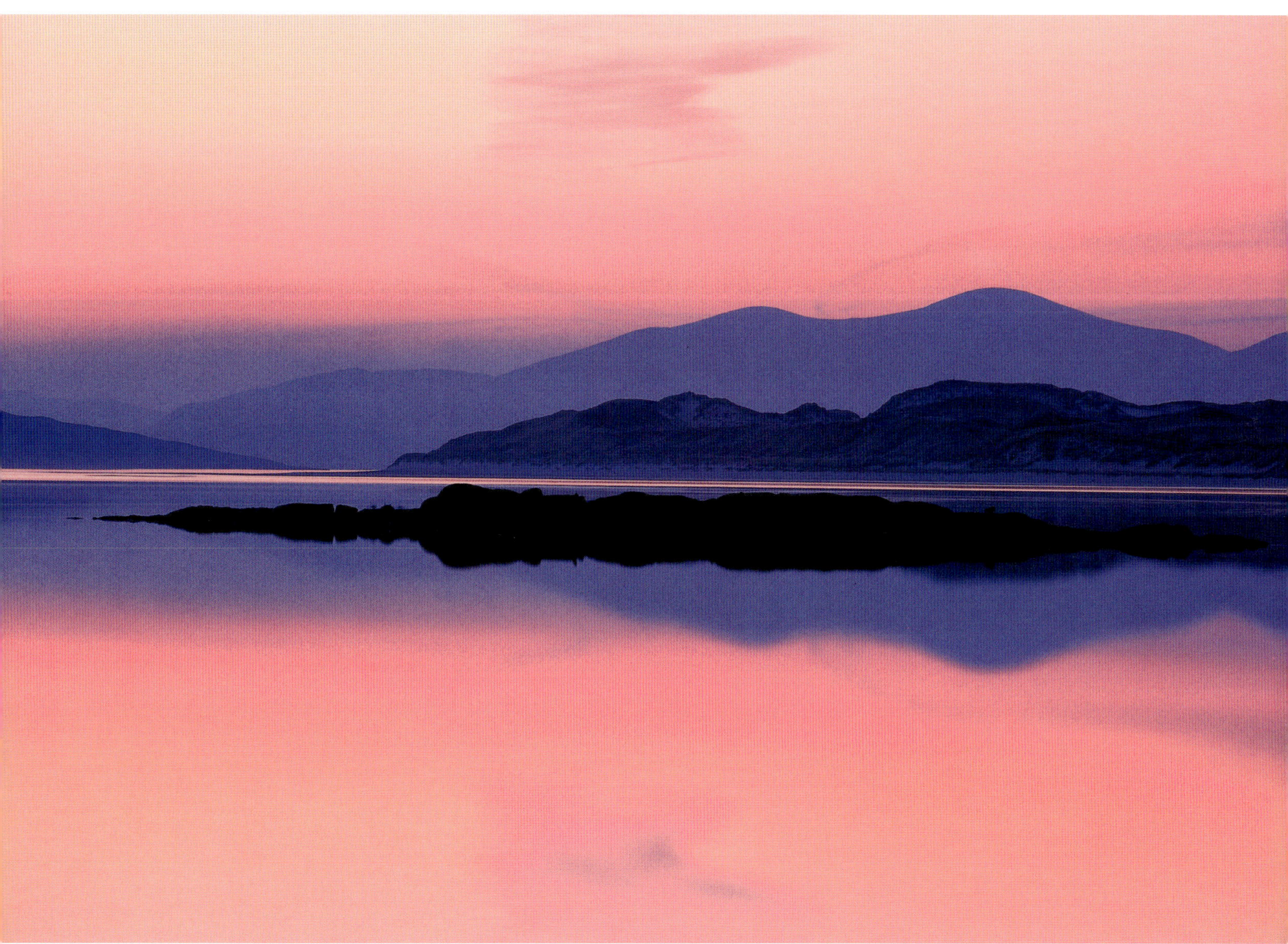

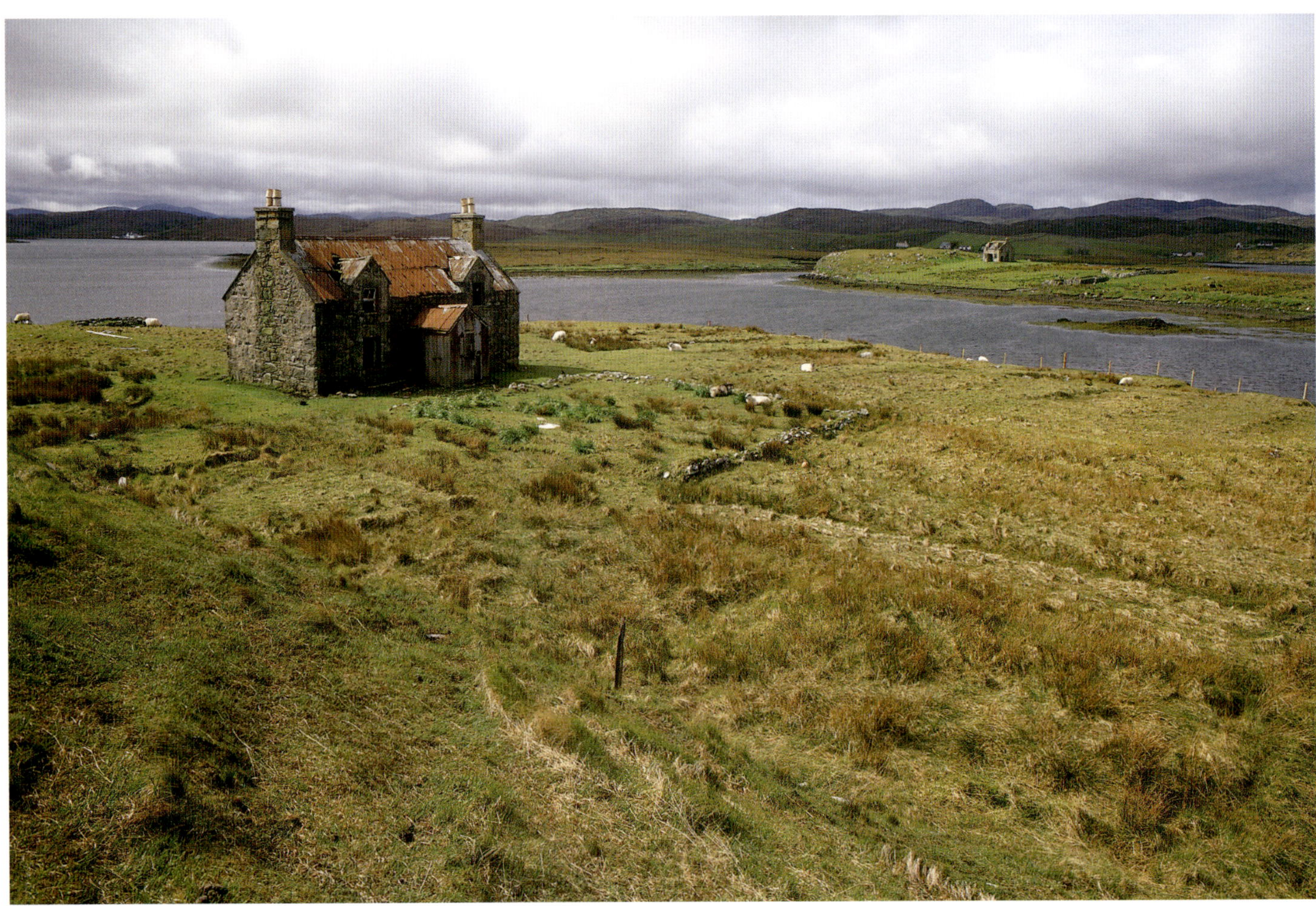

Empty cottage near Loch Roag, Callanish, Lewis. The vast peaty moorlands of Lewis spread over 70km from the Harris boundary in the south to the Butt of Lewis in the north. The very word Lewis is derived from Leogach meaning marshy. Most of the large population of over 20000 inhabitants live on or near the coast or at Stornaway, capital of the Western Isles. The interior has remained generally empty apart from a multitude of peat workings. Nearly all the townships have names derived from Norse and it is this sense of history together with its well known archaeological remains that make Lewis a place of such interest rather than its scenery. In recent years a degree of prosperity has at last reached these islands, evidenced by considerable new building in townships that display a somewhat chaotic disarray of both old and new. Much of the old now lies empty and abandoned or simply used as byres.

Peat, Rust and Stone
A HEBRIDEAN MISCELLANY

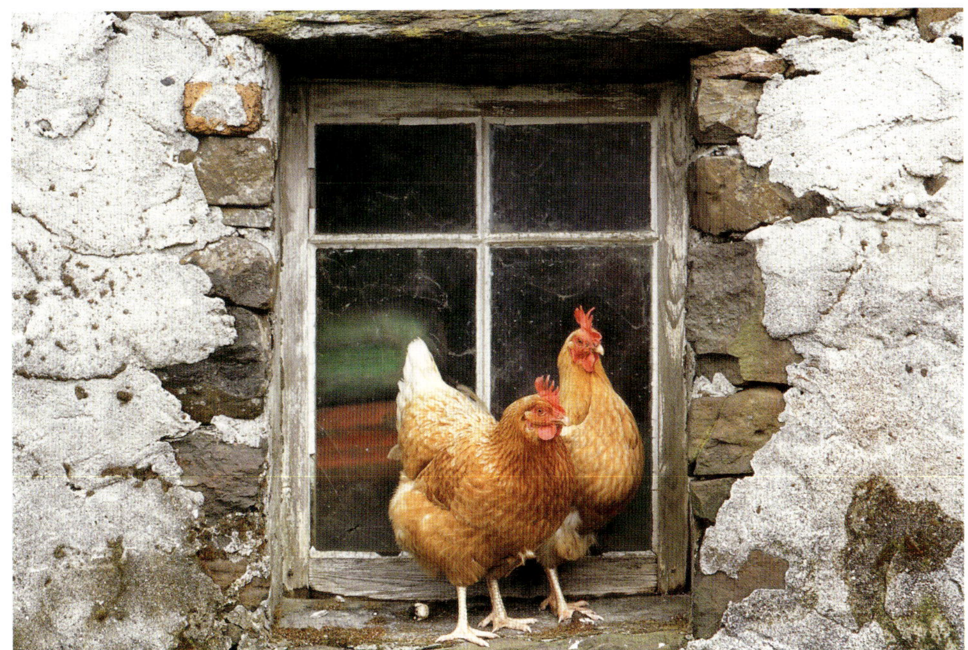

Chickens and window, Muck.

It has already been stated in the introduction that this book is not intended as a definitive study of the Hebrides or all of its islands. Instead by featuring just the islands of Skye, Eigg and Harris in some detail in the last three chapters with all their quite remarkable variety and contrast, this it is hoped, will at the very least give the reader a positive impression of the Hebridean scene. This final chapter expands that impression with images covering both small and greater aspects of further islands. The photographs are just more small parts of an elaborate jigsaw, which, when pieced together, create the final picture.

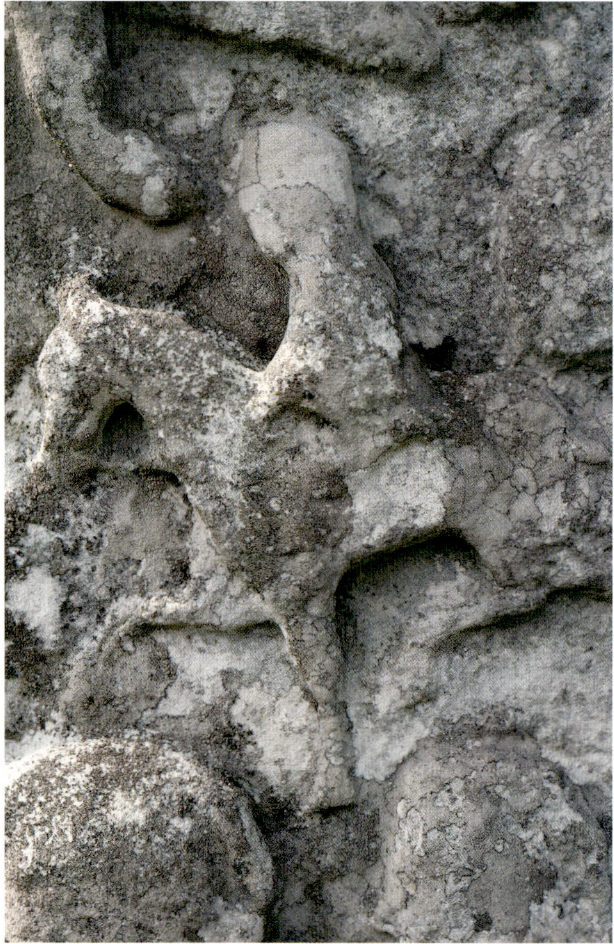

Detail of horse and rider, Canna. This detail carved on one of Canna's two stone crosses possibly dates back over 1000 years and is once again evidence of the sheer variety of interest to be found in the Hebridean islands. Canna measuring just 8km long and with a population of no more than 30 inhabitants is now in the care of the National Trust for Scotland.

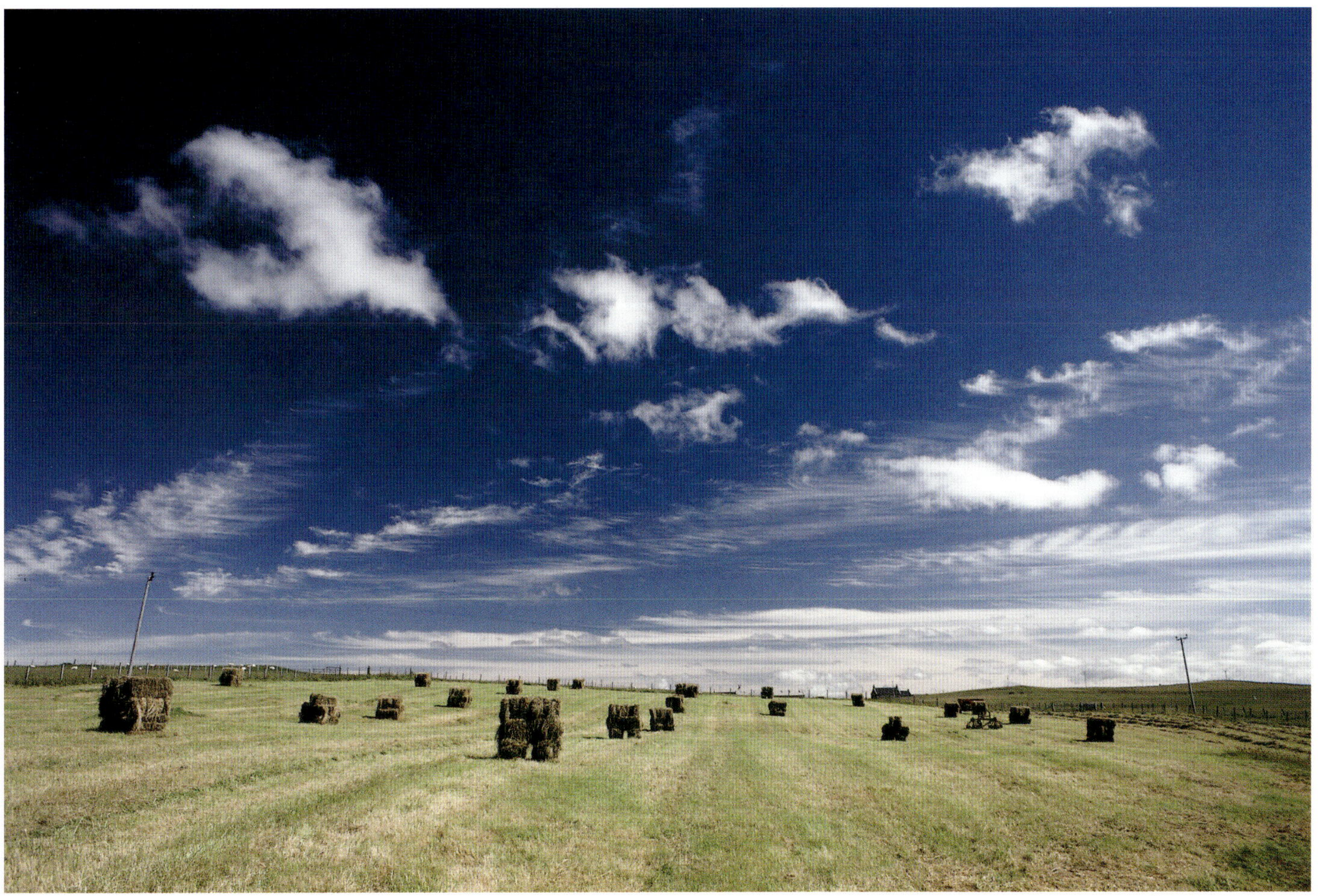

Rolling farmland under summer skies near Balmartin, North Uist. Whilst the eastern half of North Uist is mostly water – a mosaic of freshwater lochs behind a shattered coastline – the west by comparison comprises considerable areas of rich farmland used either for crops or grazing of cattle. These areas provide an interesting contrast to the moorlands of Lewis further north.

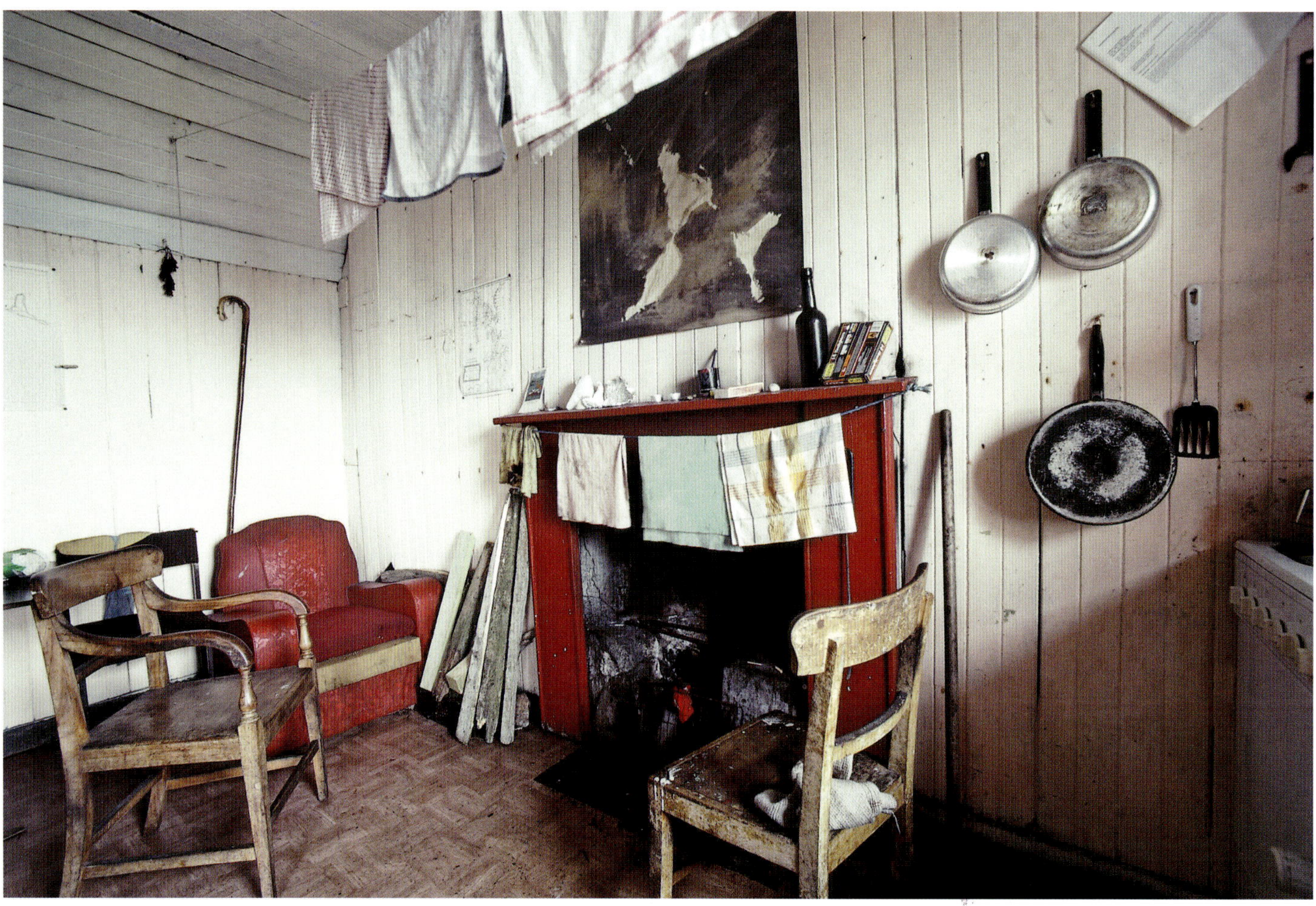

Shepherd's bothy, Eilean an Tigh, Shiant Islands. This small group of islands lie mid-way between Skye and Lewis, their stark profiles clearly visible from the passing Skye-Harris ferries. Uninhabited since 1910 they are now the home of grazing sheep (brought over from Scalpay) and countless seabirds. Sir Compton MacKenzie purchased the group in 1925 when he renovated this particular cottage to enable him to stay on the islands during the summer months to give solitude for his writing. Many of the dramatic rock formations and spectacular cliffs with their columnar basalt are similar to those found on Staffa and parts of Mull but on a much grander scale, the cliffs here in places exceeding 150m high formed of columns each up to 2m wide.

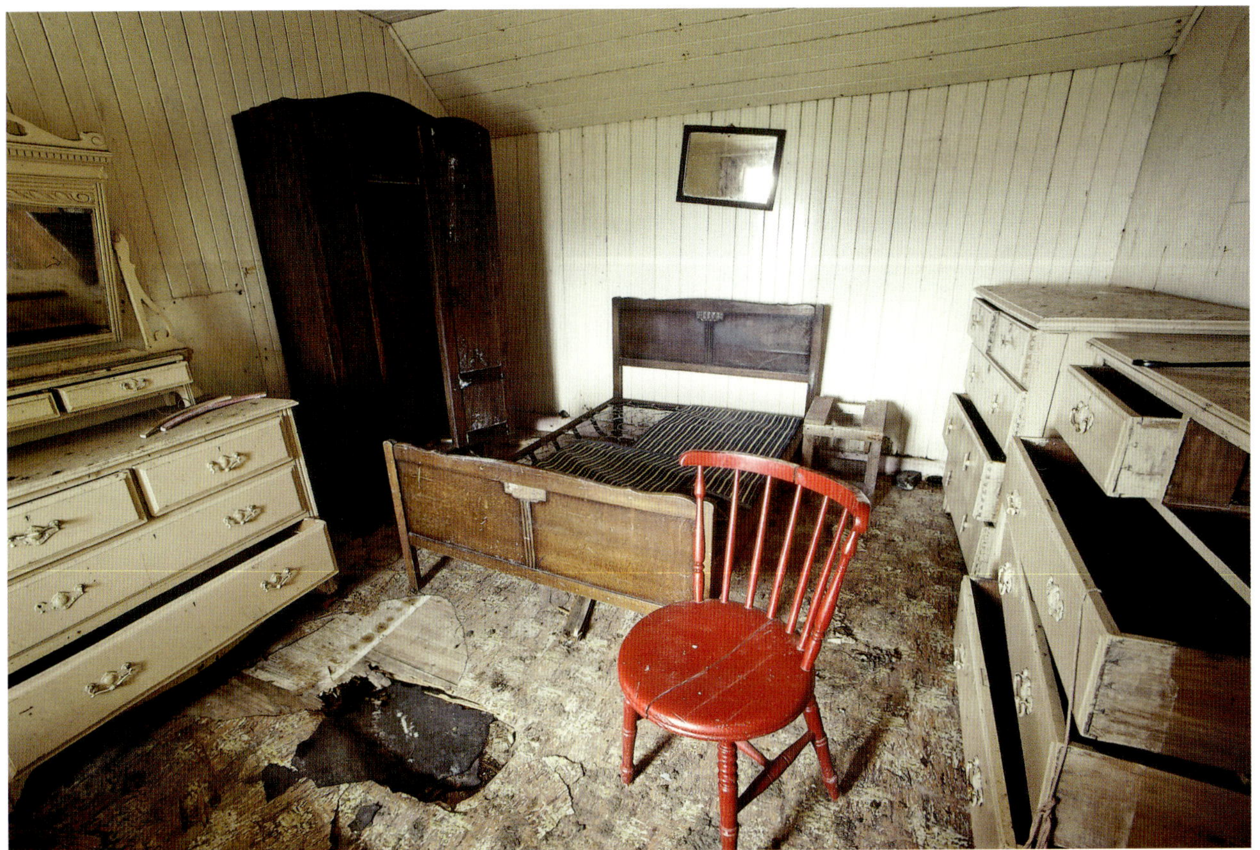

Abandoned interior, Berneray. Much has already been written earlier of the numerous empty buildings scattered throughout the Hebrides and even on the small, beautiful, relatively prosperous island of Berneray such scenes are still familiar.

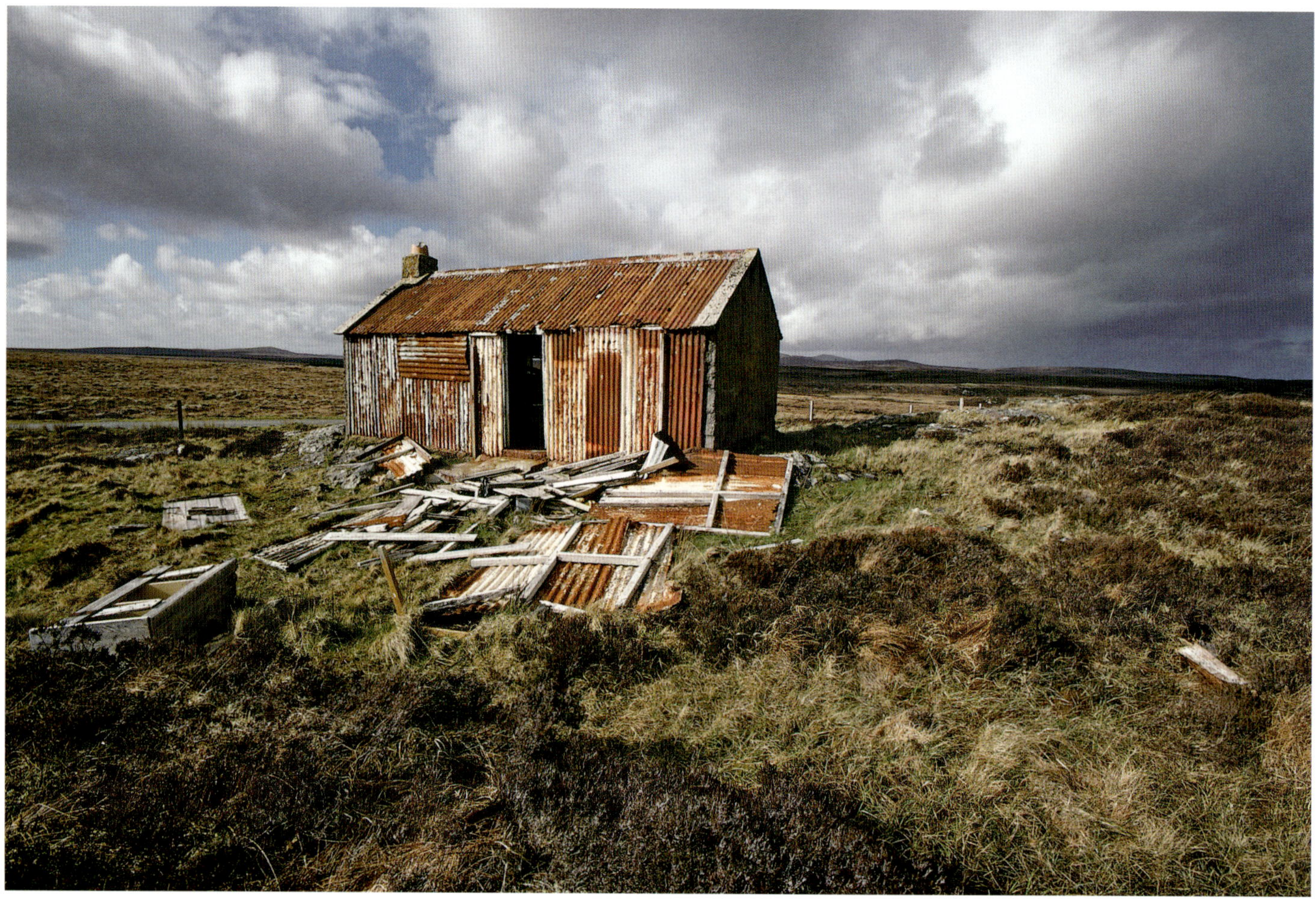

This page and opposite: Peat cutters' huts, the String Road near Stornaway, Lewis. Peat is still traditionally cut as a normal fuel throughout much of the Hebrides and in particular on the vast moors of Lewis where mechanical cutting is also carried out to a considerable degree. Cut in summer, the peats are then allowed to dry before being taken and stacked at the homes where they will be burnt during the winter months. The flimsy but sometimes colourful huts along the String Road would once have been used for the inhabitants of Stornaway attending the peats during the long summer evenings but with availability of modern transport are now rarely used and are gradually falling into total decay.

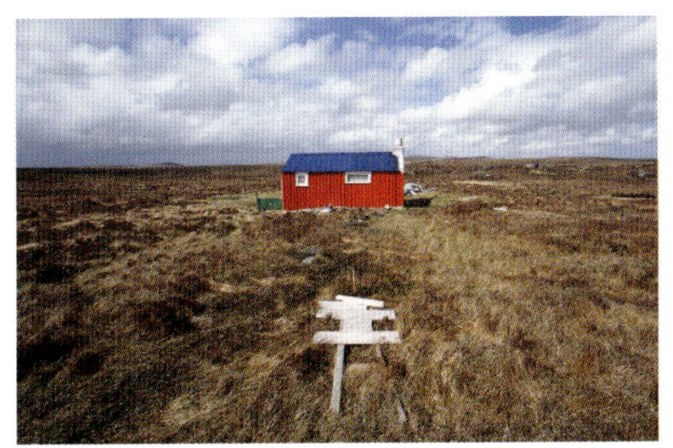
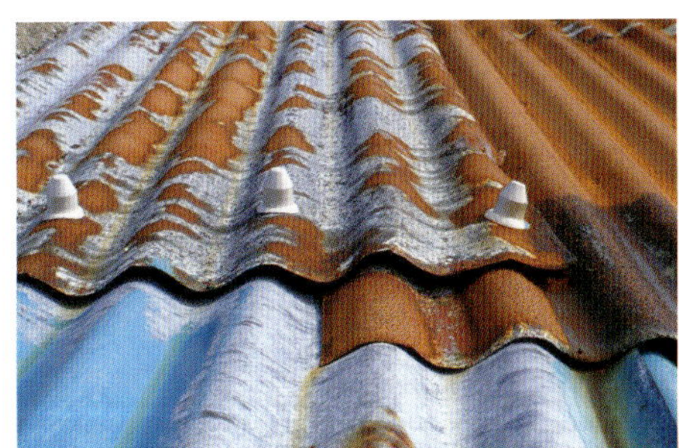
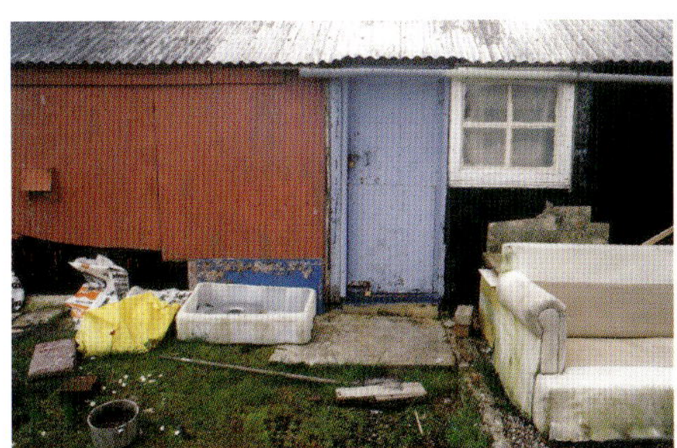
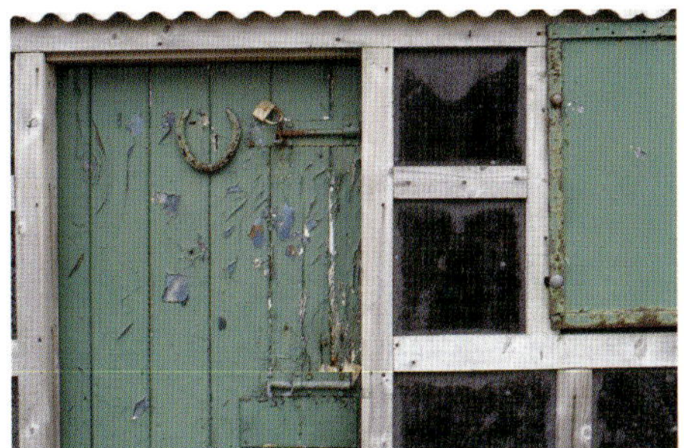
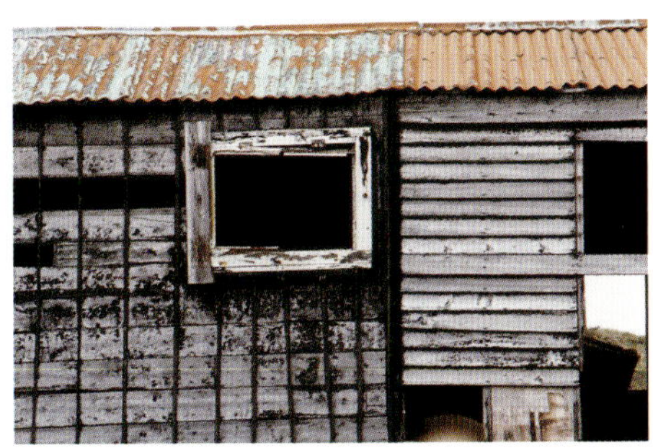
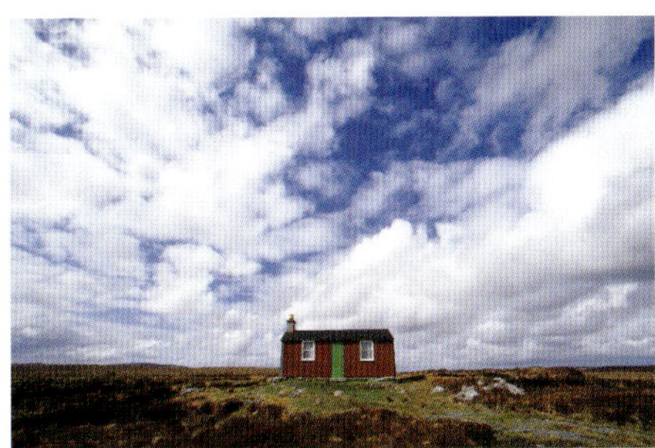
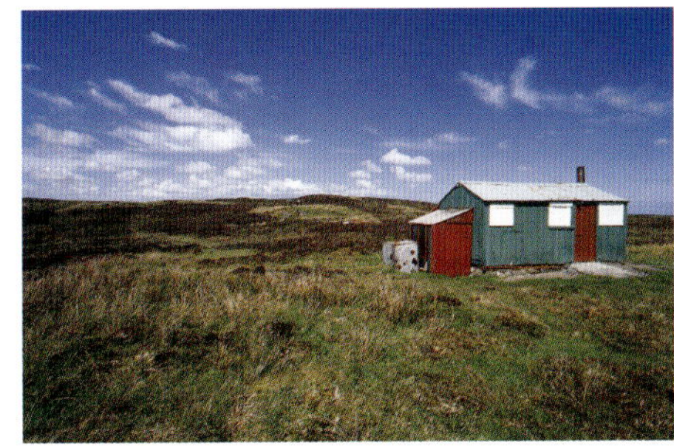
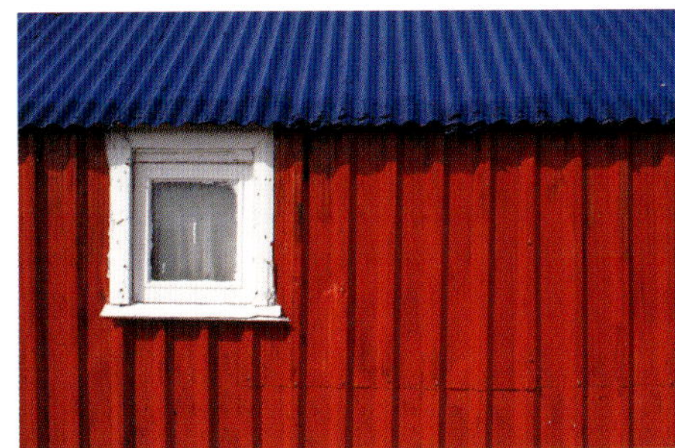
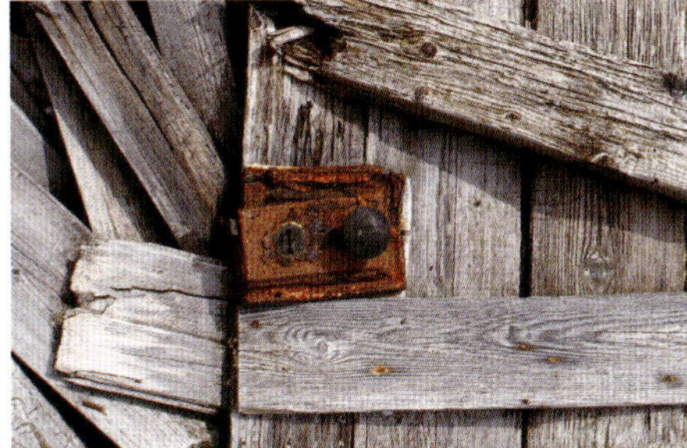

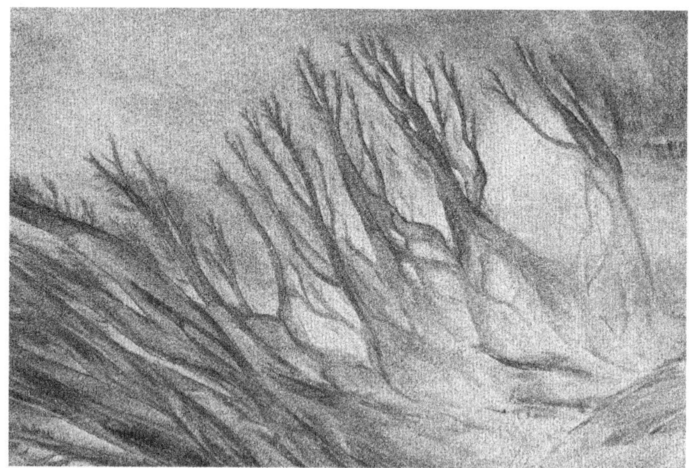

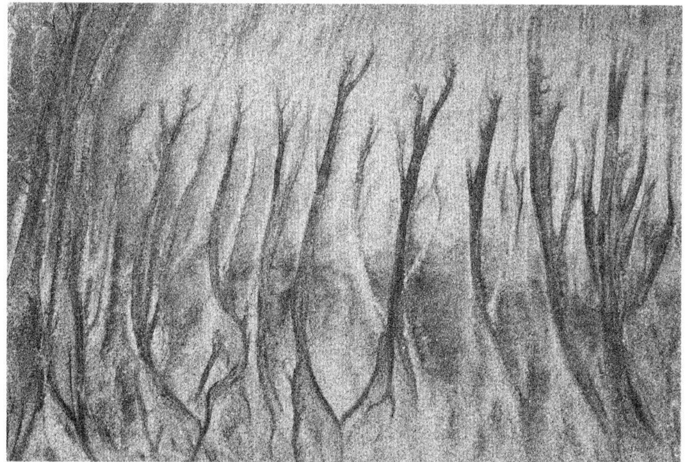

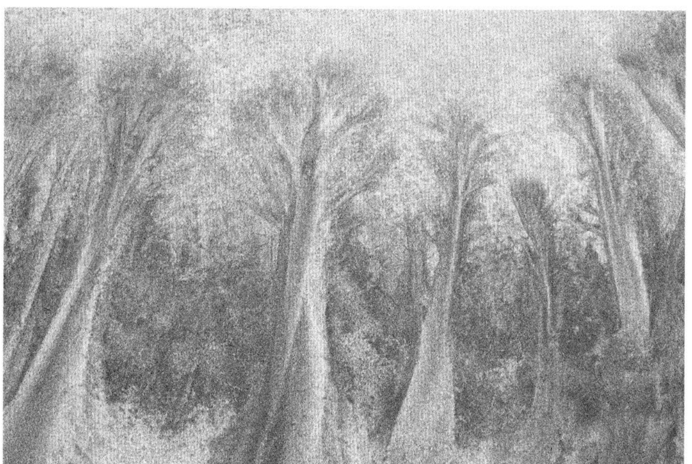

'Tree' patterns. The Hebrides are not known for outstanding woodlands and most of the trees that do exist are often stunted in their growth and bent over by the powerful winds. However, on certain sandy beaches as the tides recede, tree-like patterns and shapes are formed in the sand to give ghostly appearances of woodland, sometimes in a quite remarkable three-dimensional manner.

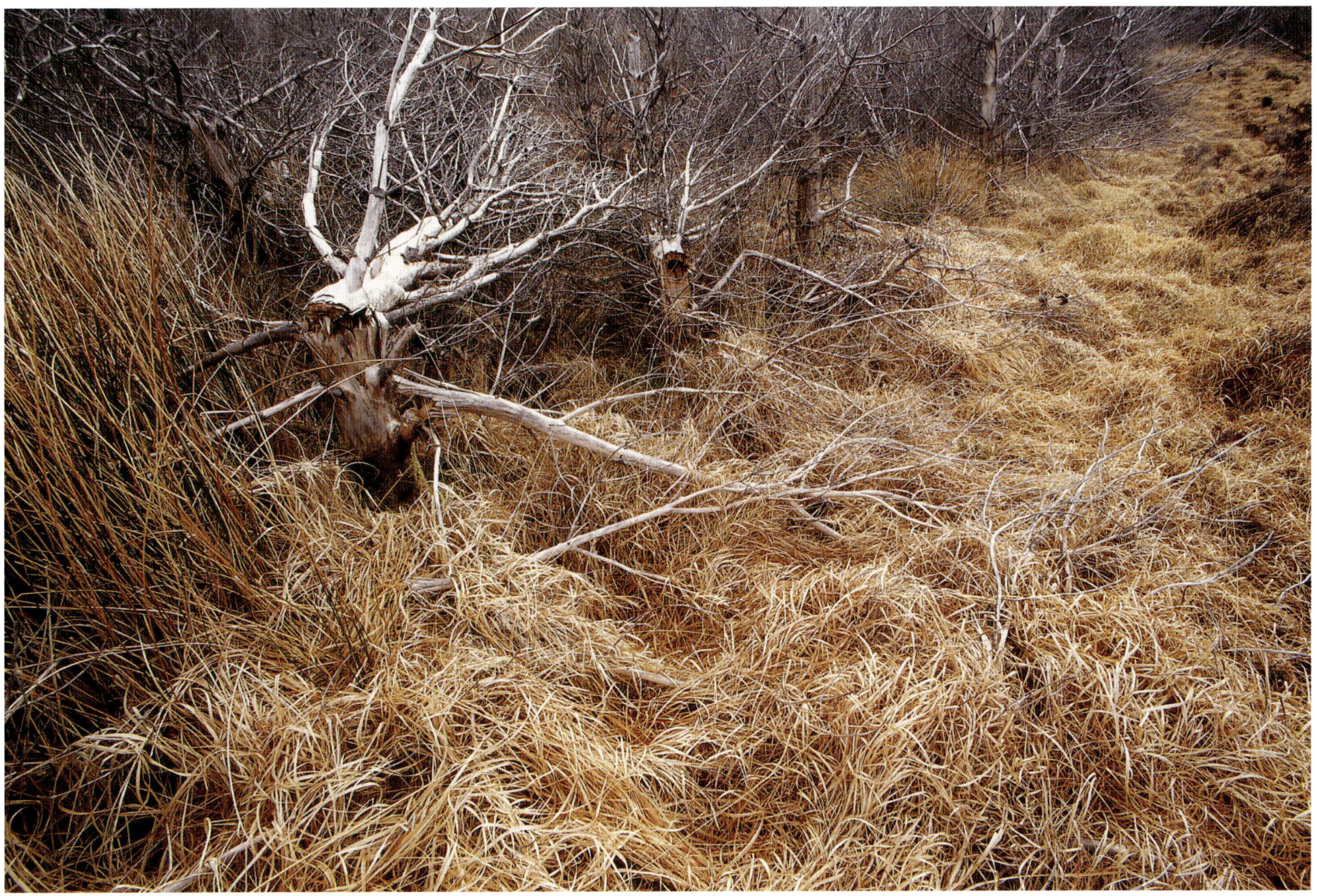

'Dead' forest near Arivruaich, Lewis. There are a few large coniferous plantations on Lewis, notably near Arivruaich and also near Garynahine. In both these areas several thousand trees now stand dead or collapsing, infected by insect born disease some years ago. The bare silvered trunks are a stark contrast to the dark green of the surviving trees.

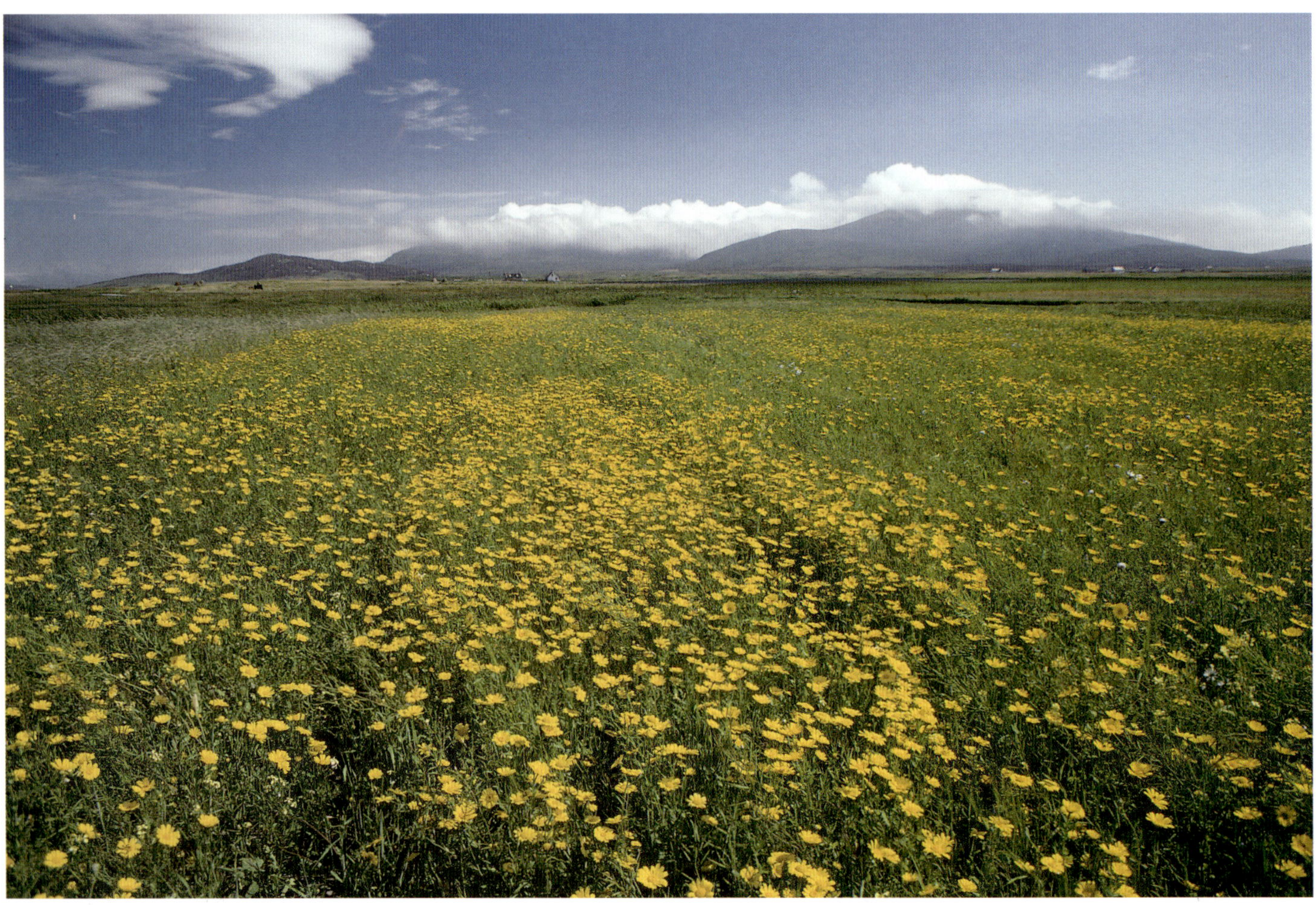

Summer grasslands, Peninerine, South Uist. Corn Marigolds spread across the grasslands of South Uist in high summer with the peaks of Hecla and Beinn Mhor beyond. This notably rich farmland stretches for about 2km inland from the long west coast beach, a carpet of flowers in summer punctuated by numerous lochans, sandy tracks and narrow roads and a haven for birds, insects and plant species.

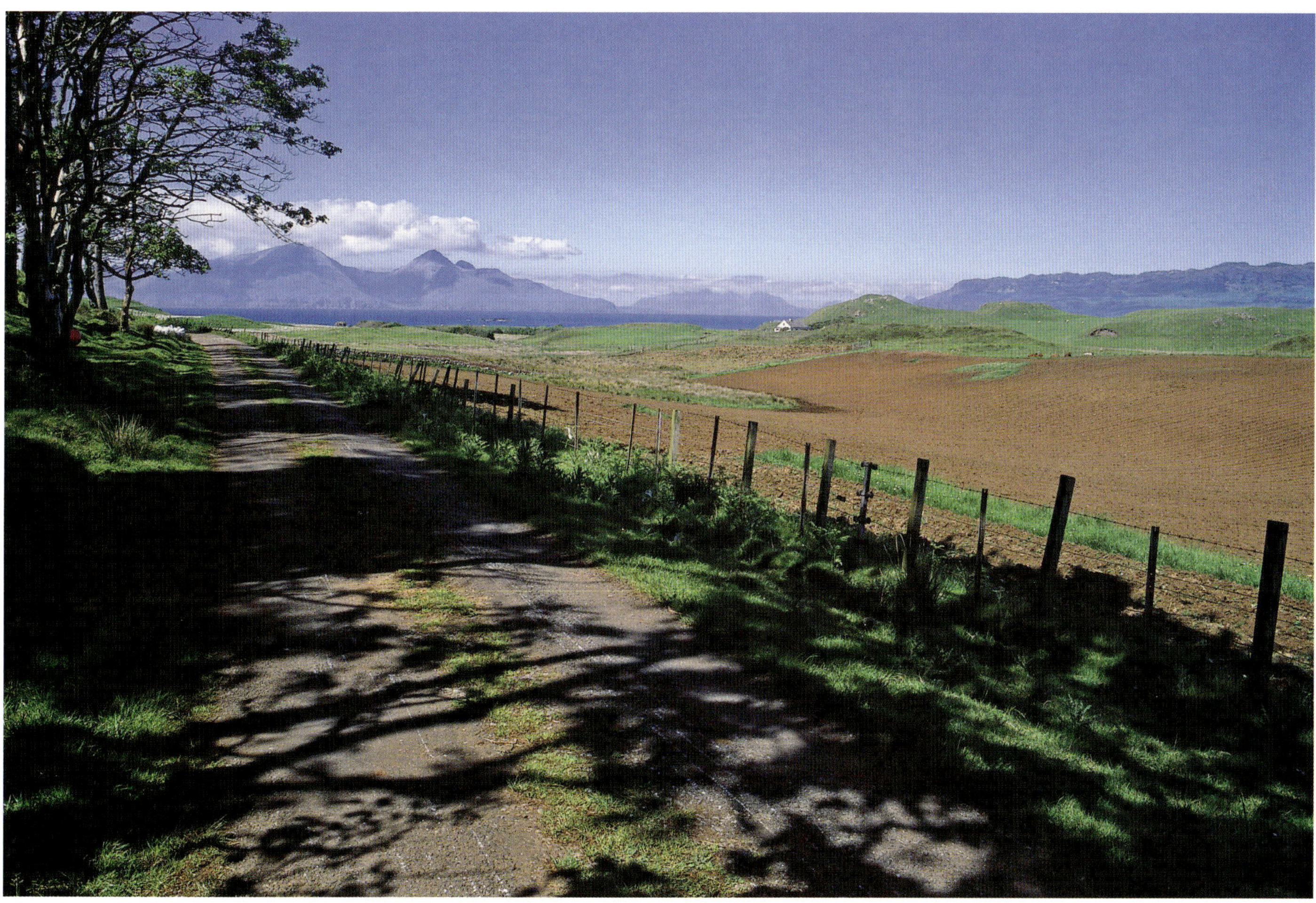

Tree shadows spread across the single 2km road of Muck (Isle of Pigs) in early spring with fields ready for planting and the islands of Rum, Skye and Eigg seen in the background. Muck, the smallest of the Small Isles group and the most fertile is still owned by the MacEwan family and with a population of some 30 inhabitants is run almost as a single farm. Beautifully tended, this peaceful island is a place to unwind and appreciate the ever-changing views of sea and sky.

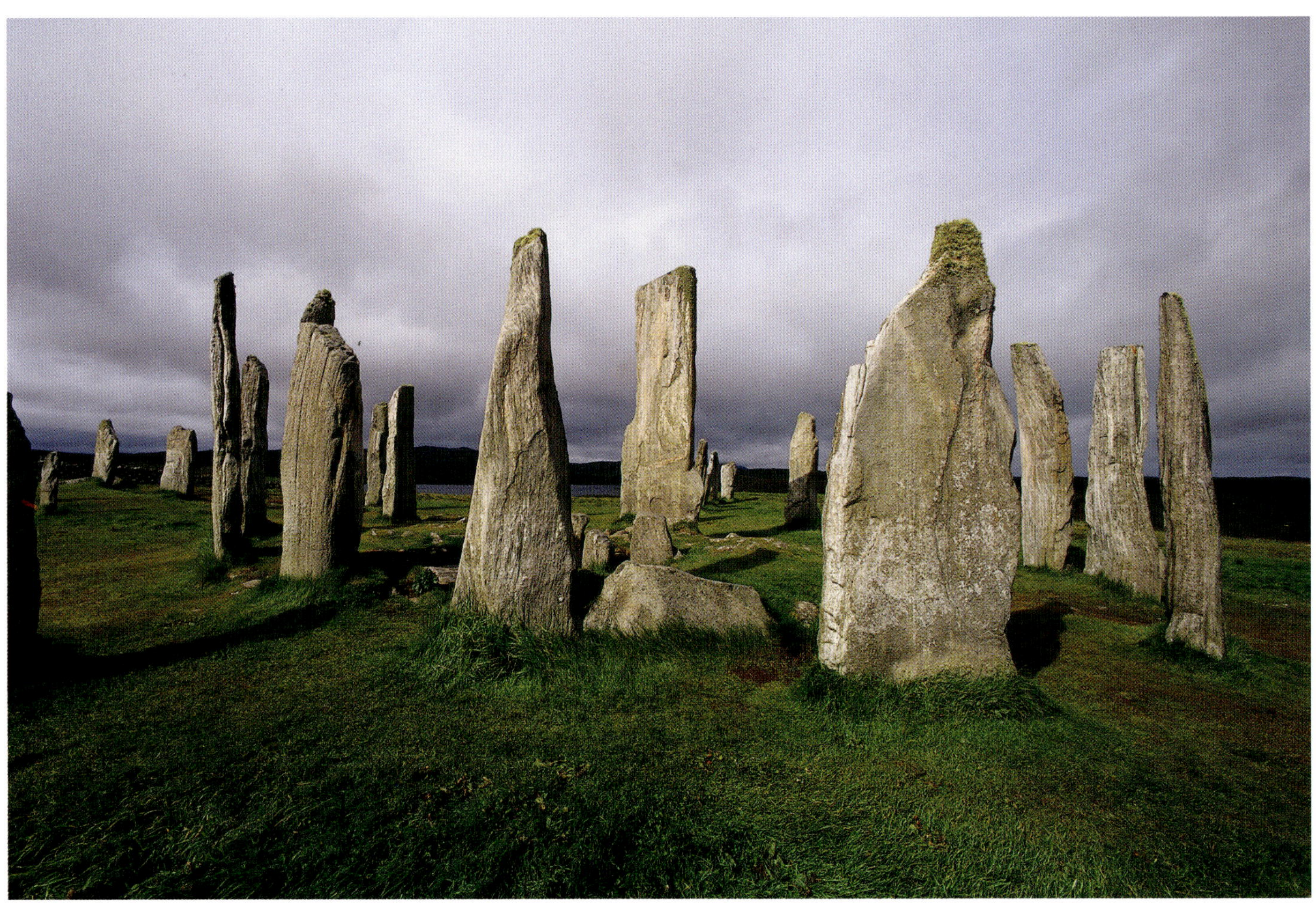

Callanish Stone Circle, Lewis. The circle stands on a low exposed hill above Loch Roag on the west coast of Lewis and is now regarded as the second most important prehistoric circle in Britain after Stonehenge. It is thought to be some 4000 years old and it was not until the 1850s, after excavation of the surrounding peat, that the true height of the Gneiss stones was appreciated – the tallest being 4.5m high. The unique arrangement of the stones, consisting of a circle within a cross formed of single and double radiating lines, and their alignment suggest its use to have been astronomical but there is no firm evidence of this and numerous other theories have been expounded over the years. Other small circles in the vicinity are possibly connected to it.

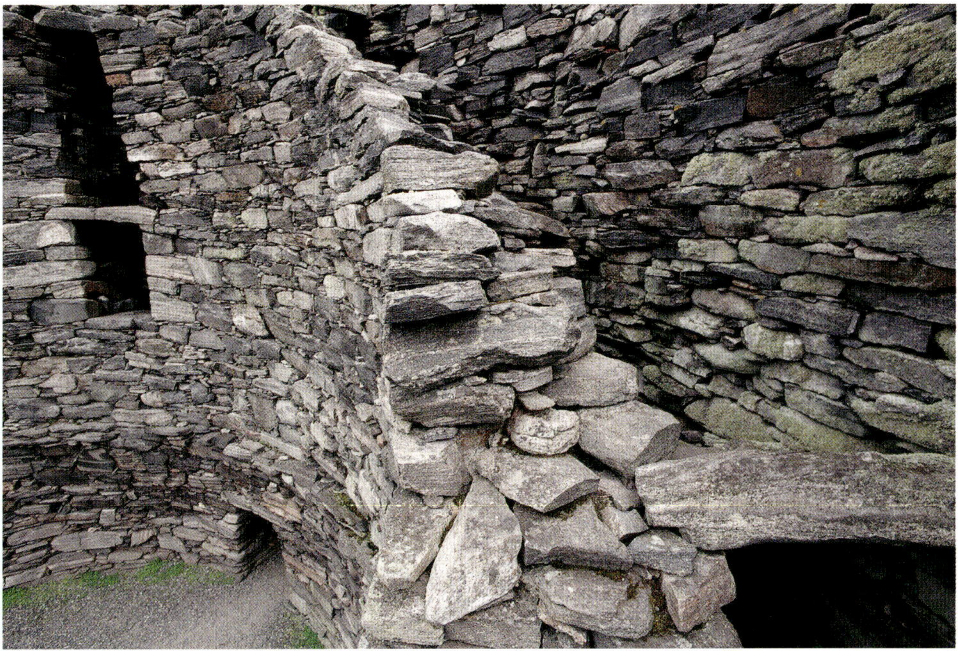

Carloway Broch, Lewis. About 8km north of Callanish, the broch at Doune Carloway is one of the finest structures of its type in Scotland. Over 15m in diameter and of a similar height, many parts of its gently-tapering double-skinned dry stone wall still survive complete in places with galleries and staircases. Its use, perhaps for defensive purposes, is still uncertain as is its age but it is likely to be at least 2000 years old.

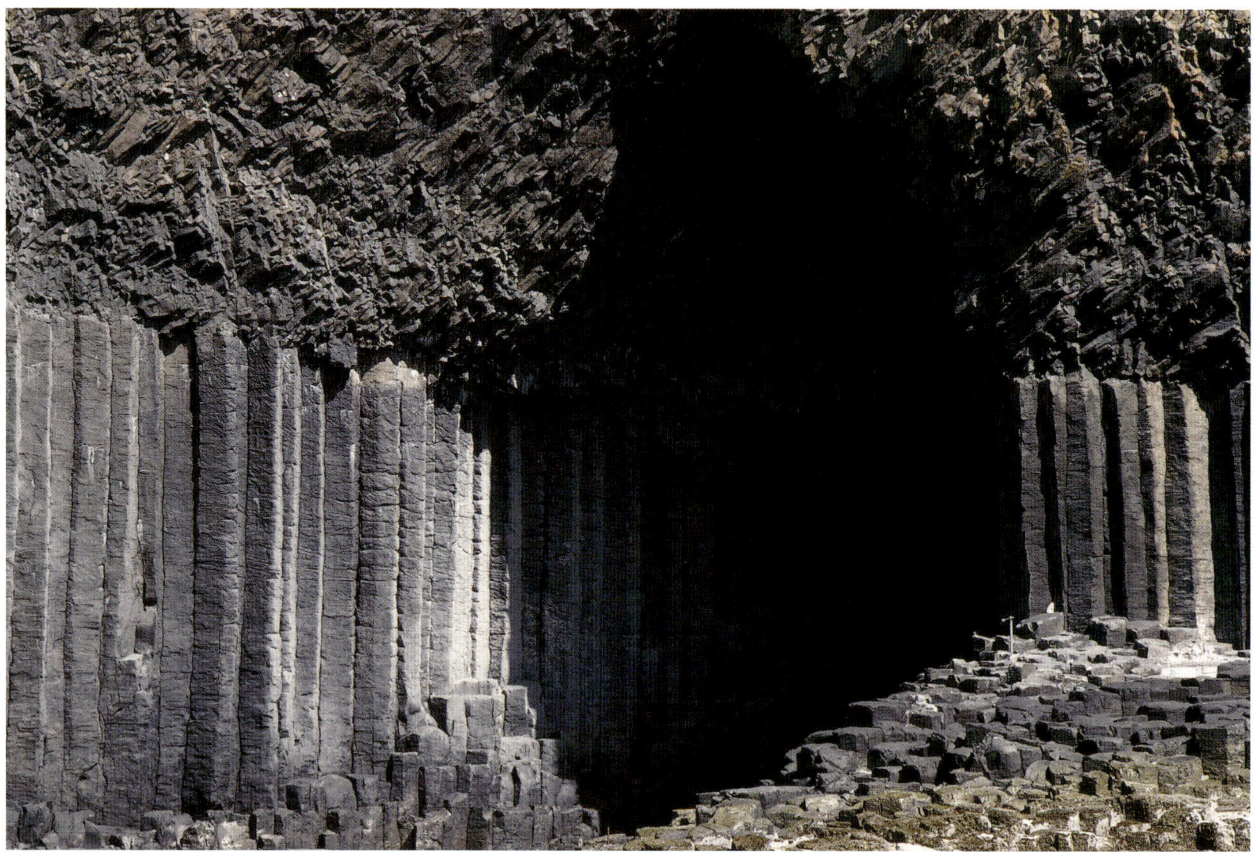

Fingals Cave, Staffa. The composer Felix Mendelssohn came here in 1829 to be inspired subsequently to write his famous overture 'The Hebrides'. As a result the tiny, uninhabited volcanic island of Staffa has become one of the best known islands in Europe receiving numerous visitors each year, weather and seas permitting, to view its caves and outstanding rock formations. Foremost of these is Fingals Cave some 25m deep and 20m high set in the Great Face of black hexagonal basaltic columns on the southern tip of the island and which boats can enter in calm conditions. Clamshell, Boat and Cormorant caves are however almost as impressive as are the basaltic pavements not dissimilar to the Giant's Causeway in Ireland's County Antrim.

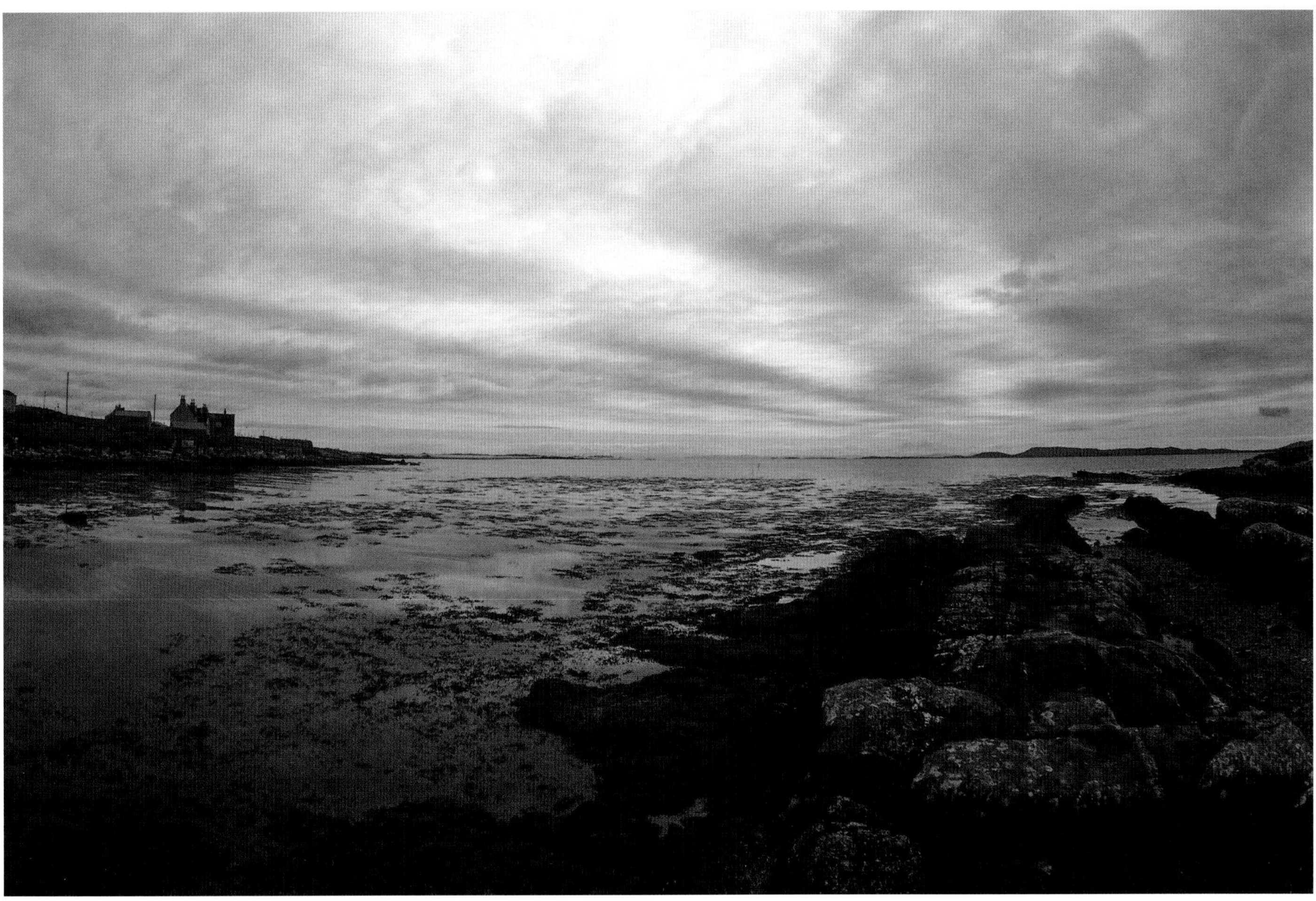

Early morning light, Berneray. Berneray is now linked to North Uist by a new causeway and also served by ferry from Harris. The ferry crossing takes about one hour, the vessel following a tortuous route through the often shallow waters of the Sound of Harris but with magnificent views to many of the adjacent islands. To arrive here as day breaks over this beautiful island is a memorable experience.

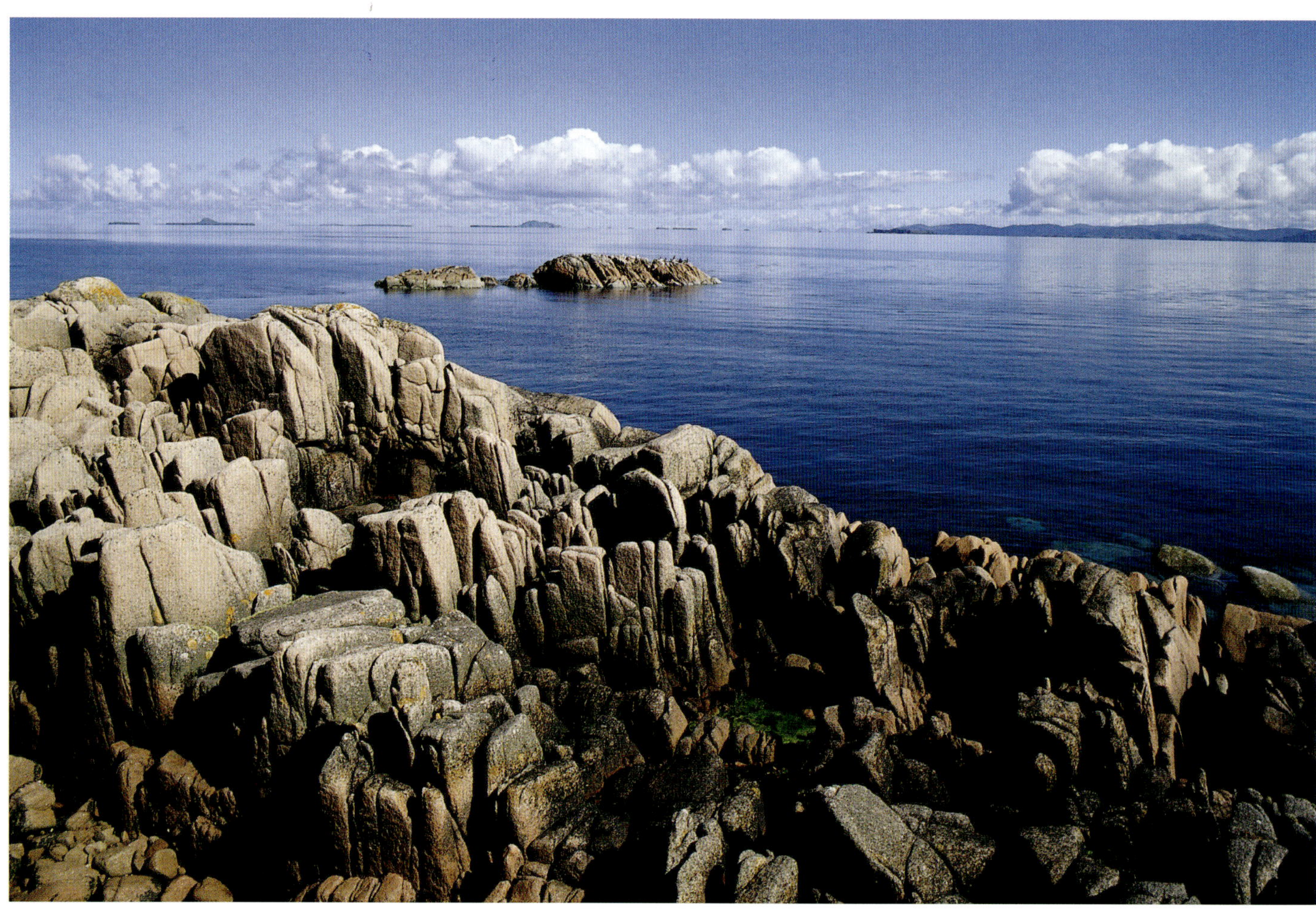

Summer calm, Kintra, Mull. On an idyllic summer's morning the view north west from Kintra at the tip of the Ross of Mull looks towards the Treshnish Isles, the islands of Staffa, Gometra, Ulva, Mull's Treshnish Point and in the very far distance the Small Isles of Eigg, Muck and Rum. Views of this nature extending at least 100km are common throughout the Hebrides in still, clear conditions.

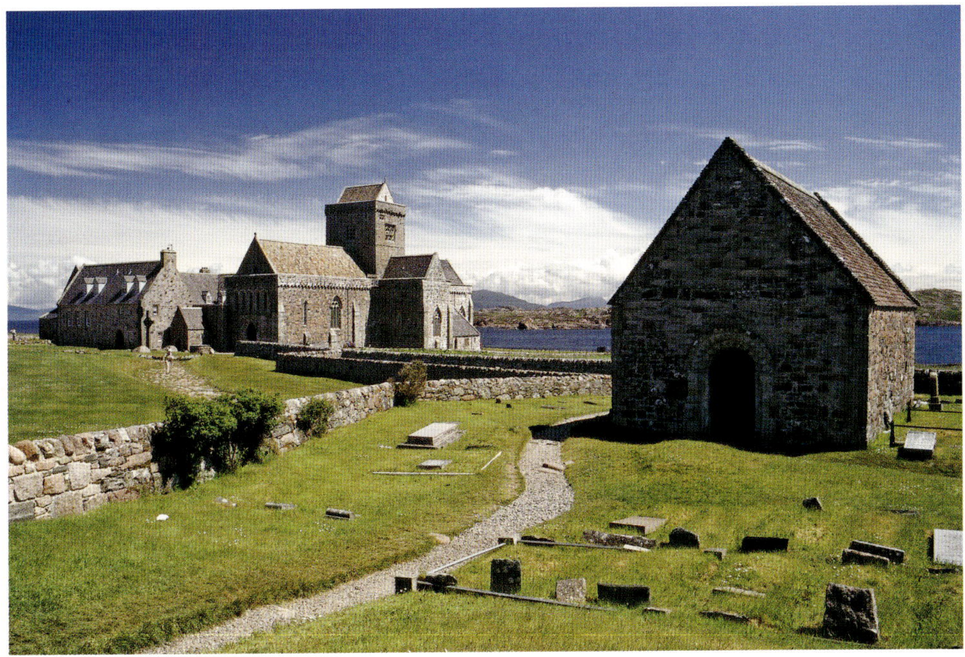

Iona. Every Hebridean island seems to have its devotees and admirers but many would claim that Iona is the most beautiful of all the Hebrides. Although only small being some 2 x 5km Iona seems to contain all the essential elements of the Hebrides – white shell sand beaches, flowering machair, glorious views to other islands, a purity of light and colour almost unmatched and of course an incomparable sense of history. Columba arrived here in 563 and in the ensuing 34 years founded a monastery and turned the island into a centre of pilgrimage and Christian learning famous throughout Europe. Following a history of numerous raids by the Norse after 795, a new monastery, abbey and nunnery were finally founded for the Benedictines in the early thirteenth century forming the foundations of the historic buildings to be seen today. The present abbey, given cathedral status, was commenced in the 1500s only to fall into decay and ruin after the Reformation but later being restored by the Church of Scotland in the early 1900s. Each year Iona is visited by thousands of people viewing the numerous ancient buildings and sacred sites, yet despite this, the island generally remains unspoilt with an uncanny sense of peace and mysticism found nowhere else in the Hebrides. The photograph shows the granite cathedral in the background and the Norman-style St Oran's Chapel on the right with the island of Mull in the far distance across the Sound of Iona.

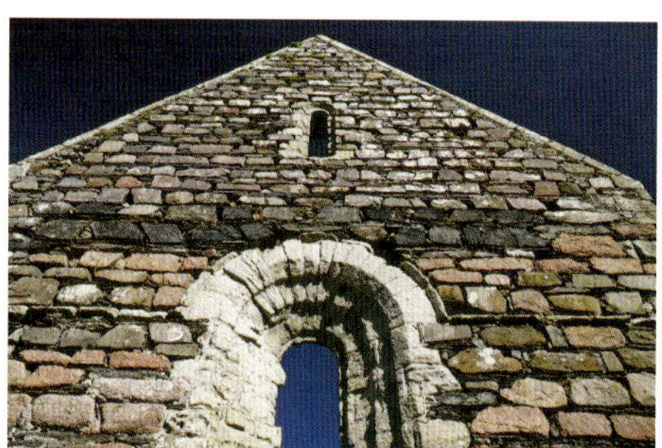

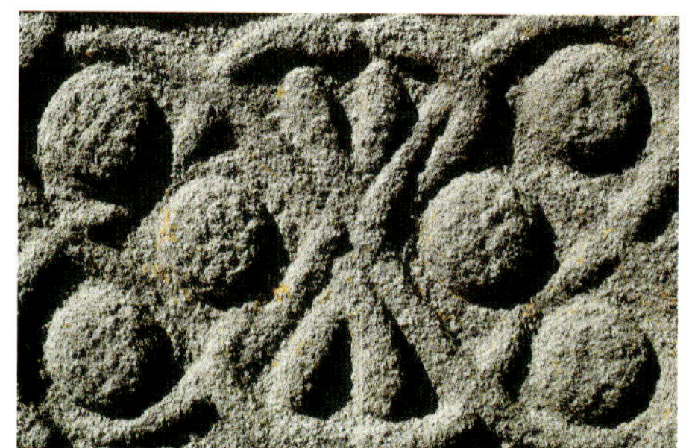

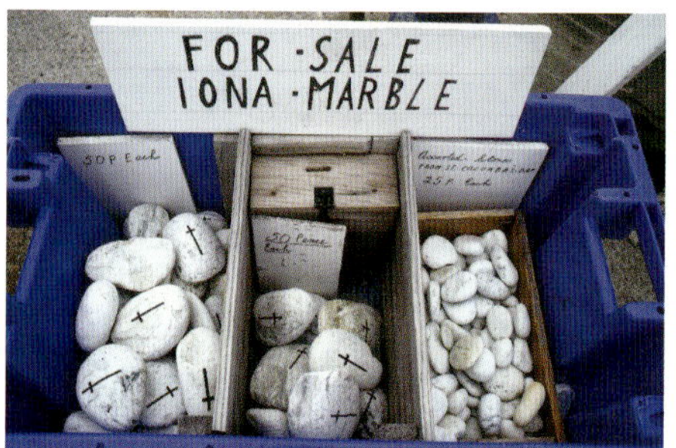

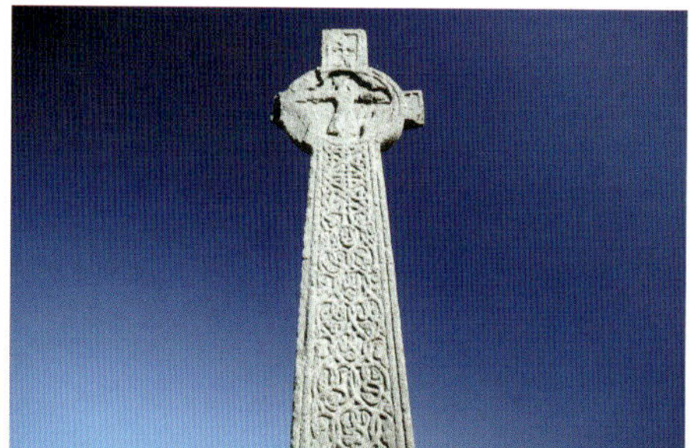

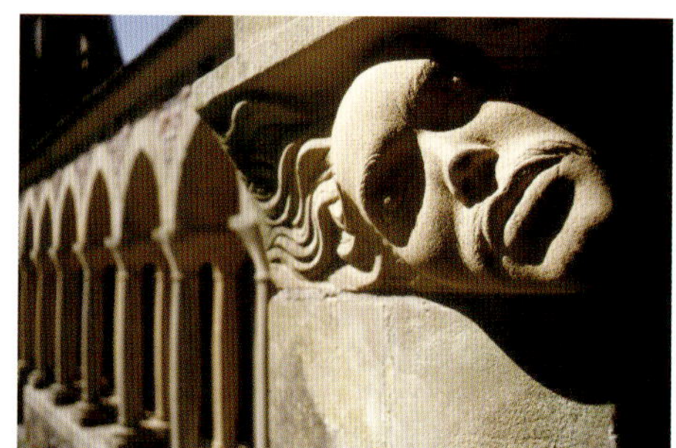

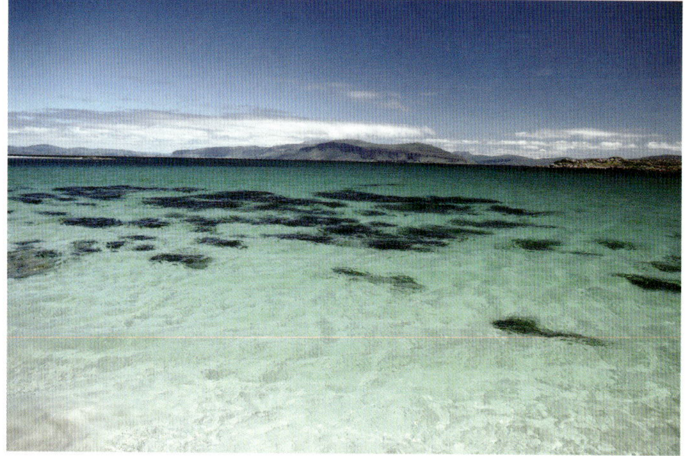

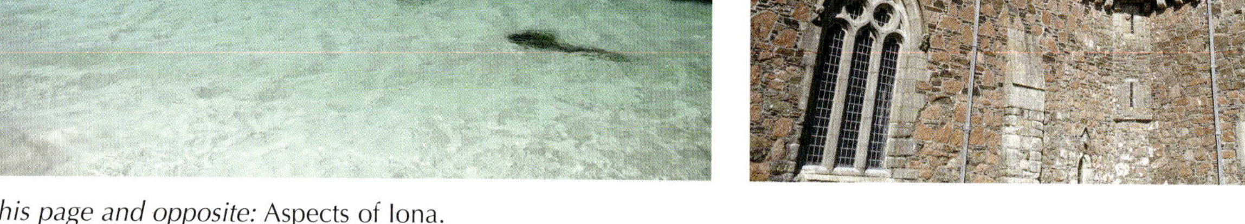

This page and opposite: Aspects of Iona.

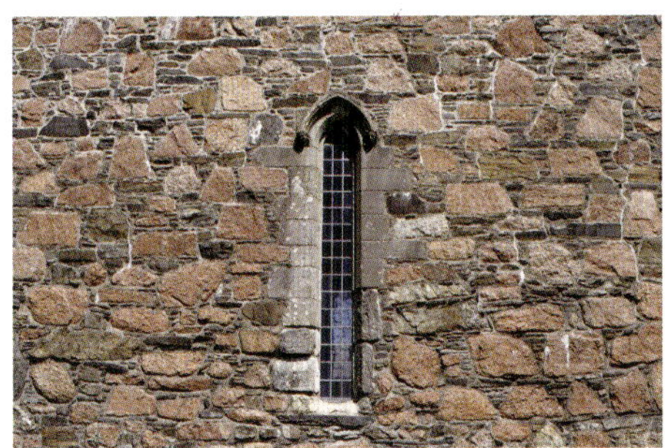

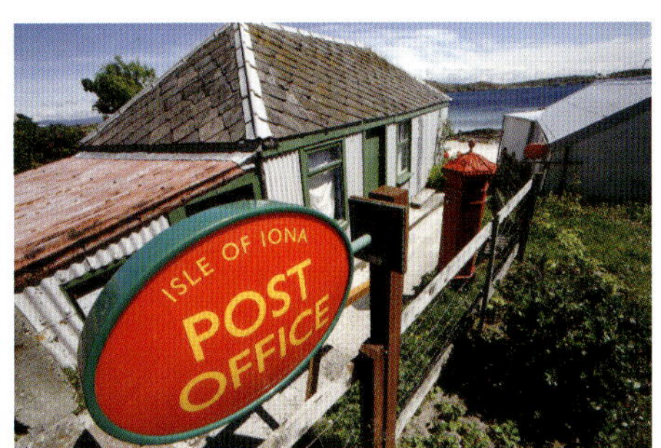
ISLE OF IONA
POST
OFFICE

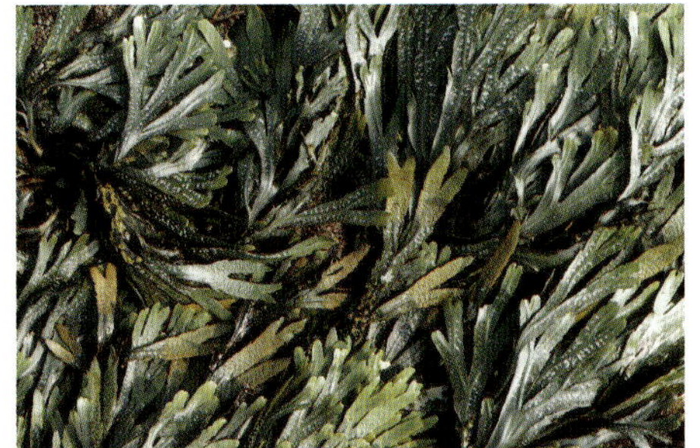

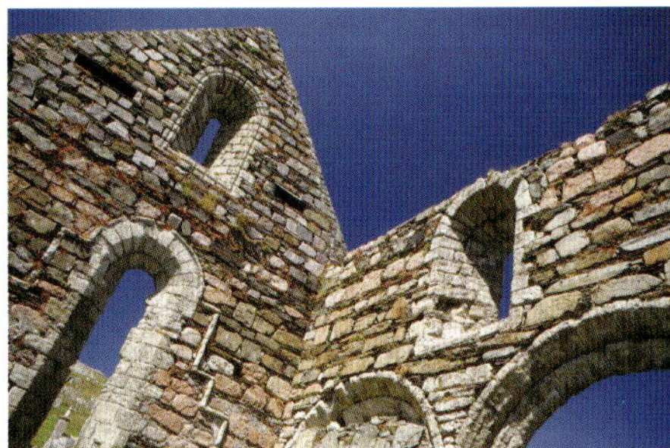

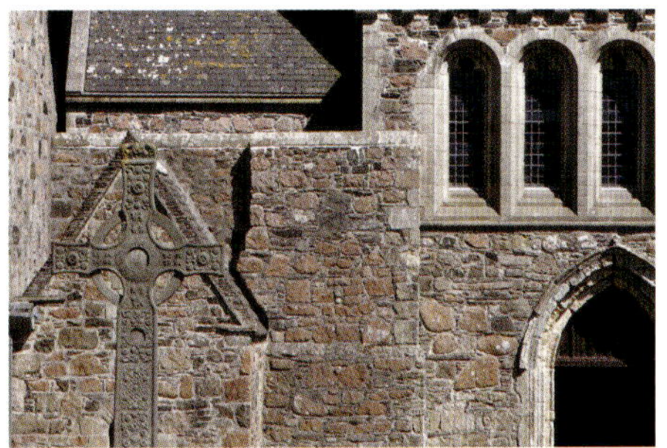

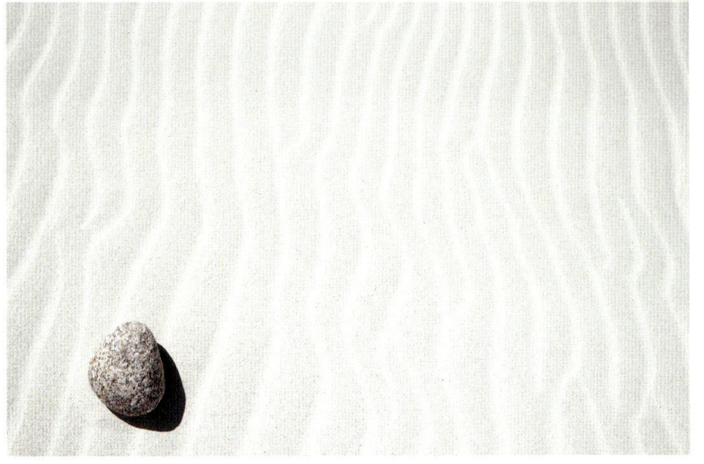

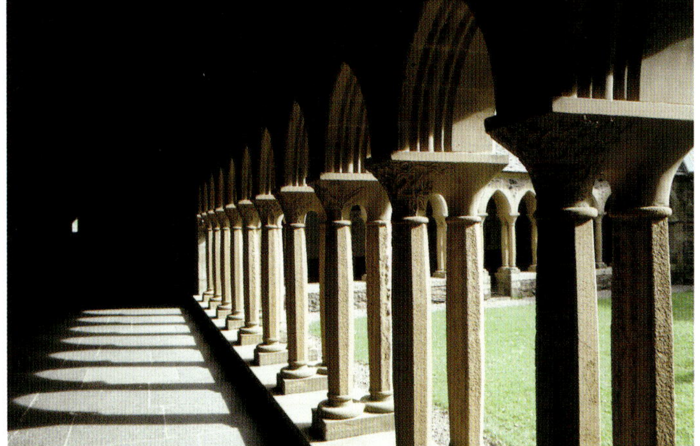

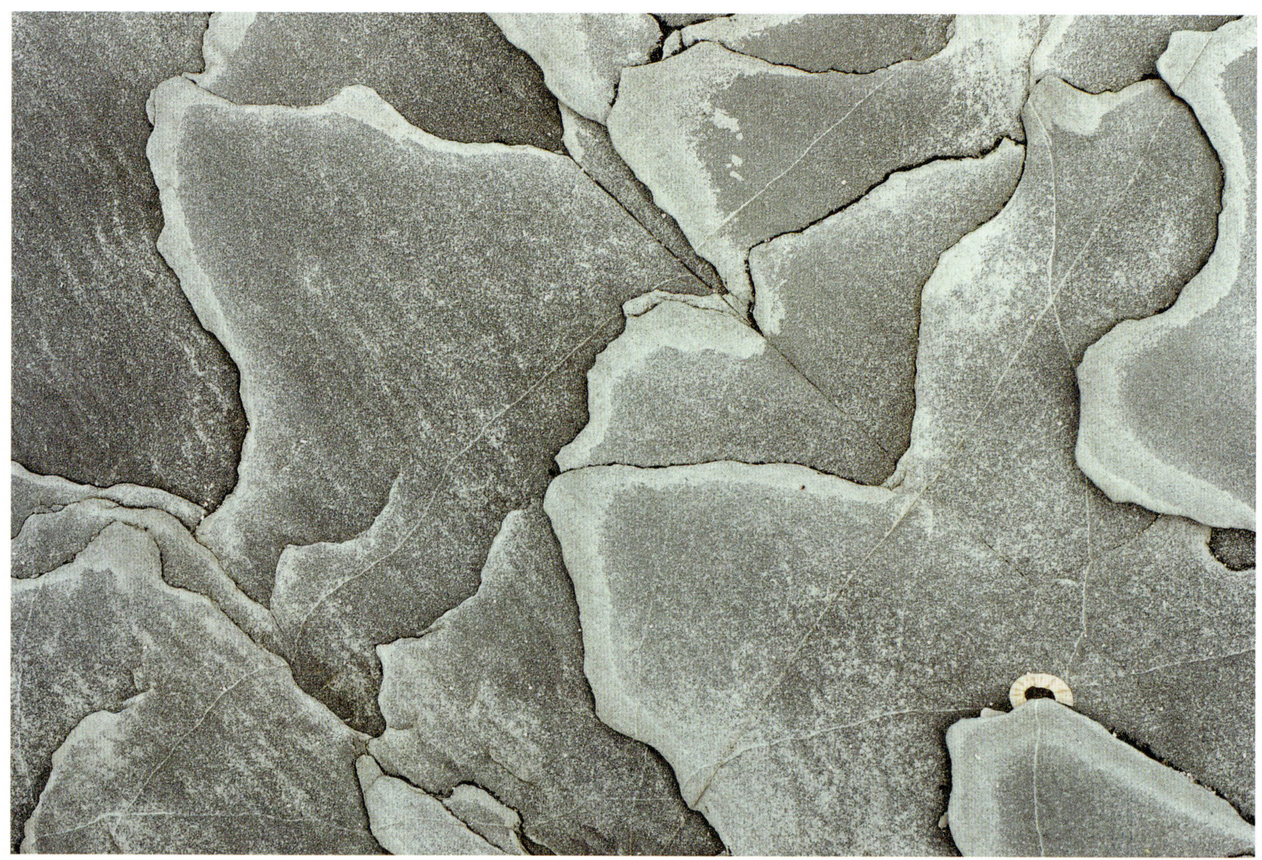

Slate design, Ardskennish, Colonsay.

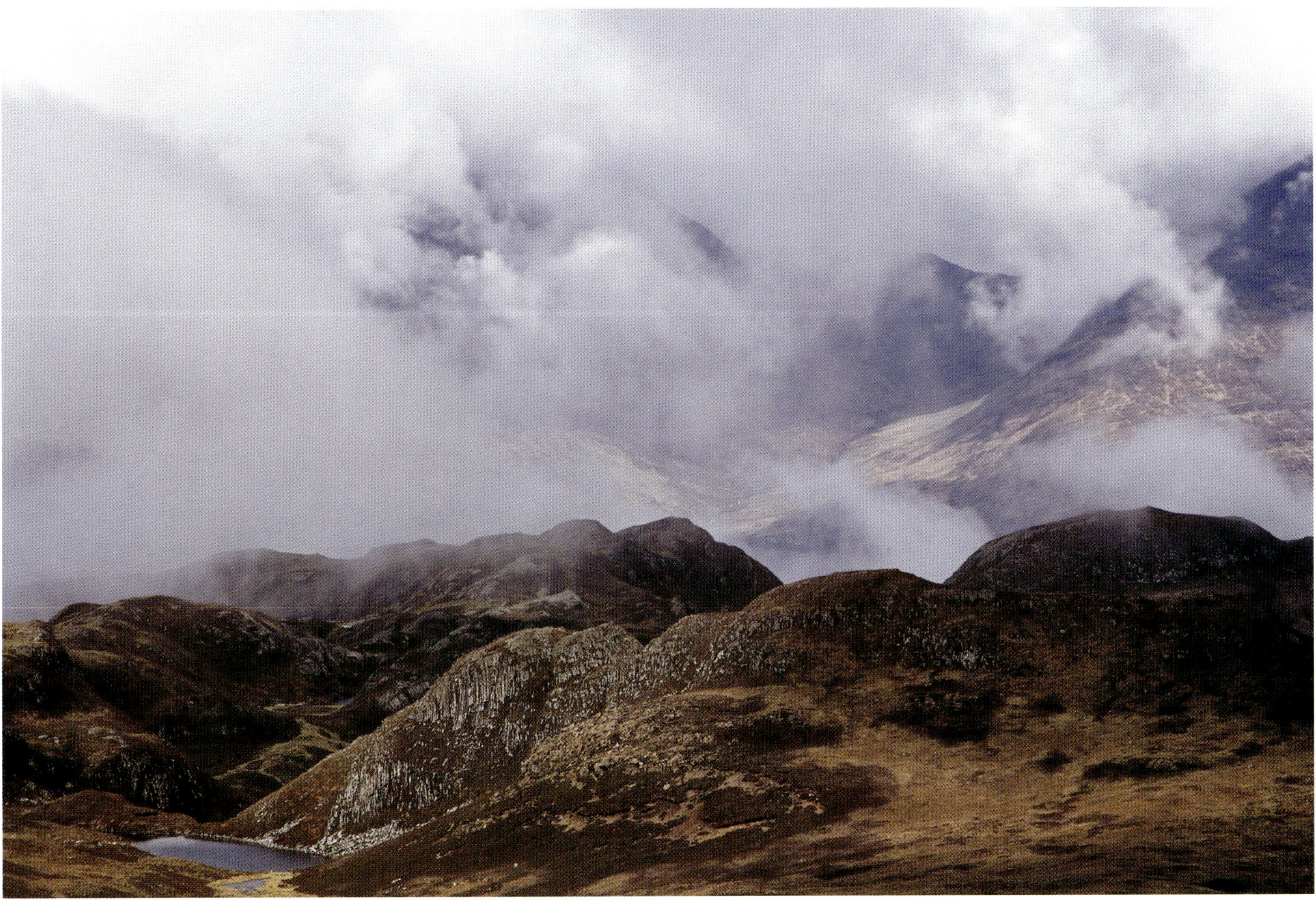

Summit of An Sgurr, Eigg. The view from the summit of Eigg's highest hill is regarded as one of the finest in the Hebrides. It was described in 1811 as 'yielding scenes unparalleled in Britain' and includes many of the mainland mountains together with the islands of Skye, Rum, Muck, the Outer Hebrides, Coll, Tiree, Mull, Staffa , the Treshnish Isles and Iona. The photograph here looking west shows the drama of morning mist and low cloud clearing from the peaks of Rum.

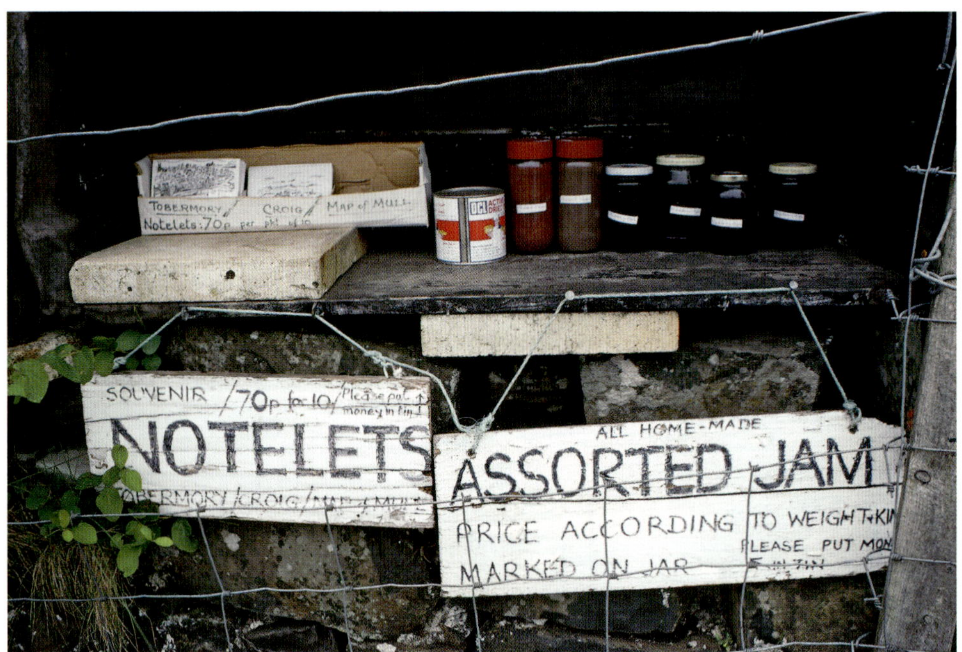

Souvenir stall, Croig, Mull.

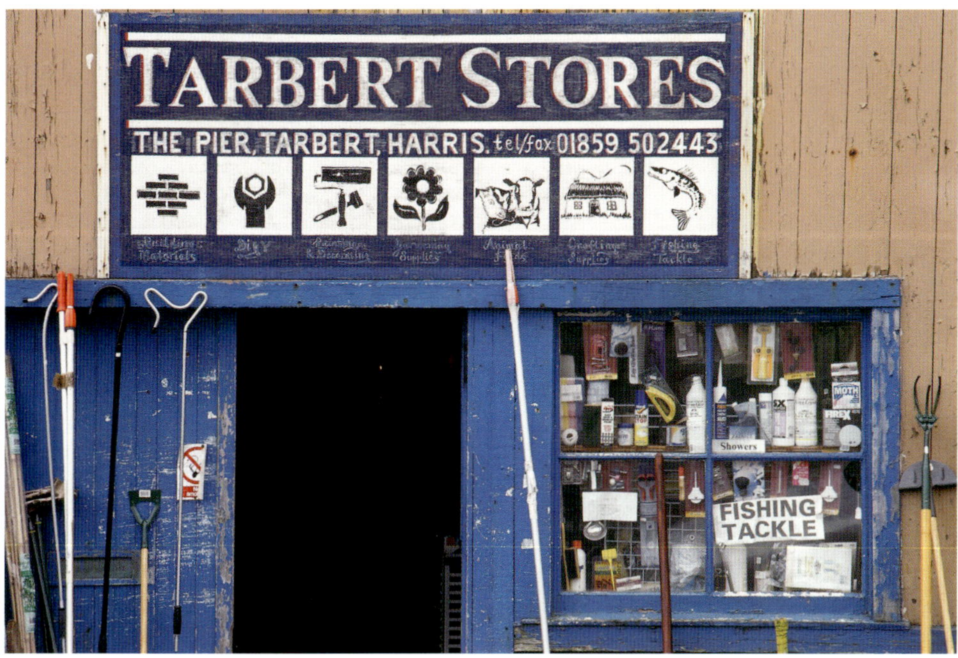

Tarbert Stores, Tarbert, Harris. The Tarbert Stores are rapidly becoming that rare commodity these days – a shop that sells just about anything apart from groceries. The fascia board more or less says it all. To go inside is one of life's great experiences foraging amongst the shelves and cupboards or in the piles of boxes, bags, sacks and containers that litter the floor. Few items here are shrink wrapped or packaged in tiny plastic bags – everything is available to handle and touch. The distinctive smells of such a shop are a reminder of days long ago in one's youth. Tarbert is the largest settlement on Harris, its narrow isthmus marking the division between North and South Harris.

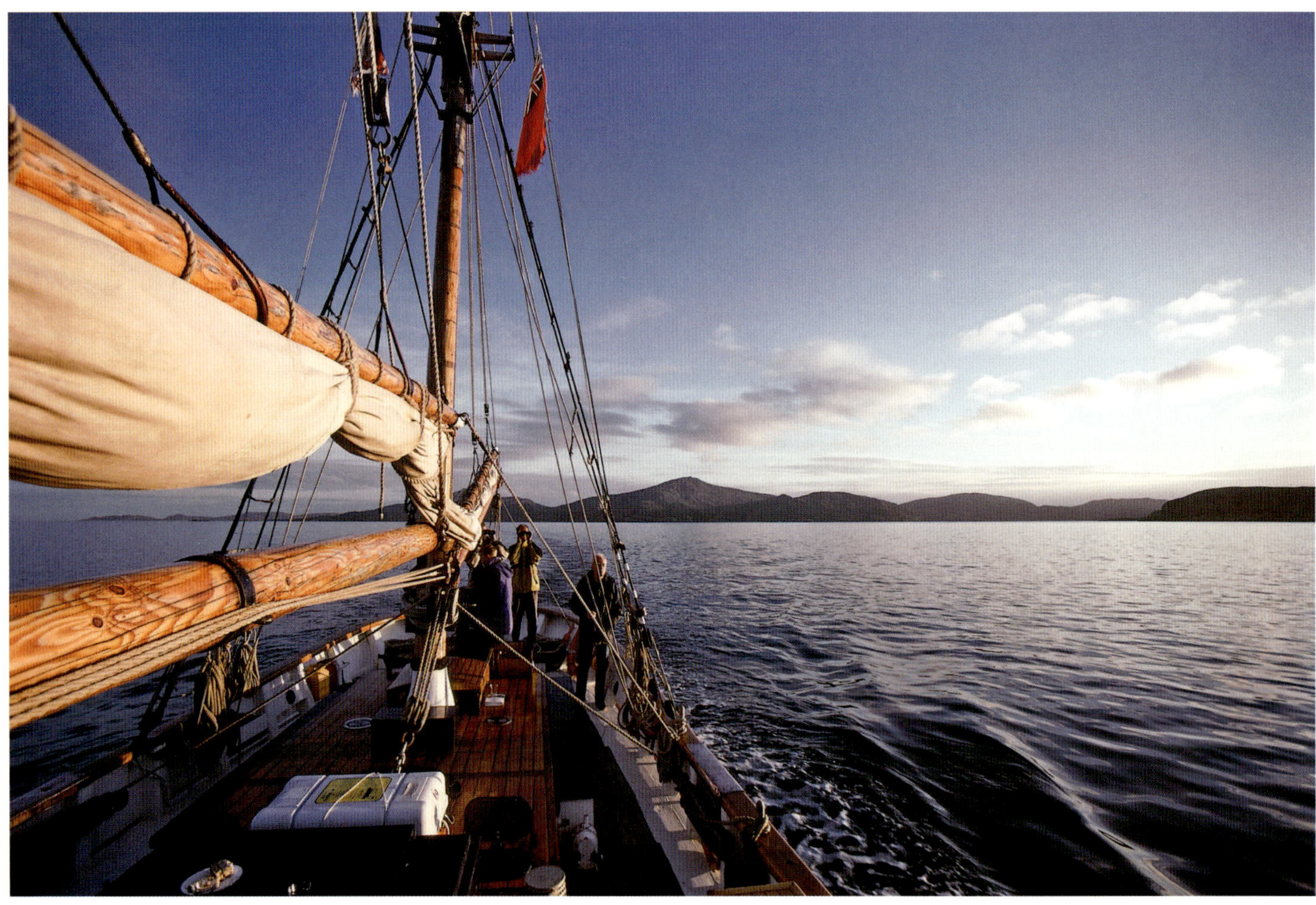

The Hebridean waters are considered to be amongst the finest sailing and boating areas in Britain subject of course to a wary eye on the often vicious tides and unpredictable weather. Not only are the islands accessible to visit but also the opportunity exists of being able to study closely the prolific bird and marine life including whale, shark, dolphin and porpoise. There is of course also the element of the ever-changing skies and sense of utter peace and solitude. The photograph here was taken on the Western Isles Sailing and Exploration Company's *Marguerite Explorer*, a traditional Danish purse seiner once familiar for its cruises around the Hebrides, at the start of crossing the Little Minch.

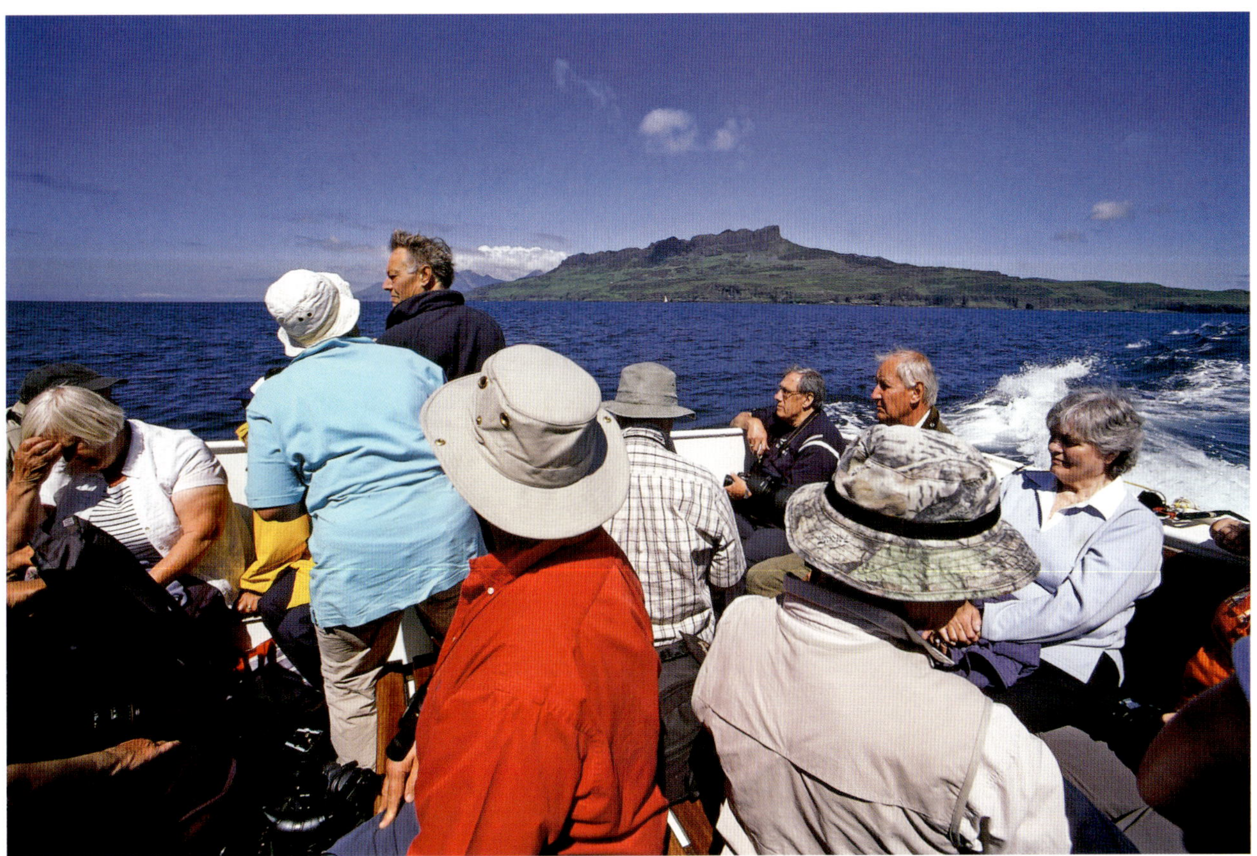

Day trip from Eigg to Muck.

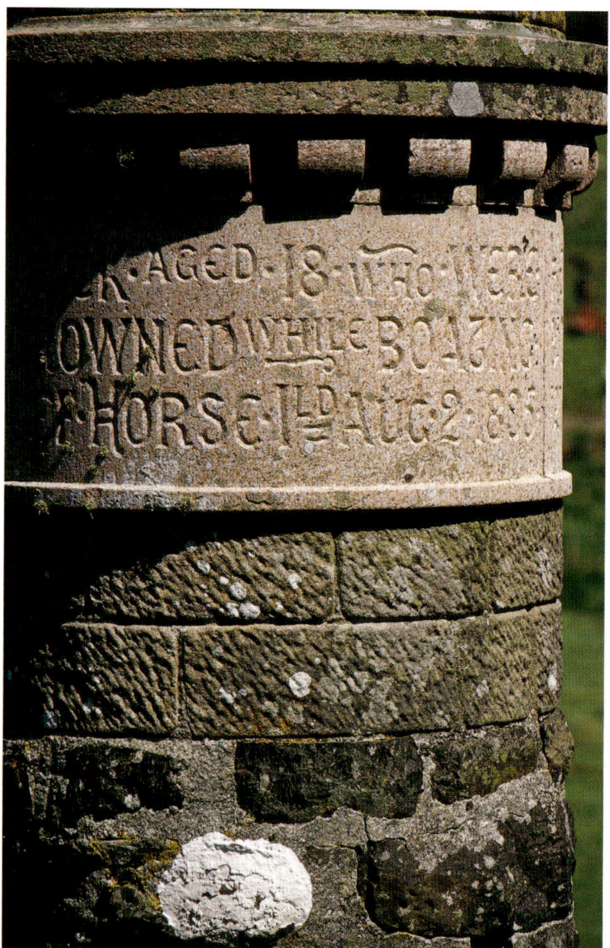

In the island graveyard of Muck below the ruins of the cleared village of Keil is this stone-built monument commemorating the two islanders and a visiting student who were drowned whilst shooting shags off Horse Island in 1885. All over the Hebrides such monuments and gravestones tell of tragic accidents that occur in island communities dependent upon the sea.

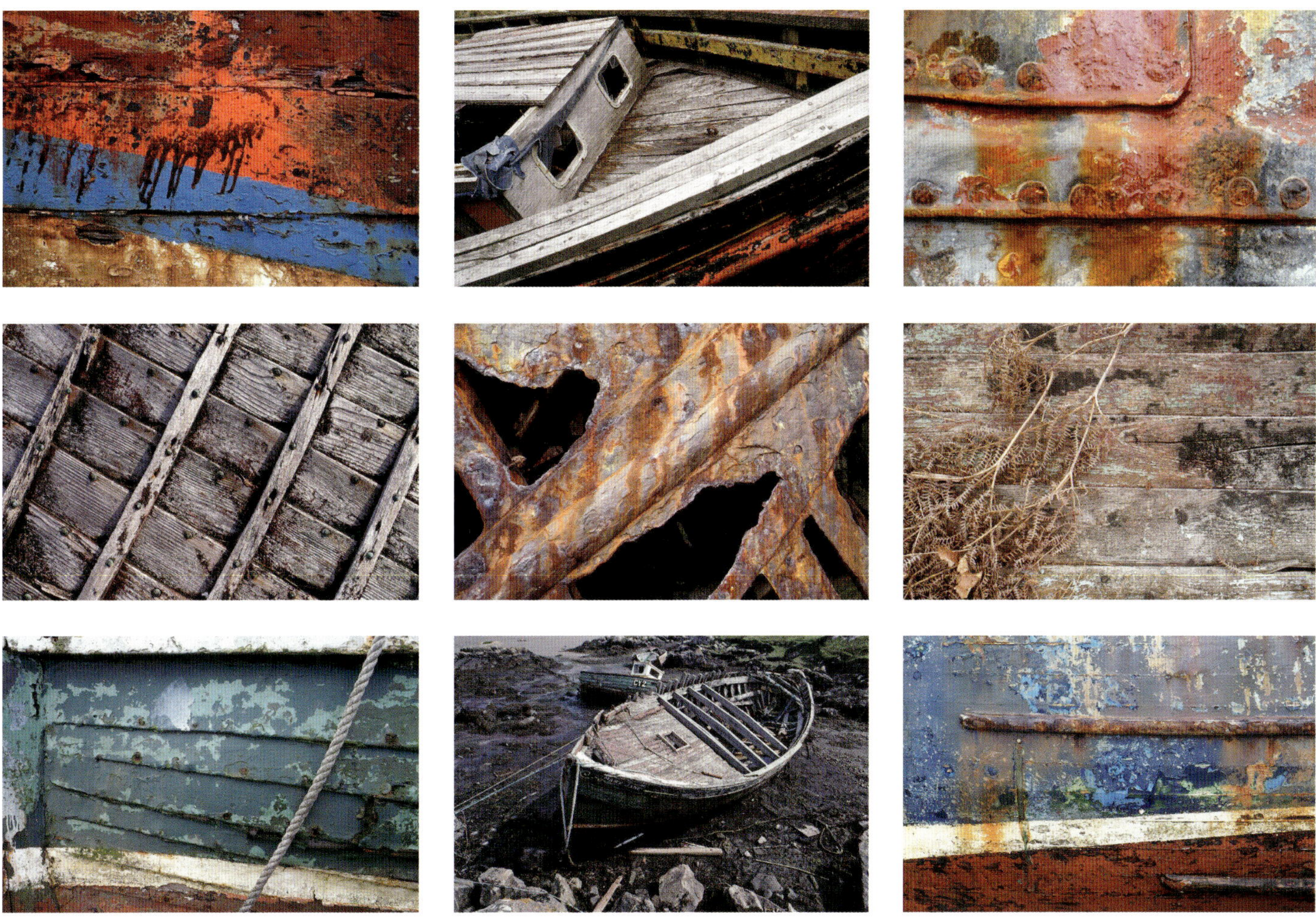

Colours and textures of abandoned and disused boats as they are left to gently rot in the salt-laden atmosphere.

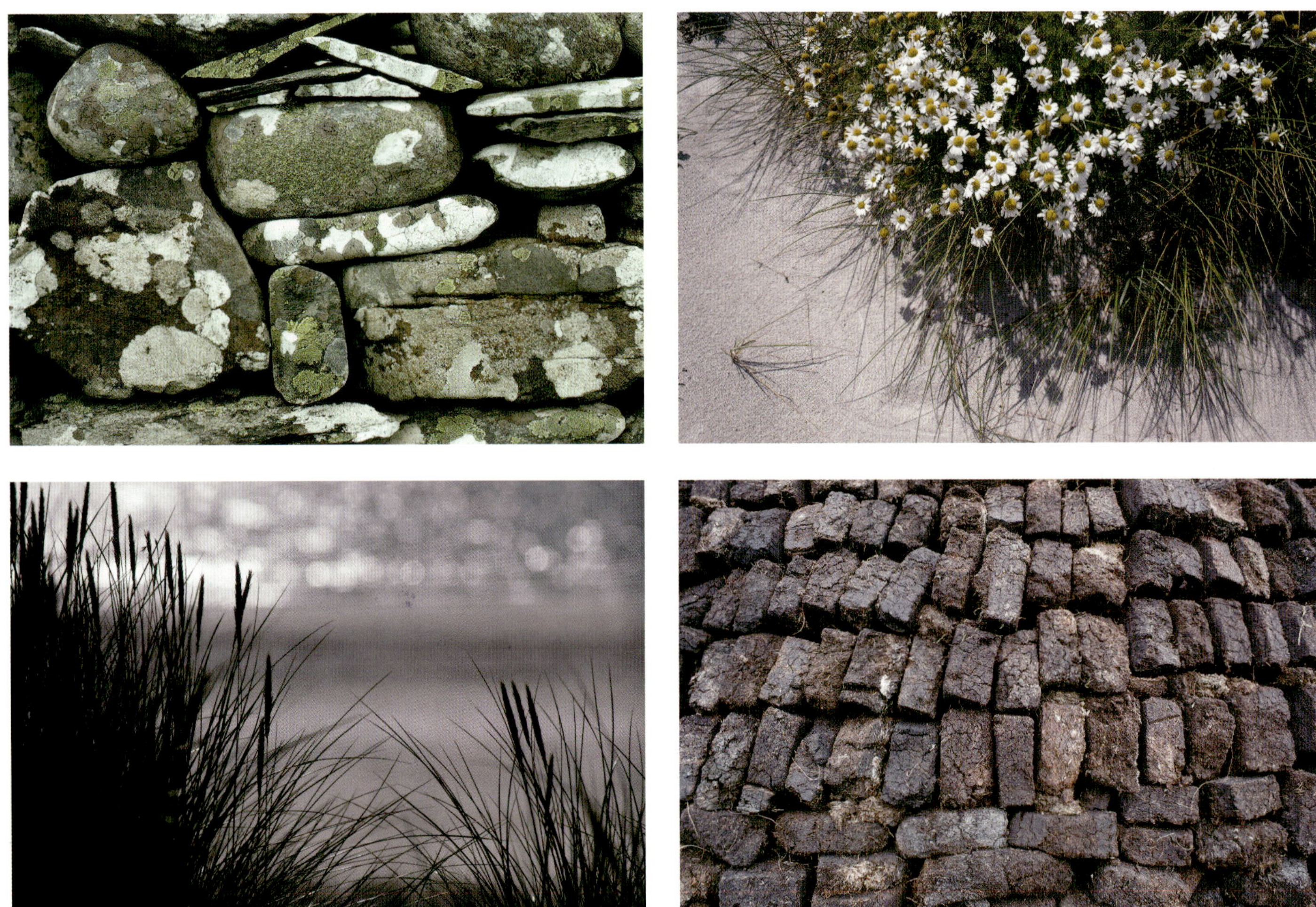

Textures of the Hebrides.

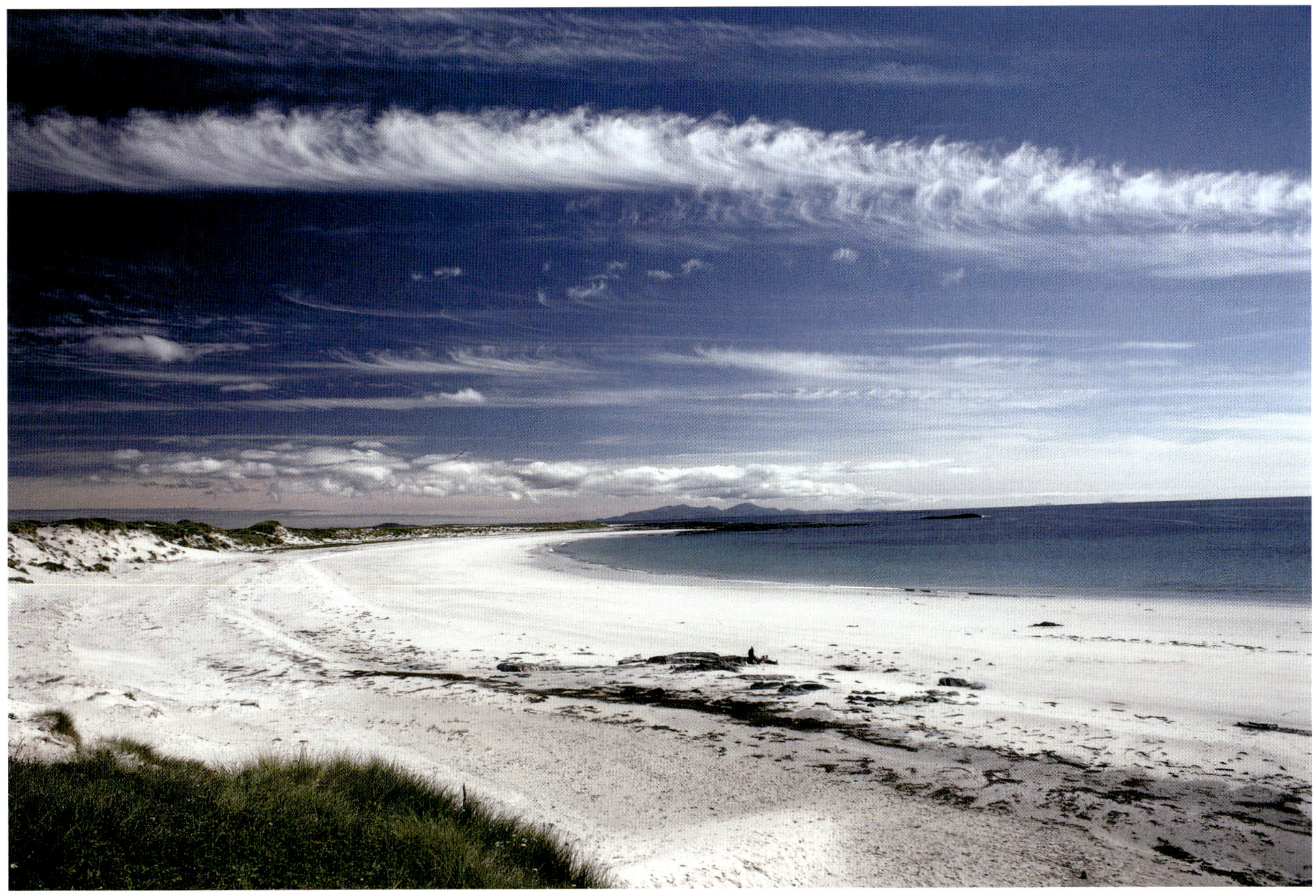

Beach near Hougharry, North Uist. A view of the dazzling white sandy beaches near Hougharry on the southern coast of North Uist under summer skies. The hills of South Uist, Eriskay and Barra can be seen in the far distance. The RSPB nature reserve of Balranald is nearby.

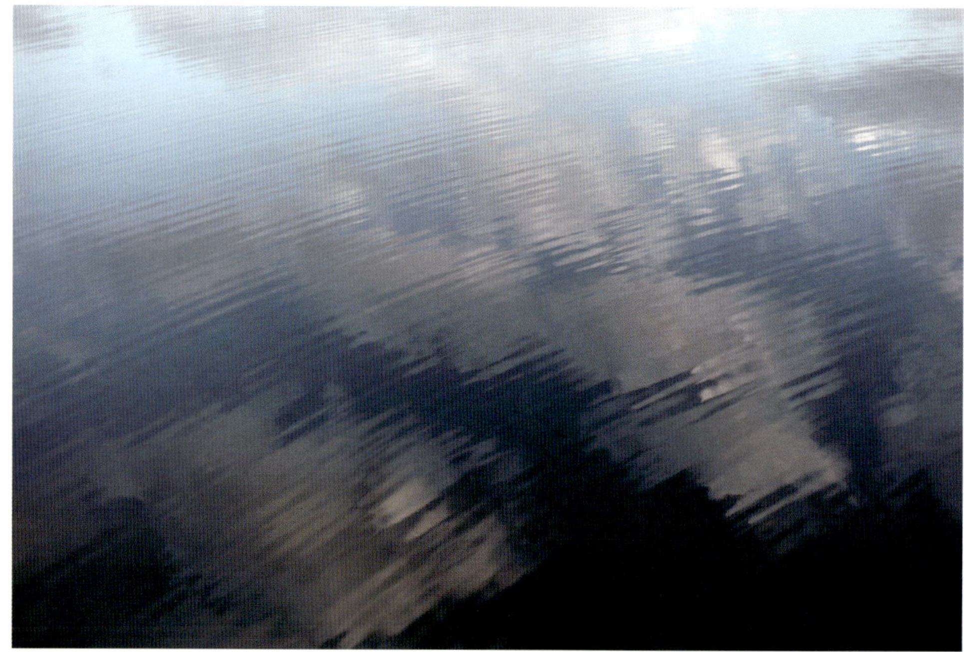

Timeless reflections. Sea and sky, the very essence of the Hebrides. John MacCulloch wrote in the nineteenth century 'time is never present, but always past or to come. It is always too soon to do anything, until it is too late; and thus vanishes the period of weariness and labour and anxiety and expectation and disappointment which lies between the cradle and the grave'.

Opposite: The classic view. The island of Rum photographed from Laig Bay, Eigg on a glorious summer's evening.

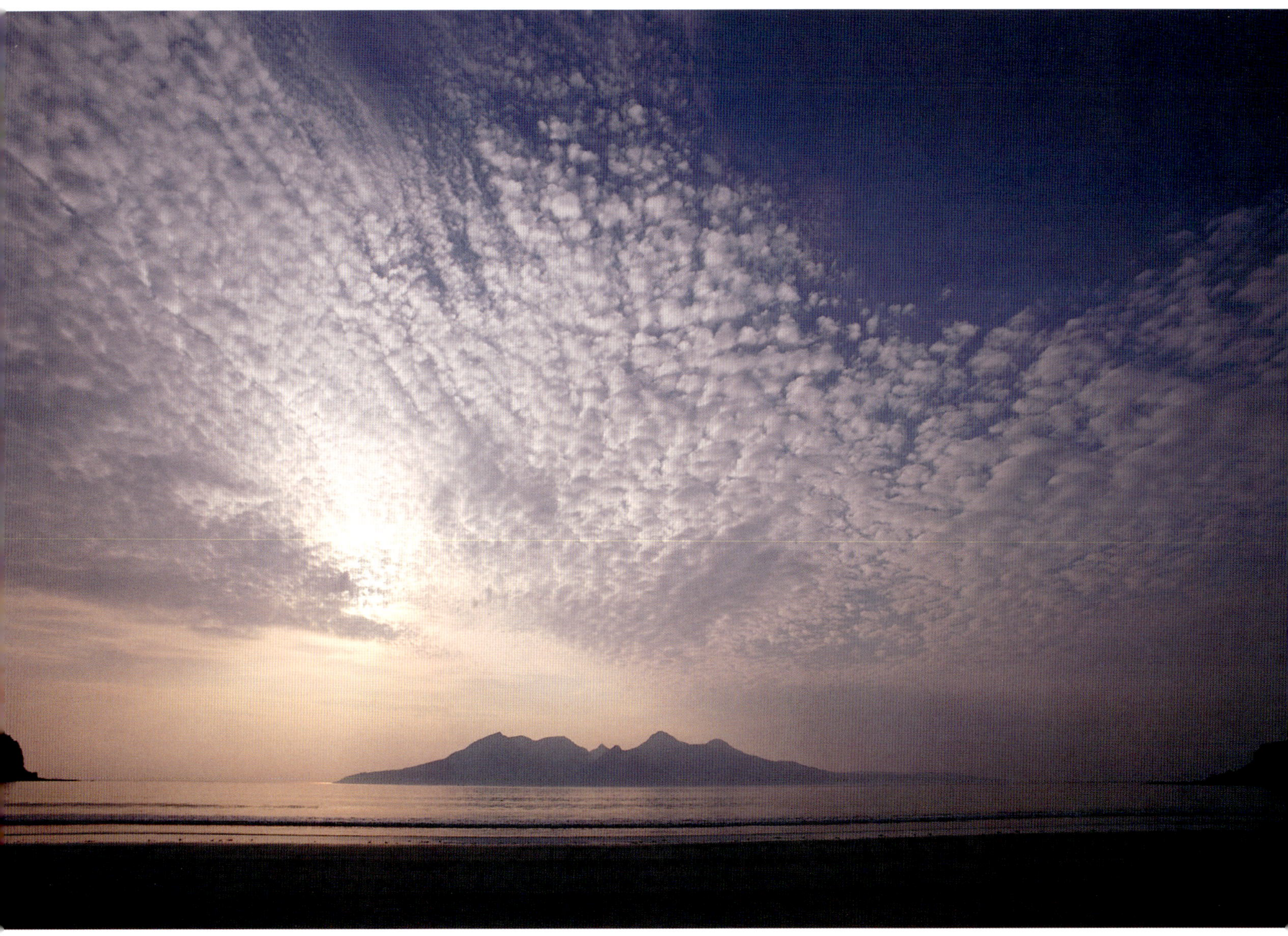

ACKNOWLEDGEMENTS

Inspiration for these photographs has come from many visits to Western Scotland and the Hebrides in the course of which I have met numerous islanders and photographers. To all of them I owe a certain debt, not only for their kindness, patience and encouragement but also for the revelation of a lifestyle where many traditional values are still appreciated, for the discovery of a landscape and environment that can only be described as unique and the realisation that 'time' is not quite so important as our modern culture leads us to believe. To all of you my grateful thanks but especially to:

Pete Bamforth; Ken and Polly Bryan; Nigel Chapman; Heather and Colin Coulson; Catherine Davies; Robert Heather; Margaret Kirk; the late Mary MacDonald; Donald John MacKay; Pat MacNab; Bill McKnight; Roger Maile; Hugh Milsom; Catherine Morrison; Pat and Cathy Myhill; the late Chris Peet; Christopher Swann; Gus Wylie.

As always particular thanks go to Joy once more for her infinite patience, support and hard work in typing the manuscript and for the provision of photographs on pages 56, 93 and 94 and finally, yet again to Steven Pugsley and his enthusiastic colleagues at Halsgrove for all their faith and assistance.

REFERENCE SOURCES

There are numerous books, booklets, papers, leaflets and guides about Western Scotland and the Hebridean Islands. It is virtually impossible to mention them all but the following have been invaluable as reference sources:

Banks, N *Six Inner Hebrides* David & Charles, 1977
Campbell, A *Island of Eigg – a short guide* 1995
Cooper, D *Skye* Routledge & Kegan Paul, 1970
Cornish, J *Scotland's Coast* Aurum, 2005
Craig, D and Paterson, D *The Glens of Silence* Birlinn, 2004
Dressler, C *Eigg, the story of an Island* Birlinn, 2007
Haswell Smith, H *The Scottish Islands* Canongate, 1996
Lawson, B *Harris in History and Legend* John Donald, 2002
MacDonald, A and P *The Highlands and Islands of Scotland* Weidenfeld and Nicholson, 1991
MacEwen, L *The Island of Muck* 1998
McGowan, I *Hebridean Images* Creative Monochrome, 1993
Milsom, H *Mood and Colour* Hugh Milsom Photography, 2007
Murray, W *The West Highlands of Scotland* Collins 1973
The Hebrides Heinemann, 1969
Nicholson, A *Sea Room* Harper Collins, 2001
Paterson, D *The Cape Wrath Trail* Peak Publishing, 1996
A long walk on the Isle of Skye Peak Publishing, 1999
A Scottish Journey Wildcountry Press, 2003
Rixson, D *The Small Isles* Birlinn, 2001
Urquhard, J and Ellington, E *Eigg* Canongate, 1987
Wade Martin, S *Eigg an Island Landscape* Countryside Publishing, 1987
Wright, A and Banning, T *Arran* 2006
Wylie, G *The Hebrides* Collins, 1978
Patterns of the Hebrides A Zwemmer, 1981
Hebridean Light Birlinn, 2003